Advance Praise for
Facebook Marketing: An Hour a Day

Not only does FBMHD provide a practical framework for Facebook marketing, but it also offers a 360-degree perspective on how social media connects with a cross-section of marketing disciplines. By reading and using FBMHD, social-savvy marketers gain the strategies, tactics, and tools to cross the chasm from a hope-it-works community to a well-performing channel for marketing and communications.
> —ADAM WEINROTH, VP of Strategic Marketing, Demand Media

Facebook is a powerful new marketing platform and thanks to this book it, just got a whole lot easier to understand and tap.
> —JOHN JANTSCH, author of *The Referral Engine*

This is the only book that walks you through every step of creating, implementing, measuring, and optimizing a successful strategy for engaging on Facebook. Featuring proven strategies and techniques, this approachable guide walks the walk. It shows marketers at all levels how to roll up their sleeves, jump in, and get winning results quickly.
> —BRIAN GOLDFARB, director, Microsoft

The best marketing engages buyers with valuable information at the precise moment they are receptive. That's why my chiropractor shares video exercises with me on Facebook! And it's darned effective, too. If you want to learn how to tap the communications tool of choice for hundreds of millions of people around the world, study Facebook Marketing. The real-world examples from organizations of all kinds are especially valuable for those who still need to be convinced (like your boss).
> —DAVID MEERMAN SCOTT, bestselling author of *The New Rules of Marketing & PR*, now published in 24 languages

Even though (or perhaps because) it's transforming the way businesses interact with customers and prospects, Facebook is often confusing and counterintuitive. Not anymore. Chris and Mari have created the Holy Grail, a book where nearly every page is worthy of an underline, highlight, or dog ear. With some companies posting to Facebook twice a month, and others posting banalities four times daily, the content strategy guidelines alone make this book indispensable. Buy two copies—keep one for yourself and mail one to a company whose unfocused Facebook approach drives you crazy.
> —JAY BAER, Convince & Convert

Mari Smith quickly became THE *go-to expert before the crowds flocked to Facebook, realizing how powerful this channel is for business. Mari, teamed up with Facebook analytics expert Chris Treadaway, have created an absolute masterpiece! Facebook*

Marketing: An Hour a Day is long overdue, and every reader is lucky to have this book at their fingertips so they can tap into the mind of these pioneers and accelerate their success on Facebook by applying these tips. If you want to know exactly how to position yourself as the go-to expert among the millions of users on Facebook and drive droves of paying clients to your website, you must get a copy of this book!

—DEBORAH COLE MICEK, aka: @CoachDeb, founder of QuanSite.com and author of *Twitter Revolution* and *Secrets of Online Persuasion*

The social media world is full of people saying they know this tool or that tool. But there's a reason "Mari Smith" is the first name people think of when they think "Facebook marketing." This book shows you how the world's largest social network can be leveraged for your business. And it's written by one of few people out there who actually has shown companies how to succeed on Facebook. If you're trying to leverage Facebook to reach your customers, this book should be on your shelf. It's on mine.

—JASON FALLS, Social Media Explorer

Every marketer knows they need to be on Facebook and other social networks, but few know how to do it right. Chris and Mari have created what is essentially a user's manual for anyone managing a brand or advertising a business on Facebook. Whether you're new to social networking or a savvy user, this book provides the tools every marketing professional needs, from getting set up the right way to managing successful, targeted advertising campaigns. The book's step-by-step format makes what many consider a daunting undertaking seem more like a manageable process for even the busiest marketers by helping you prioritize your time online.

—PETER VANRYSDAM, Chief Marketing Officer, 352 Media Group

Mari and Chris have written an excellent, easy-to-read guide on using Facebook to grow your business. Chapter 7, "Advanced Tactics and Campaign Integration" is alone worth well more than the price of this book.

—DAVE KERPEN, CEO, theKbuzz

I love books that start with strategic planning. Just about every Facebook title I've seen is obsessed with secret tips and tricks, without ever encouraging the reader to identify what they're trying to accomplish in the first place. Chris and Mari have done a splendid job putting those tips and tricks into a meaningful context, and I know I'll be studying my copy to improve my own Facebook presence. If you're looking for the full picture—the "why" along with "what" and "how"—then this is your book.

—DAVE TAYLOR, online entrepreneur, AskDaveTaylor.com

Mari and Chris have a unique gift in that they can take the very complex and sophisticated paradigm of marketing on the world's largest social networks and present it in a way that anyone can understand and, more importantly, put into practice.

—BRIAN SOLIS, author of *Engage: The Complete Guide for Businesses to Build and Measure Success in the New Web*

Facebook®
Marketing

An Hour a Day

Chris Treadaway

Mari Smith

WILEY

Wiley Publishing, Inc.

Senior Acquisitions Editor: WILLEM KNIBBE
Development Editor: ALEXA MURPHY
Production Editor: LIZ BRITTEN
Copy Editors: JUDY FLYNN AND KIM WIMPSETT
Editorial Manager: PETE GAUGHAN
Production Manager: TIM TATE
Vice President and Executive Group Publisher: RICHARD SWADLEY
Vice President and Publisher: NEIL EDDE
Book Designer: FRANZ BAUMHACKL
Compositor: KATE KAMINSKI, HAPPENSTANCE TYPE-O-RAMA
Proofreader: WORD ONE, NEW YORK
Indexer: TED LAUX
Project Coordinator, Cover: LYNSEY STANFORD
Cover Designer: RYAN SNEED

Library of Congress Cataloging-in-Publication Data:
Treadaway, Chris, 1974–
  Facebook marketing : an hour a day / Chris Treadaway, Mari Smith. — 1st ed.
     p. cm.
  Includes bibliographical references and index.
  ISBN 978-0-470-56964-1 (pbk. : alk. paper)
  1. Internet marketing. 2. Social networks—Computer network resources. 3. Facebook (Electronic resources) I. Smith, Mari, 1966- II. Facebook (Firm) III. Title.
  HF5415.1265.T74 2010
  658.8'72—dc22
                    2010004712

Dear Reader,

Thank you for choosing *Facebook Marketing: An Hour a Day*. This book is part of a family of premium-quality Sybex books, all of which are written by outstanding authors who combine practical experience with a gift for teaching.

Sybex was founded in 1976. More than 30 years later, we're still committed to producing consistently exceptional books. With each of our titles; we're working hard to set a new standard for the industry. From the paper we print on to the authors we work with, our goal is to bring you the best books available.

I hope you see all that reflected in these pages. I'd be very interested to hear your comments and get your feedback on how we're doing. Feel free to let me know what you think about this or any other Sybex book by sending me an email at nedde@wiley.com. If you think you've found a technical error in this book, please visit http://sybex.custhelp.com. Customer feedback is critical to our efforts at Sybex.

Best regards,

Neil Edde
Vice President and Publisher
Sybex, an imprint of Wiley

For my mother, Mary Ellen Treadaway, who taught me the values of honesty, integrity, and sincerity that help me every single day. I love you, and I miss you.

—Chris

For my awesome Facebook friends and fans and you, our readers— it's an honor to share and create this journey with you to a whole new frontier!

—Mari

Acknowledgments

Writing a book on a topic as dynamic as Facebook is perhaps one of the most difficult things I've ever done. It wouldn't have been possible without my co-author, Mari Smith, whose contributions certainly turned a good idea into a great book. Thank you also to Giovanni Gallucci who contributed several of the anecdotes that appear in this book.

Special thanks also goes out to the world-class team at Wiley that I've had the pleasure of working with for five years now. In particular, I should mention Ellen Gerstein, Jennifer Webb, Katie Feltman, and others at Wiley who, among other things, encouraged me to write this write this book. I'd also like to thank the editorial staff at Sybex. Without hands-on help from Willem Knibbe, Alexa Murphy, Pete Gaughan, Liz Britten, and countless others, this book would have been obsolete by the time it hit the shelves!

This book is a collection of thoughts and ideas from hours upon hours of experience spent with clients who have different interests, different motivations, and different levels of expertise. I'd like to thank all the people at Microsoft, the City of Austin, Land Rover, and other organizations that I've supported in the two years I've done consulting work. Interactions with you have made this book a better product and a true "practitioner's guide" to using Facebook for marketing purposes.

I'd be remiss if I didn't thank the different people who have taught me valuable school and life lessons along the way. In particular, I'd like to thank teachers from St. George Catholic School in Baton Rouge, Louisiana, and Northwest Rankin High School in Brandon, Mississippi. They all, in their own ways, instilled enthusiasm, confidence, and (tough as it may have been at times) grace in me throughout the formative years of high school. I'd also like to thank Jim Nolen and Dr. John S. Butler of the University of Texas, two instructors from the business school, whose ongoing support and interest in me and my career continues to help in countless ways.

Special thanks also to my business partner at Notice Technologies, Robert Starek, who has been patient and supportive despite long hours of writing, editing, and improving this book.

Most importantly, I'd like to thank my parents and grandparents for raising me in a healthy, happy, and supportive home; without your sacrifices for and undying confidence in me, I'd be ill-equipped to deal with life's difficulties, and I wouldn't be the person I am today. I'd like to thank my wife, Kimberly Toda Treadaway, for her love, support, and patience. I love you dearly. And finally, I'd like to thank God for all the opportunities and blessings he shares with me every day.

—Chris

First, huge props to my awesome coauthor, Chris Treadaway—it's a delight to team with you, and I look forward to a long and lasting friendship! I'm also grateful to the exceptional team at Sybex (big virtual hug to Willem Knibbe!).

A special mention to my wonderful mentors, teachers, and friends, all of whom have directly or indirectly helped shape my successful career in the social media industry over the past several years: John Assaraf, Jim Bunch, Jack Canfield, Ali Brown, Lorrie Morgan Ferrero, Alexis Martin Neely, Ann Handley, Joel Comm, Ken McArthur, Yanik Silver, James Malinchak, Fabienne and Derek Fredrickson, Adam Urbanski, Lisa Sasevich, Carrie Wilkerson, Kevin Nations, Larry Benet, Nick Nanton, Scott Martineau, Chris Knight, Gary Goldstein, Ellie and Charlie Drake, Kim Castle, David Tyreman, Scott Hallman, Gary Gil, Greg Habstritt, Peggy McColl, Stephanie Frank, Stefanie Hartman, T. Harv Eker, Bill Glazer, Dan Kennedy, David Finkel, Rick Calvert, Dave Cynkin, Dan O'Day, Paul Lemberg, and Declan Dunn. Thank you for your support, your friendship, and the opportunity to speak on your stages and contribute to your peeps!

I am also indebted to my business partner, Mark Eldridge, and our team at the International Social Media Association—Lyn-Dee Eldridge, Elsom Eldridge, Tripp Eldridge, Sica Martin, and all our founding members and grads of Mentor With Mari.

A huge acknowledgment to my friend and social media partner, Michael Stelzner—it's a true joy to collaborate with you. Thank you for the opportunity to contribute my best Facebook posts to your subscribers!

I'd also like to thank these social media professionals whom I admire greatly for leading with heart, soul, and integrity: Chris Brogan, Guy Kawasaki, Gary Vaynerchuk, Jeremiah Owyang, Charlene Li, Brian Solis, Lee Odden, Pete Cashmore, David Armano, Erik Qualman, Liz Strauss, Jason Falls, Jay Baer, Dave Kerpen, Louis Gray, Loic LeMeur, Jesse Stay, Nick O'Neil, Laura Fitton, Sarah Evans, and Beth Kanter.

My deepest gratitude goes to my spiritual mentor, Esperanza Universal, who opened a door for me and changed my life forever in the spring of 2009. To my dear girlfriends for always believing in and encouraging me: Ashley Mahaffey, Dorcy Russell, Baeth Davis, DC Cordova, Laura Rubinstein, Amy Porterfield, Angie Swartz, and Deborah Cole Micek, aka @CoachDeb (you encouraged me to write a Facebook how-to book for years!)—I heart you all!

Finally, my dear Facebook and Twitter community—I am blessed to be connected to you.

And, if I missed anyone, it was unintentional—send me a tweet or write on my Facebook Wall, and I'll happily acknowledge you!

—Mari

About the Authors

Chris Treadaway is the founder and CEO of Notice Technologies, a provider of local, real-time advertising platforms for newspapers, television, and technology companies. He is also managing director of Ultrastart, a social media consulting firm that has consulted for major companies such as Microsoft, Land Rover, Wiley Publishing, and the City of Austin, Texas. Prior to his work at Notice Technologies, Chris spent almost four years at Microsoft Corporation where he was the group product manager for web strategy in the Developer division and the business lead on the first launch of Silverlight. Chris has worked in the Internet marketing field for more than 15 years and in three start-ups— Cruising Speed, Infraworks, and Stratfor.com, where he built the company's first portal, which was profiled in *Time Magazine* and other international publications. He has an MBA from the University of Texas at Austin and a BA from Louisiana State University. He blogs regularly about entrepreneurship and social media issues at http://treadaway.typepad.com and on Twitter at www.twitter.com/ctreada.

Mari Smith is the president of the International Social Media Association, an organization dedicated to providing cutting-edge social media resources, training programs, certification classes, and a collaborative community. FastCompany.com dubbed Mari "the Pied Piper of Facebook," and ClickZ named Mari one of the 20 Social Media All-Stars. Mari is an in-demand international social media keynote speaker and trainer, and she runs her own vibrant social media consultancy specializing in helping business owners, authors, and celebrity clients increase their profits with Facebook and Twitter integration. She has a popular Facebook fan page at http://facebook.com/marismith, blogs at http://marismith.com, and is very active on Twitter at http://twitter.com/marismith.

Contents

Introduction

Over the past five years, the social media business has grown from a sleepy, sophomoric way for college kids to communicate to perhaps the future of how people will share information and bring their offline lives online. It's truly been amazing to see how much the Internet business has evolved as a result of Facebook, MySpace, Twitter, and other social media technologies.

I originally took a great interest in social media in business school at the University of Texas in 2003. A classmate, Cory Garner, and I had just heard of this new thing called LinkedIn, and we were instantly captivated by the possibilities. Social relationships were becoming more and more transparent, and they were moving online. We worked like crazy to encourage classmates to get on the social network. Our fear, at the time, was that we would lose the opportunity to get people to sign up, and in so doing we'd lose our captive audience. We succeeded in the "membership drive" of sorts, but it didn't turn out to be that important in the end. We had no appreciation for the fact that social media was a tsunami that would eventually encourage just about everyone to create a profile and establish relationships—even the Luddites in our class.

That same tsunami hit consumers in 2006 with MySpace and later with Facebook. I was at Microsoft running Web 2.0 developer strategy and messaging when Facebook had a mere 40 million users. Even then, it was apparent to me that this Facebook thing was poised to redefine the Web, Internet advertising, and possibly even web development. I worked aggressively inside Microsoft to shed light on the new paradigm. I looked around and saw a variety of business opportunities in and leveraging social media. So, I left Microsoft to start a new company in March 2008, where I could spend all my time thinking of new business opportunities and helping clients with their social media problems.

Over the past 18 months, I've interacted with countless entrepreneurs, visionaries, and managers and executives of large corporations in an attempt to learn about how people view and want to utilize social media. That experience alone has been rewarding—the best and brightest people from a variety of disciplines are redefining the Web in their own little way with social media at the forefront of those changes.

Interestingly, since leaving Microsoft, I've also reviewed and edited books on Facebook and social media marketing. The one common theme across all these books is that, to date, they've all been heavy on the ideas, the theory, and the trends that social media brings to bear. That's great, but now there are perhaps far too many books that explain social media marketing from an "academic" perspective.

Conversely, there aren't many books that actually tell people how to conduct a social media marketing campaign. I looked around for books that would help people with the day-to-day tasks associated with Facebook marketing, and I was disappointed to find very little that would help a panicked middle manager navigate the breadth of the Facebook platform. So, I had a quick conversation with the people at Wiley, who I had helped with their Facebook presence, and next thing you know, I, along with Facebook marketing expert Mari Smith, am writing this book for Wiley.

It is in that sense that this book is written strictly as a "practitioner's guide" to Facebook marketing. Mari and I wanted to get down on paper all the tips and tricks that we employ when marketing products and services for ourselves or for clients. We specifically did not want to create a feature walk-through like those that appear in so many other Facebook marketing books. We also did not want to write another book about the shift to social media, what is possible in the future, or what it means for society. This book is about the here and now and what you can do for your organization using Facebook today.

This book is a summary of all the little things necessary to make a marketing campaign work. It's specifically for people who get a mandate from a manager, investor, or whoever who says, "This Facebook thing is important—go figure out how to make it work for us!" Those can be stressful situations, and the last thing you need is pressure along with a vague directive and no idea of how to make it work. This book does not provide the creativity necessary to resonate with your customers in clever and unique ways, although we do provide examples in different parts of the book to give you ideas and show you how other people have solved tough problems.

—Chris Treadaway

Who Should Read This Book

This book is for anyone who is charged with the responsibility of owning some part of Facebook marketing for an organization, whether it be a business, a nonprofit, a government agency, and so on:

- A middle manager who needs help executing a marketing campaign on Facebook
- An employee who needs ideas for how to best utilize Facebook for marketing purposes
- A business owner who wants to engage better with customers but doesn't have a lot of time to learn on their own
- A manager or executive who needs to know the possibilities and the challenges that employees face when executing campaigns

Much of the content of the book is geared to the tactics of building, measuring, and monitoring a Facebook marketing campaign. People who are not directly responsible for executing a campaign will also learn about the possibilities of Facebook and other social media products.

What You Will Learn

Facebook has attracted hundreds of millions of users in just a few years. This book will help you learn how to tap into this wealth of consumers for whatever marketing purposes you have. You may need to drive traffic to a web site. You may want to use Facebook to drive awareness of another type of marketing campaign. You may just want to get the word out about your own Facebook presence in what is an increasingly crowded space. This book will teach you how to mine Facebook for the very people you need in order to have a successful marketing campaign, regardless of the goals.

What You Need

Although we cover Internet marketing basics throughout the book, it will be easier for you to pick up the skills and demands of effective Facebook marketing if you have a basic understanding of Internet marketing metrics and measurement. The only other thing you need is something to market—a product, a service, a brand, and so on. Without it, you won't be able to run a real campaign.

What Is Covered in This Book

Facebook Marketing: An Hour a Day is organized to turn you into a social media marketing powerhouse while attracting people in your target market to your organization cost effectively.

Chapter 1: Internet Marketing 1985–2010   Walks you through the evolution of Internet marketing, from closed services to portals to search and now social media.

Chapter 2: What Is Facebook?   Summarizes the Facebook phenomenon, the basics of how Facebook works, and how Facebook fits into the social media landscape.

Chapter 3: Develop a Facebook Strategy and Measure Success   Helps you frame your approach in terms of success metrics that will drive your work and inevitable adjustments to your campaign.

Chapter 4: Month 1: Create the Plan and Get Started   The first chapter with "hour a day" content, designed to create your first Facebook marketing campaign.

Chapter 5: Month 2: Establish Corporate Presence with Pages and Groups   Summarizes the two primary means by which organizations create an "official presence" that is used to communicate with consumers and other target audiences.

Chapter 6: Month 3: Create Demand with Facebook Ads   Highlights the wide range of opportunities in promoting a website or Facebook presence using Facebook's self-serve advertising system, one of the best values in Internet marketing in 2010.

Chapter 7: Month 4: Advanced Tactics and Campaign Integration   Includes information on a variety of Facebook platform extensions and features designed to help the marketer create better and more engaging social network marketing campaigns.

Chapter 8: Customized Experiences via Facebook Applications A detailed overview of opportunities in custom applications on Facebook and how applications may be used in the future.

Chapter 9: The Analytics of Facebook Summarizes all the metrics that are discussed throughout the book to make it easier for you to understand how to keep score and monitor success.

Chapter 10: Organizational Considerations Helps frame Facebook marketing opportunities, risks, and threats as it pertains to specific types of organizations that see the opportunities in Facebook.

Contacting the Authors, and Companion Websites

One thing is constant with Facebook and life alike: change. The Facebook platform is, to be polite, a moving target. The behavior of Facebook changes, the rules change for communications/notifications and the News Feed, and developers are allowed to do things today that they aren't allowed to do tomorrow. Facebook makes changes rapidly and sometimes without warning. So if you'd like to keep up with these changes, feel free to check out one of the following:

> www.facebookmarketinganhouraday.com includes information on the book, links to destinations on Facebook, links to blog posts that will cover hot issues, contact information for any questions you may have, and information on vendors that can help you with sticky social media marketing problems.

> www.twitter.com/FacebookMktg links to interesting articles and developments in Facebook marketing, case studies, statistics, and so on.

Both sites are operated by the authors and will include updates, podcasts, tips and tricks, and other helpful information that you may need. They're also places for you to provide feedback. As long as you are respectful and constructive, we'll answer just about any question. But we won't do your job for you.

Sybex strives to keep you supplied with the latest tools and information you need for your work. Please check its website at www.sybex.com, where we'll post additional content and updates that supplement this book if the need arises. Enter *Facebook marketing* in the Search box (or type the book's ISBN, **978-0-470-56964-1**), and click Go to get to the book's update page.

Final Note

This book is really one part social media marketing, one part Internet marketing. As hot of a topic as social media is, in some ways it is just the next iteration of things that have evolved over the past 15 years. It is Internet marketing with social context. Throughout the next several hundred pages, I will do my best to help you learn what you need to know to succeed with Facebook marketing. Good luck, and let's get to work!

Internet Marketing 1985–2010

Today, computer usage is a pervasive part of our lives. It's hard to believe that wasn't so just a little more than a generation ago. Even so, Internet marketing and social media aren't exactly new concepts. Even the earliest online services included a variety of marketing options to help businesses tap into this vast new marketplace of consumers. How did the industry evolve over the years?

1

Chapter Contents

The Humble Beginnings of Social Marketing

We all enjoy life through a series of defining experiences with friends and loved ones in our social circles: people who attend the same school, live on the same street, work in the same company, or root for the same team. The jeans they wear, the phones they use, and the brands they favor to some extent encourage us to think positively or negatively about ourselves and others. They're consumers just like us, and they shape our thoughts and opinions in profound ways that we rarely notice.

All of us have been pitched products in advertising from memorable spokespeople: Spuds McKenzie, Joe Isuzu, the lonely Maytag repair guy, Max Headroom, Charlie the Sunkist Tuna, the California Raisins, to name just a few. We remember catchy phrases and sayings like "Just Say No," "Where's the Beef?" "Kibbles and Bits and Bits and Bits," "Calgon, Take Me Away!" and "We thank you for your support." We respond to their honesty, their humor, and their brute force and take on their marketing messages by making subtle, subconscious changes to how we live, what we consume, and what we think.

For years, experiences were lived largely "offline." Our interactions have been in person, in front of a television, or through headphones. But times are different. Internet technologies and social media have enhanced our online experiences. We enjoy interactivity, video, audio, and pictures just as much from computer screens as from offline experiences. We want to learn, share, and interact from the comfort of our computers and mobile devices more than ever.

For me, it started when my parents bought a Commodore 64 in 1984 along with a 300 baud modem. Connecting to other users in the "online world" was a novel concept at the time—it was 1985 after all! But we wanted to experience the future firsthand. Our first taste of social computing was on a service called Quantum Link (Figure 1.1). Q-Link was one of the very first online services that combined electronic mail, public file sharing, and games. It was fascinating. To play games, I didn't need to get permission from my parents to invite people over. I could do it from the comfort of my own bedroom and at any time of the day or night. The only problem was the pesky usage fees. Mom and Dad didn't seem too excited about a big bill for "plus" services. Nonetheless, I got my first taste of social computing on Q-Link.

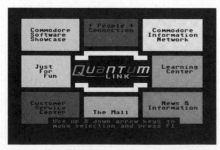

Figure 1.1 Quantum Link home page

Online Services v1

Three major competitors—Prodigy, CompuServe, and America Online (AOL)—
evolved over the following few years. All three took online services to an entirely
different level with improved user interfaces made possible by advances in computer
hardware and operating systems. Some of the first real-time online services were made
available via Prodigy in the early 1990s—news, sports scores, weather, and so on. It
was the primary way I kept up with my favorite baseball team, the Chicago Cubs, for
a few seasons. Prodigy also offered premium content from the Mobil Travel Guide and
Zagat's Restaurant Ratings, to name a few. But perhaps most important, Prodigy had
very well-integrated message board and e-mail services that allowed people to meet,
discover similar interests, and communicate with one another. These were the "killer
apps" behind the growth of the Internet in the early 1990s. They were, in effect, the
first generation of modern social networks. Figure 1.2 is a screen shot of the Prodigy
login screen, which may be familiar to those of you who used the service many years ago.

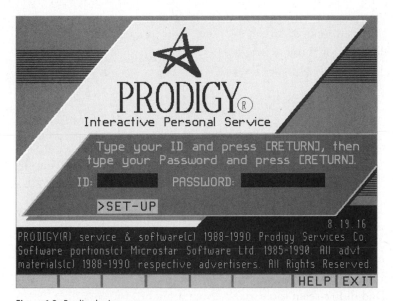

Figure 1.2 Prodigy login screen

    While Prodigy, CompuServe, and AOL were pioneers in the online services busi-
ness, none of them were particularly interesting channels for e-commerce or Internet
marketing. Most notable was Prodigy's classified ad experiment with *USA Today*,
whereby Prodigy offered advertisers the opportunity to reach parts of the Prodigy
user base for as little as $60/month for an approximately 250-character text advertise-
ment. Prodigy also made screen space available to advertisers through "teasers," or
what would be viewed today as banner advertising, at the bottom of each screen. If a
consumer was interested in the advertisement, they could click the advertisement to

get more information via a larger version of the ad and then buy the product or service being offered. But neither advertising option became sufficiently popular and effective for Prodigy or any other online service. Internet advertising was only a $55 million industry worldwide in 1995; it was just too early for people to respond well to the advertising of goods and services on the Internet. Compare that to the $25.7 billion Internet marketing business in 2009 and it probably seems a lot smaller. Because Internet advertising was so ineffective early on, Prodigy, CompuServe, and AOL focused primarily on growing consumer subscription revenue by increasing subscribers in the mid-1990s.

Emergence of the World Wide Web

The proliferation of proprietary first-generation online services came to a stunning halt with the emergence of Mosaic, the first widely available web browser. In 1994, with Mosaic and a web connection via an ISP (Internet service provider), a user could spend an unlimited amount of time surfing the Internet and send an unlimited number of e-mail messages. This was a departure from existing services that relied upon tiered hourly service and other usage upcharges for profitability. Fueled by the wealth of new online services, applications, and a proliferation of websites, consumers moved to the World Wide Web en masse starting in 1995.

As users flocked to the Internet, the first experiments in Internet marketing were already underway. HotWired, an online Web magazine, was the first company to sell banner advertising to corporations, in late 1994. Figure 1.3 is the first banner ad ever sold, an AT&T advertisement. Banner ads were long, rectangular advertisements usually 468 pixels wide by 60 pixels tall with information and/or graphics designed to entice a reader into clicking them to visit another website. They were sold for a flat rate per 1,000 impressions or views, which is now referred to CPM (cost per mil). Around the same time, a number of experiments popped up to guarantee clicks and not just impressions. The idea was that advertisers wanted visitors and not just views.

Figure 1.3 The first banner ad ever displayed on the Internet

The mid-1990s was a revolutionary period for the Internet as millions of people got online. The possibilities were endless, as were questions about how advertising could be used to build new businesses, new opportunities, and new communities. How would people interact with each other? How much would the Internet change purchase behavior? How would business be conducted differently in the age of the Internet? What new business opportunities would be possible? All of the possibilities led to an unprecedented level of entrepreneurial activity from both new companies and established corporations. Everyone wanted an opportunity to participate, to reap the spoils.

As a result, the Internet advertising business grew tremendously through banner advertising. Sites could devote a certain amount of space to banners to generate revenue. It was a good deal for advertisers as well because at the time it was the best way to reach people and get them to learn about another site on the Internet or a product, service, or other offer. For no less than five years, banner advertising was the best Internet marketing opportunity available to people who wanted to connect with consumers on the Web. This dynamic led the developers of many early popular websites to turn their sites into *portals*, sites that would help users get a wide range of information that would be helpful in a personal and sometimes professional context. By building an effective portal, a company could create a thriving and growing Web property that would generate revenue and profits through banner advertising.

Search and the Decline of Banner Ads

The number of websites continued to proliferate well beyond people's expectations. Consumers needed a way to sort through all the noise to find exactly what they needed at any given time. A number of companies built sites to help with this exact problem. Yahoo! indexed sites by subject matter and added a rudimentary search function that helped users find resources quickly. Others didn't rely on a proprietary directory but instead depended on scanning the full text of web pages to determine relevance for a particular search term. Popular search engines from this period included Magellan, Excite, Inktomi, AltaVista, and Lycos. Later, other search engines such as MetaCrawler and Dogpile emerged, combining search results from individual search engines to provide more accurate and complete results to users. Over time, these search engines became the "starting point" for many users. Rather than logging into a portal like Go.com or MSN to get information, users began to frequent search engines.

Before long, it became apparent that users preferred an effective, powerful search engine to all other means of finding relevant information on the Internet. Enter Google. I remember the first time I used Google in early 1999. I was stunned by how it so easily and quickly pointed me to the exact information I needed at the time and, more important, how consistently effective the search engine was regardless of the search term used. It took just a few times for me to realize that Google was revolutionary. Like a lot of other Internet users, I ditched every other search engine I had used before and converted to Google. Contrary to popular belief, Google did not immediately revolutionize Internet advertising. It was primarily a great search engine for several years while the company experimented with a variety of different business models.

The world continued to buy and sell banner advertising as the primary means for generating demand on the Internet, although banner advertising certainly peaked in the late 1990s for a few reasons. For one, the proliferation of websites meant that the number of advertising options increased significantly. Less scarcity = lower prices. Negotiating power shifted from the publisher to the advertiser, who now had more available options for ad spend. Second, the novelty of Internet advertising wore off to some extent. Click-through rates on banners dropped from as high as 2 percent to well below 0.5 percent, and with that drop came a reduction in prices. No longer were companies blindly sinking thousands of dollars into banner advertising. Advertisers demanded results, which was increasingly working against banner advertising. Third, consumers experienced some level of banner ad fatigue. These ads were everywhere on the Internet by 1999, which also made them somewhat easy to ignore. This created an environment ripe for the emergence of a new, effective, and trackable way to reach consumers.

The Rise of Google and Clickthrough Ads

Around this time, Google emerged as perhaps the world's greatest and most accurate search engine. In just a few years' time, it launched a search engine that was superior to rivals such as HotBot, AltaVista, Lycos, and others. It quickly gained market share but ironically launched an impression-based advertising business in 2000.

Advertisers were tired of spending a lot of money on ineffective banner ads, and consumers were ignoring them. Realizing this, Google abandoned its impression-based advertising program in favor of experiments with click-through advertising, text-based ads for which the advertiser would only pay if a user clicked the ad (Figure 1.4). This invention was named Google AdWords, and the rest is history.

Figure 1.4 Google AdWords click-through ads appear at the top and down the right side of the search results pages.

Google AdWords was a self-serve advertising service similar to services offered around the same time by competitor GoTo.com, later renamed Overture by Yahoo!. Advertisers would enter the text for a relevant ad that adhered to style guidelines and character limitations. The advertiser would then add the search terms that would trigger these ads along with the highest bid they would be willing to pay for the click. The final step was setting a daily budget; without a budget, a lot of money could be spent on these ads! Using an automated auction system, Google would serve ads based on the total bid and the amount remaining in the budget for each bidder.

It may seem simple now, but this was a revolutionary shift in Internet advertising for a few reasons. First, an advertiser could effectively guarantee traffic to a website by simply bidding high enough and devoting enough budget on a daily basis to the advertisement. Now this wasn't particularly difficult in 2002—many click-throughs cost as little as a nickel a piece, so 100 new visitors for a website per day could cost as little as $5.00. Not a bad deal. But more importantly, Google realized that the folks clicking on these ads weren't just any users. They were highly targeted users by virtue of the fact that they had searched for a specific term in a search engine. This was a stark contrast from banner ads, which generally were not targeted to specific users looking for specific things. So in summary, Google took an increasingly large audience and made it available to advertisers on a relatively inexpensive, self-serve basis. It was pure genius.

As with any auction model, prices increased significantly as more people jumped in. I remember first getting into Google AdWords in the fall of 2002 with my third startup, a lead generation business that found qualified leads for consumer products from Google. I could buy tons of clicks, send these visitors to a website where I qualified them and converted them to leads, and then resell them to customers who wanted incremental business for 5 to 10 times the cost of generating the leads. But in less than a year, I started to see the bids increase substantially as larger corporations, ad agencies, and other entrepreneurs had discovered this "new" opportunity. This trend continued for years as Google maintained and grew its search share. From 2003 to 2008, Google was the one place to go to tap into large numbers of Internet users interested in a particular subject matter or topic.

The Emergence of Social Networks

As Google asserted its click-through dominance, a number of social networks began to emerge and reach mainstream consumer audiences. There wasn't anything particularly new about social networks. Online communities had formed at every evolution of the Internet, dating back to well before the World Wide Web. The difference by 2003 was the fact that people had grown increasingly comfortable with interacting with one another on the Internet, and at times in plain view of other users. Social networks, after all, work better with a larger number of engaged users sharing more and more details about themselves.

The first notable companies from the social networking era were Classmates.com and Friendster. Classmates.com allowed people to associate themselves with certain graduating classes to keep in touch with friends from various schools and points in their lives. The concept of *profiles* on Classmates.com was very basic, and many features of the site were ultimately hidden behind a paid subscription. Friendster emerged six years after the launch of Classmates.com and exposed more features to users. Friendster was the first social network to successfully integrate the profile concept whereby a user could enter personal data, preferences, and so on. Friendster grew aggressively just after its launch in 2002 but endured a number of technical problems that disenfranchised early adopters and new users alike. Further, Friendster exposed profile data and actions to people within several degrees of separation from a user, which later, more-successful social networks did not do. Despite the fact that neither Classmates.com nor Friendster achieved mainstream worldwide success, both sites continue to operate today, each with a large user base. Table 1.1 summarizes the top social networks from 2000 to 2009—note how the early pioneers have faded as Facebook and MySpace now dominate the social media market.

▶ **Table 1.1** Popular social networks as of July 2009

Social Network	# Users	Notable Facts
Facebook	350 million	Most users of any social network in the world.
MySpace	125 million	Most popular social network from June 2006–April 2008.
Twitter	75 million	
LinkedIn	55 million	Most popular social network for business.
Classmates.com	40 million +	As much as 10% are paid subscribers.
Friendster	90 million	90% traffic comes from Asia.

Source: comScore, Compete.com, ComputerWorld.com, official statistics released by each company

MySpace in many ways was the beneficiary of Friendster's inability to turn into a mainstream global phenomenon. The service launched in mid-2003, not as a new startup but rather as a side project of parent company eUniverse. With support and resources from a larger company, MySpace was able to scale from a handful of users to several hundred thousand very quickly. MySpace and Friendster had many of the same features, such as profiles, friends, blogs, and comments, but MySpace did not always share data with friends of friends. A direct friend connection was required to view specific information about a person. Care over sensitive data created an environment in which users were much more willing to add personal information to profiles. MySpace also allowed users to customize their profiles with different types of information, special layouts, and unique background images.

All of this had the impact of fueling the growth of MySpace in a relatively short time. MySpace went from launch in mid-2003 to being the most popular social network in the world in 2006. It became very popular with younger demographic groups in that period of time. comScore estimated that over 60 percent of users of MySpace were under the age of 34 in 2005. As such, it became an essential marketing tool for musicians and bands that sought to engage with fans through the site. Over and above that, users of MySpace got more and more comfortable with the idea of living their lives online—communicating important life events and mundane details to friends on the Internet. See Figure 1.5 for a sample MySpace profile.

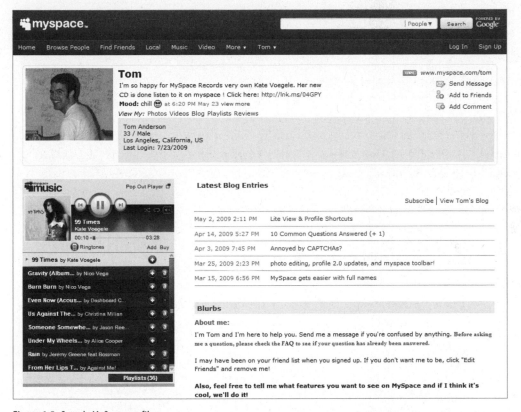

Figure 1.5 Sample MySpace profile

Having collected information on users through profile data, MySpace became the "next generation" way to target consumers. Google pioneered learning about consumer interests through search. MySpace did the same in 2006 to 2008 through information such as profile data and interests. Think for a moment about the types of information available through a social media profile:

- Hometown
- Current home
- Date of birth
- Interests
- Likes/dislikes

- Hobbies
- Marital status
- Activities
- Education
- Political views

Access to this amount of information about a person is a marketer's dream! All of it was unlocked by social networks that created a relatively safe and fun environment in which people were encouraged to willingly share this information with friends. This data has not, to date, been used by advertisers to communicate directly with individual users, but it has been used in the aggregate to target groups of people interested in a certain thing. For example, through social networks, a marketer can do the following:

- Send banner ads to the 47,000 users interested in bowling in Ohio
- Update 2,809 fans of the fictional band Orangebunny Wahoos about a new concert tour
- Tell 13,287 single New Yorkers interested in kite flying about an upcoming event in Central Park

For more information on this phenomenon, I recommend reading "To Aim Ads, Web Is Keeping Closer Eye on You" by Louise Story of *The New York Times* (www.nytimes.com/2008/03/10/technology/10privacy.html). The article does a great job of explaining how different online services compare to each other when capturing consumer data and making it available to advertisers.

Emergence of Facebook

While MySpace continued to grow between 2004 and 2008, Facebook emerged as its chief rival in dominating the consumer social network industry worldwide. Conceptually, Facebook was very similar; it had just about the same profile data as its predecessors. But it did not allow data and profile backgrounds to be customized by users as MySpace did. This had the impact of providing some standardization to data and the overall experience of browsing profiles. Facebook did offer users a rich set of tools to limit or expose data to only certain people: friends or people in particular networks. But aside from this, the design philosophy behind Facebook was to make experiences consistent. Users could expect similar data and the same look and feel when browsing profiles.

Facebook initially launched at Harvard, where its founders originally used it to encourage classmates to get to know each other better. Check out Figure 1.6 for an early screen shot of the Facebook home page. At that time, many colleges actually provided printed facebooks to students that included biographical information, interests, areas of study, and so on. After getting half the undergraduate class at Harvard to create profiles, Facebook expanded to other Ivy League schools. The company later expanded to other colleges and universities, high schools, and finally major corporations before releasing to the general public in late 2006. This strategy of exclusivity in the early years gave Facebook the advantage of gaining critical mass within networks of people who were likely to keep in touch with one another. A high concentration of people interacting inside Facebook provided great insight into what people would do and how they would share information with one another, and most importantly, it provided an idea of the features and enhancements that would help Facebook compete with rivals.

Figure 1.6 Early Facebook home page

The battle between Facebook and MySpace became yet another in a long line of "Coke vs. Pepsi" battles throughout late 2006 to 2008. In early years, MySpace had a loyal following in younger demographics, but Facebook slowly gained the attention of college students. The visual customization aspects of MySpace made some profiles very difficult to read, while the lack of data standardization meant that users could say anything they wanted without necessarily making it readable for the viewer. Others believe that the Facebook/MySpace preference fell along class lines. One such critic was danah boyd, a fellow at the Berkman Center for Internet and Society. In her June 2007 essay, "Viewing American Class Divisions through Facebook and MySpace" (www.danah.org/papers/essays/ClassDivisions.html), Ms. boyd argues that Facebook's origins in Ivy League schools and its original "by invitation-only" method for signing up new users set it down a path to be the preference for affluent and upper-class early adopters. MySpace was positioned as a place for young people interested in bands and those who were not particularly popular or into extracurricular activities in high school and college. MySpace users were not likely to become Facebook users because their friends were not on that network and vice versa. *Forbes* (www.forbes.com/2007/07/20/facebook-myspace-internet-tech-cz_ccm_0723class.html) and other major publications covered Ms. boyd's observations in great detail. It was, and remains to be, a compelling argument.

A Researcher's Perspective on Social Networks

danah boyd, Ph D, is a researcher at Microsoft Research New England and a fellow at the Harvard University Berkman Center for Internet and Society. She maintains a website at www.danah.org where she blogs and includes links to her latest academic research and essays.

Dr. boyd's dissertation, "Taken Out of Context: American Teen Sociality in Networked Publics," focused on how American youth use networked publics for sociable purposes. She examined the role that social network sites like MySpace and Facebook play to develop her theories on how social networks reflect social structure and norms.

Q: *Do you still think the choice between Facebook and MySpace is dictated mostly by class identification? Has the situation changed significantly?*

A: Choice was never dictated by class identification. Choice is and continues to be dictated by social relations. People choose to go where their friends are. That said, people's connections are not random. There's a concept in sociology called "homophily" which means that "birds of a feather stick together." People are friends with people who are like them. There are all sorts of social divisions in friend networks and these are reproduced online.

Q: *You've pointed out that class differences are arguably the main difference between Facebook and MySpace. Is there anything necessarily wrong with this? Or does it simply mirror the differences that already exist in society?*

A: My argument is that Facebook and MySpace are making visible everyday social stratification based on the patterns by which American teens have adopted these two sites. Self-segregation is a part of everyday life and it is not particularly shocking. But when we treat social network sites as public places, when we expect everyone to be present, we've got a problem. For example, when universities only do college recruiting on one site or when politicians only reach out to constituents on one site, we have to think about the ways in which they are biasing the population they're connecting with.

Q: *Where do you think we're headed with the use of social media? I know you don't have a crystal ball. But knowing what you know about Facebook, MySpace, Twitter, and other emerging technologies, will people connect better or will divisions in society be even more apparent as social media matures?*

A: Technology is not going to magically solve social ills, but it will continue to make visible divisions that exist in society that we may be uncomfortable addressing. As for where things are going ... mobile. And social media will continue to be about friends, not strangers.

After expanding beyond education, Facebook slowly began to eat into MySpace market share for a few reasons. Applications such as Photos, Notes, and Gifts were easy to understand and very well executed—and all three helped encourage users to interact with one another. Status updates and news feeds gave users the opportunity to passively keep in touch with friends. But perhaps the most important development was the May 2007 release of the Facebook Developer Platform, a framework that allowed developers to write custom applications that ran inside Facebook.com and took advantage of each person's unique social graph. All of a sudden Facebook made its audience available to third-party developers. This opportunity led to a quick proliferation of new applications on Facebook. Games were most popular, but all sorts of applications were created over the subsequent 12 months. Two main things contributed to Facebook's success in this arena: valuable supporting applications and the elegantly executed strategy to encourage developers to write applications for Facebook. Finally in early 2009, Facebook overtook MySpace in several key usage metrics and was poised to be the dominant player in social networking.

Rise of the Real-Time Feed and Beyond

It's likely that 2009 will go down as "the year of the real-time feed." Early in 2009, Facebook redesigned its home page to highlight the News Feed, which is made up almost entirely of status updates, links, photos, and other updates from Friends and Fan pages. This turned Facebook into more of a real-time communication channel for friends to communicate with one another.

The change was initially met with major resistance. Reportedly as much as 94 percent of Facebook users did not like the change at first. In fact, several Facebook pages were created to protest the new home page design. One such page has over 810,000 members as I'm writing this chapter! That said, the fury over the site redesign quickly dissipated as people became more familiar with the new approach.

A new competitor, Twitter, also began to gain significant customer traction in early 2009. Twitter is a lightweight social network that is built around simple 140-character messages that are ordinarily shared for anyone to read. Figure 1.7 shows these real-time messages from other Twitter users. It is ostensibly the Facebook Status Update, turned into a product with limited functionality and a slightly different policy for becoming a friend of a particular user. According to Compete.com, Twitter increased its unique users by 400 percent over the first few months of 2009. The success of Twitter has already resulted in a series of changes for Facebook, and it's likely to result in further adjustments over time. We'll talk more about these changes and Twitter later in this chapter.

Overall, the Web has evolved into a significantly more transparent and social technology with the evolution of social media over the years. Over time, users have gotten increasingly more comfortable with sharing personal information online and in social networks. People live their lives offline and report on what happens online. Yesterday's privacy intrusion is today's opportunity to share life's intimate details with friends, acquaintances, and sometimes strangers alike. From a marketer's perspective, we've never had an opportunity like this, where so much information is available about consumers. Information that was once trapped in databases is now accessible in aggregate form from Facebook and its competitors. We have an unprecedented opportunity to use these technologies to share the value of our products and services not with the general public, but rather with people who are very likely to be interested in hearing from us. So let's turn our attention to a snapshot of what we know about social media usage and how we may be able to use social media most effectively when marketing products and services.

Figure 1.7 Twitter home page

Social Media by the Numbers and by Feel

Let's take a moment to consider just how pervasive social media and particularly Facebook has become for Internet users. An April 2009 study by Harris Interactive revealed that 48 percent of all American adults had either a Facebook or a MySpace account. It took Facebook eight months to go from 100 million to 200 million users. Contrast that to the growth of the United States—it took the good ol' USA 52 years to go from 100 million to 200 million inhabitants! If Facebook were a country, it would be the fourth most populous country in the world ahead of Brazil, Japan, and the populations of Germany, France, and Spain combined.

But these aren't just casual users. According to Nielsen Online, people spent 13.9 billion minutes on Facebook in April 2009, up from 1.7 billion in April 2008 for a stunning annual growth rate of 699 percent. In terms of usage, this makes social networking the third most popular computing activity now, ahead of using e-mail. Facebook reaches an estimated 29.9 percent of the global Internet user community. It has clearly become a mainstream phenomenon and the numbers are sure to get bigger from here. For the full Nielsen report, check out this page:

www.docstoc.com/docs/5830948/Nielsen-Report-on-Social-Networkings-New-Global-Footprint

The rise of social media has coincided with a decline in consumer use of traditional media. Social media usage numbers are up while newspaper circulations are down. In many cities, the number of social media users surpassed the stated circulation of venerable newspapers in 2008. eMarketer reports that Internet users consumed far less traditional media in 2008 than 2006 (www.emarketer.com/Article.aspx?R=1006892/). It's safe to say that today, people get far more news, information, and commentary from their friends than from traditional media.

It's great that people are using Facebook and social media, but do these products and services impact purchase decisions? It's probably too early to tell how social media marketing and advertising will compare to search engine optimization and click-through search advertising. But we do intuitively know that we all personally have friends we ask for recommendations: the sports enthusiast, the wine lover, the tech geek, the foodie. We rely on friends and people we trust for feedback and information every day. We similarly listen to our friends when it comes to music, things we do for fun, responses to politics and world events—you name it. We're influenced on a regular basis by people we know and love. Social media records all those recommendations and makes them visible for friends and friends of friends to see.

The history of computing also tells us that opportunity lies in the first place people log in to every day. In the early 1990s, marketers sought ways to take advantage of Prodigy, CompuServe, and AOL. The mid-1990s was dominated Microsoft, when installed client software was the major opportunity. Companies fought to get a presence on consumers' desktops. The late 1990s was dominated by the portals such as MSN, Excite, and Yahoo!, where eyeballs were most concentrated. We talked earlier in this chapter about Google and how it created a center of gravity for the Web that captured consumer attention and marketing dollars. Today, many people start their day not by going to google.com, but rather by logging into Facebook.

What Social Media in 2010 Tells Us about the Future of Marketing

So what does all this mean for marketing in 2010 and beyond? The biggest change in marketing has been the shift from "push marketing" to more of a conversation with customers. In the past, companies were limited to communicating directly with us through radio and television commercials, print advertising, billboards, and other "old media" ways of marketing. But somewhere along the way, we got cynical. We realized that our friends and colleagues were probably more honest about products and services than the self-interested companies that marketed to us. So we started listening to our friends and social networks more and traditional advertising less.

At the same time, technology has marched forward relentlessly. TiVo and digital video recorders made it easy for us to bypass and ignore commercials in live television. MP3 players helped us listen to music and podcasts on demand, which similarly marginalized radio advertising. Online retailers realized that they could increase sales by allowing visitors to their site to offer personal recommendations about products they were selling. And, of course, the social media industry was very successful.

So how should we frame our thinking when setting the stage for marketing plans today? Five years from now? And how should long-term strategy be structured to give social media a competitive advantage? Allow me to suggest five broad themes that I think will define social media and marketing for years to come:

The need to share information. If the rise of mainstream social media has proved one thing, it is that a lot of people have an intrinsic need to share things about themselves. Maybe it's self-importance, maybe everyone needs to feel like a celebrity. I don't know. But social media today captures a lot of mundane information about users. Sometimes that mundane information can include an experience, positive or negative, with your brand or with your company. Today, everyone can broadcast to their own little social media network of usually a few hundred people. For more on this topic, I recommend reading Brad King's book *The Cult of Me* (Carnegie Mellon, 2010), which discusses these themes in great detail. Word-of-mouth marketing has become both a threat and an opportunity to modern businesses—social media provides the loudspeaker.

Immediacy is here to stay. All of the tools provided in social media give people an opportunity to respond immediately to things and share those reactions with friends in real time. It could be a great experience with a restaurant, a terrible interaction with an airline at the airport, you name it. With immediacy comes human emotion—powerful feelings once shared only in the presence of friends can now be shared immediately with friends, colleagues, acquaintances, and the general public through social media. Sometimes this can work for your business/brand; sometimes it can work against you. Some companies are already seeking ways to communicate with angry or satisfied customers in real time through social media. So far, it is proving to be a differentiator for a lot of brands that deal proactively with negative social media publicity.

Everyone is a source of information, and everyone is biased. It's 2010, so people don't just hear about news, events, and so on from the local TV news broadcast and/or newspaper. People (not to mention your customers) hear about things from blogs, Twitter, articles, casual conversation. Some people's opinions on politics are influenced by *The Daily Show with Jon Stewart* and the Fox News Channel! Let's face it: The line between fact and opinion is muddy. People today don't have the interest or the time to learn the difference between the two.

Think about this from your own personal perspective. Which friend of yours is known among friends as an expert on food, drink, nightlife, or politics? Do you have friends who *want* to become known among friends as being an expert? What about the ones who think they are influential about certain topics yet nobody wants to hear from them? One thing is certain about all three groups: They can use social media to say whatever they want. Oftentimes, one opinion is just as good as another, as informed or uninformed as one may be.

Noise level. Everyone is now a publisher and a celebrity in their own world. So it takes a lot of effort to keep up with it all, if you choose to do so. This can work two ways for marketers—some people will respond to direct engagement that cuts through the clutter. Others will instead ignore your noise alongside everyone else marketing a product or service. So the challenge is twofold: A marketer must fit into the noise with interesting things for one segment of their customer base while grabbing the attention of the other. The worst thing you can do as a marketer is say something wholly uninteresting or something that doesn't serve to engage with customers in a meaningful way. The bar is as high as ever today, and consumers don't have significantly more spare time these days.

Melding of worlds. Like it or not, the openness of social media means that it is almost impossible for users to keep different parts of their lives distinct. Things done offline invariably find their way online—and it may not even be your doing. And all those things are available for your personal and business contacts to enjoy!

Think about how this happens—it's all too innocent. You get a friend invite from a coworker. You probably don't want to offend this person, so you decide to accept them as a friend. Now this "friend" is on equal footing with your other friends: college buddies, people you knew in elementary school, and your closest friends. Any one of them can comment on your Facebook profile or send you a tweet, and that comment is out in the open. Any one of them can post embarrassing pictures of you, comment inappropriately on your status or links you share, and so on. Now some people simply don't care what happens. But others obsess over their personal or professional image. Customers today live with and accept a degree of transparency into their lives that simply wasn't there just a few short years ago. Marketers need to remember this when putting together campaigns and customer engagement programs.

We are starting to see elements of "social commerce" emerge on the Internet, whereby purchasing decisions are directly influenced by other people and sometimes friends. Epinions was one of the first companies to emerge (in 1999) with a platform for helping consumers share experiences with certain products on the Internet for other consumers to consider. Yelp does similar things for local businesses, and many retailers are now integrating reviews on their websites to increase sales. Similar products have not yet emerged on mainstream social networks, although integration with these third-party websites is gradually increasing. Web Strategist and former Forrester analyst, Jeremiah Owyang, sees the Era of Social Commerce as the last phase of a gradual shift from the anonymous Web to a social Web through maturing social media technologies. For more information, check out his insightful report at

www.web-strategist.com/blog/2009/04/27/future-of-the-social-web.

It's a great framework for considering where customers and technology will be in coming years.

Realistic Social Marketing Expectations

Now that we've reviewed the background and the trends of where we are, how do you put together a plan that takes advantage of the opportunities? Where is the low-hanging fruit? What should you expect when starting a social media effort or campaign?

First, let us set the expectation properly: Social media marketing, and particularly Facebook marketing, takes time. It isn't something you just turn on overnight to gain followers, fans, friends, and hoards of consumers saying good things about your brand and/or your company. Facebook will not do your job for you, it won't sell for you, and it won't make you creative. Facebook is a set of tools that, if used properly, can give you a way to reach people in a new and exciting way. If it's used improperly, you are sure to spend a lot of money, get frustrated, and ultimately lose faith in a channel that could be very, very good to you. Every situation is different, so you'll have to assess how different parts of Facebook could be used in concert to solve your business problems. We will discuss this more in Chapter 3 and other parts of this book.

Effective execution on Facebook generally starts with an honest assessment of the metrics you are trying to drive. For example, consider the following questions:

- Do you want more direct revenue for your e-commerce effort?
- Are you primarily trying to reach new customers? Or are you trying to communicate better with existing customers?

- Do you want to improve your customer engagement or image metrics?
- Are you establishing a base from which you can market future products and services over coming months and years?
- Do you need to connect better with people in different demographic groups?
- Are you interested in a set of customers on social media that you can benchmark against other customer lists (e-mail, newsletter subscribers, show/conference attendees)?
- Do you want to increase referral business?
- Are you trying to reposition your business or brand?

The answer to these questions will help determine your tactics, how aggressive you should be, and perhaps most important, the things you want consumers to do. Remember, this is an interactive medium, so you aren't necessarily just blasting messages to your customers. You can get them to communicate with you and with their friends. This is the power of the medium, and it's at your fingertips.

In terms of workflow, you'll first have to come to grips with the fact that managing social media will take time, and quite frankly, you have a lot of work to do. You first have to decide what you will promote—a company, a brand, a product? These decisions are typically driven by organizational dynamics, such as what a manager owns or how a company views social media. These conversations can take a lot of time, and the outcome can be based as much on politics as the right thing to do for the customer. Once you've determined what you want to do, you need to have the resources set aside to establish the presence. So in summary, you'll need to ask yourself the following questions as you begin.

- What do you want to say?
- How will you say it?
- Do you need your own content or will you point to other content on the Internet?
- Who will post the content?
- What creative is necessary (logos, icons, ongoing graphic design work, custom applications) to fulfill the business objectives?

Depending on priorities, these tasks are generally assigned to full-time employees, interns, or even consultants who know the business well and understand how to establish a social media presence quickly. The best situation is to have a trusted employee manage your social media presence. You don't want to invest time and money in all the learning only to have the person responsible work for someone else or end a contract and take the knowledge with them.

After the basic presence is established, you'll have to maintain your new property. I like to think of this responsibility as a social "editor-in-chief," someone who is responsible for making sure the presence is fresh with updates on a regular basis. This should be a person you trust implicitly; words and thoughts shared on social media can in some cases be permanent! I've typically recommended at least one update per day per social network for clients, and no more than 7 or 8 per week. Remember, you don't want to annoy people.

This person is oftentimes the person who will monitor outcomes and manage analytics for a social media project. In an ideal situation, each business goal you've identified will be mapped to a specific success metric. Those metrics should be measurable and recorded in a spreadsheet on a daily basis once your project is established. Social media projects are relatively new, so you'll probably have to go above and beyond to ensure that management is supportive of your effort. We've had a lot of success when we are able to show data, charts, and details on how the effort results in increased awareness, improved image, or higher revenues.

All told, you are trying to create a presence and tweak it into optimal performance. Very few web properties were perfect upon launch. The optimal combination of design and content for your business goals is determined only after a lot of experimentation. Get comfortable trying things out. It's a common characteristic of the Web, and social media is no different. If you have metrics to back up your assertions, you'll be a lot more confident because numbers rarely lie.

A Few Thoughts Regarding Consumer Engagement

Finally, you're going to have to think deeply about how customers will interact with your company or brand on social media. Put a different way, you have to remember that consumers aren't necessarily eager or ready to buy from you at all times. So while you may be interested in promoting an offer or a product, doing so over and over again is likely to alienate your customer base.

Take, for example, one case that I witnessed recently. I partnered with a marketing company that was helping a sandwich franchise with their social media presence. Their job was to identify opportunities on Facebook and Twitter that would help the franchise reach more customers, and they managed the client's Facebook and Twitter accounts in the early stages of the project. Over the first few months, they posted status updates such as these:

"Enjoy a meatball sandwich today!"

"Our shakes are fantastic!"

"It's hot outside—come enjoy a cold beverage!"

What's consistent across all of these messages? Well, for one, they aren't particularly informative. Worse yet, these messages were sent out with the franchise's marketing goals in mind, not the needs/desires/wants of the customer base. Needless to say, this wasn't a particularly effective campaign. The number of Twitter followers and

Facebook fans didn't increase significantly, which led the franchise to distrust the marketing company before it could show its capabilities. To say the least, the marketing company got off on the wrong foot! The company would've been better served to mix it up a bit by including an occasionally important or informative message alongside its marketing messages, such as these examples:

"Bring your umbrella—storms expected this afternoon in town!"

"Get a free drink with any of our great meatball sandwiches today only when you mention Facebook!"

"Festival downtown this weekend—get your early-bird tickets at www.earlybird.com."

When in doubt, you should remember the golden rule of social media marketing:

"Do unto your customers as you would be happy to have them do unto you."

There is a fine line between informing and annoying your customers—make sure you are providing value to your community through social media. Be thoughtful and informative with everything you share on social media. When someone chooses to become a fan or follower of your company, it's a privilege and not a right!

What Is Facebook?

2

So what is this Facebook thing all about anyway? In Chapter 1, we talked about what social media means at a high level and how consumers are changing behavior to share life's details online. In this chapter, we'll break down the different social networks and talk about how the individual parts of Facebook come together for a user.

Chapter Contents

Social Networking and Social Media Defined

Before we discuss the other websites that I want to call to your attention, it is important that you understand some nuances and some issues in the vocabulary that I will be using when uncovering these topics. In particular, I want discuss a few terms: *social media*, *social networks*, and the *social graph*. Figure 2.1 is an illustration of how all of these fit together.

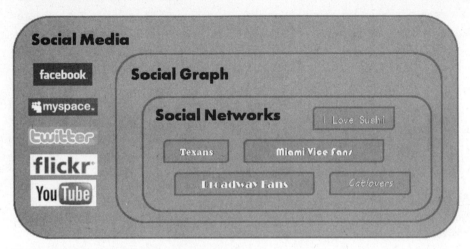

Figure 2.1 Social media, social graph, and social networks

The term *social media* refers to the collection of technologies that capture communication, content, and so on across individuals, their friends, and their social networks. Examples of social media include social networking sites like Facebook and Twitter, blogging technologies like TypePad and WordPress, crowdsourcing products like Wikipedia, photo and video sharing sites like Flickr and YouTube, and others. These technologies help users easily create content on the Internet and share it with others. Social media is the infrastructure that helps users become publishers of content that is interesting to them and their friends.

Social networks are groups of people, or communities, who share a common interest, perspective, or background. As much as we like to talk about social networks in the context of popular online services such as Facebook, these networks exist offline just as much as they do online. So whether you are talking about Pink Floyd fans, people who attended the University of Texas in 2004, people who enjoy fly-fishing, or Brazilians, these networks exist regardless of whether or not the individuals in them share information and life experiences on social media.

The *social graph* is the broad collection of people, places, and interests that makes us individuals. It's how and why we're connected to other people. Think about it—a lot of who we are is defined by who we know, the associations we have made over the years, the schools we've attended, the interests that captivate us, and so on. Before social media, information about our social graph was largely difficult to find, lost when we moved to a new place, lost touch with old friends, or stopped participating. Social media keeps us connected to our interests, our past, and our old friends. For this reason, many experts believe that Facebook may emerge into a "next generation social operating system" similar to Windows and the Web. Logging into Facebook and other social networks is the first thing a lot of people do every day, and it will only get more important as it attracts more users, more friends, and more data on the social graph of individual users. Facebook CEO Mark Zuckerberg popularized the term *social graph* in 2007 when first describing why the company was able to grow so rapidly.

For example, I am an entrepreneur, so I'm part of the social network of entrepreneurs. But because I worked at Microsoft for three and a half years, I'm also a member of the social network of Microsoft alumni. I am a member of hundreds of networks from various associations in my life to date, and I'll likely join others in the future. The collection of my networks is my social graph, and it is as unique to me as my own fingerprint. All of the information across my social graph, including the social networks to which I've subscribed, is captured in social media sites such as Facebook and Twitter. These sites collect, organize, and disseminate that information to me and other users in consumable ways.

Social Network Landscape

So what other social networks compete with Facebook? And how are all of them used? It can be very confusing to navigate the world of social media, especially if you are not an active user or if you've just been tasked with becoming an expert in your company. What's the difference between Flickr and Facebook Photos? What are the differences between each social network? Which social networks are in decline and which are growing? When building a campaign, how much can (and should) you depend on Facebook? And do certain types of campaigns lend themselves to one social networking strategy over another?

The answers are going to depend entirely on the business metrics you are trying to drive and the demographics you seek. There are no hard-and-fast rules that dictate what you should do. Worse yet, social media preferences and usage changes so fast that there's a good chance that anything I say in this book will be out-of-date by the time you read it! While qualified consultants can probably help you learn quickly, this isn't an argument for going that route at all. I think you can educate yourself on social media in a few hours a week, otherwise I wouldn't write this book!

Facebook Is Not Forever

In 2009, this statement seems ridiculous. But in 2007, there was no question that MySpace was the king of the social networks. Additionally, few people saw Twitter as the future of social media when it made its debut. However, Twitter has experienced a growth of almost 1,200 percent growth year over year as compared to 250 percent for Facebook, according to Compete. com (`http://siteanalytics.compete.com/Facebook+bebo.com+hi5.com+orkut.com+Twitter`).

Considering Twitter's growth, Facebook must be looking in its rearview mirror at Twitter coming up fast from behind. For these reasons, I always recommend to those who ask that they pick a least a couple if not several different social networks as targets for their marketing campaigns, so they don't get caught spending all their time on yesterday's social network before they realize it.

First, let's quickly discuss the differences between the different social networks so you know how they differ and how they may evolve in the next few years.

While many social networks appear to be independent, most are run or influenced by major media or technology companies. Google, Microsoft, Yahoo!, AOL, and other large companies have a stake in the game as they either own the major social networks or work with them officially or unofficially. Maybe you are thinking that this doesn't matter, but if you are going to create a social media competency in your business, you'll want to pay attention. Why?

Each of the major players has distinct advantages and disadvantages in the marketplace, all of which will also play out in social media.

Microsoft Microsoft, for instance, operates a number of Web properties, such as Windows Live Messenger, that are used by millions of people. Data from Windows Live Messenger is used in its social network, Windows Live Spaces. Windows Live Messenger also pulls data from other social networks to make the user experience richer. Figure 2.2 is an example of how Windows Live Messenger pulls in status updates from another social network in the What's New area.

Google Google has millions of users of their applications, Google Mail, and YouTube. Google uses login data for these users to enable the quick creation of profiles on other Google properties, an important fact given that many industry experts believe that Google will need to diversify beyond search advertising revenue soon.

Yahoo! Although Yahoo! is currently second place in search, perhaps more importantly it owns a network of sites that are used by over 500 million people worldwide. Yahoo! representatives have stated many times that they want to integrate more social features into Yahoo! Mail to make it a de facto social network.

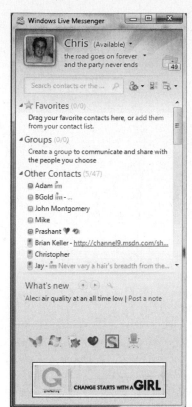

Figure 2.2 Windows Live Messenger displays status updates from a social network.

It's important to understand the major technology companies because their sites and properties are visited by millions of people and they are as interested in marketing and advertising as you are. Some of these social networks are frequented by the same people, so to reach more people, you may need to do things in more than just one place. New opportunities will emerge to market your products and services effectively. You will want to know what is on the horizon to better plan your marketing strategy and budget.

Three Types of Social Networks

There are three types of social media sites: the one size fits all, the one-trick pony, and the hybrid.

One Size Fits All

The one-size-fits-all social network provides the user with one-stop shopping for all of their online community, entertainment, communication, and social media needs. These websites not only let you connect with friends, they let you upload photos from your family's vacation and videos of your daughter's second birthday party. They let you update your "status" so the world knows that you woke up feeling grumpy or that you are thankful for a new day. They let you join groups associated with your political affiliation, hobbies, or career. In short, these websites want to be your everything online.

MySpace, although in its decline, is Facebook's nearest competitor in the United States. Other sites in this category include QQ.com, Bebo.com, Hi5.com, Friendster.com, and Orkut, among others.

The One-Trick Pony

These types of social media sites try to do one thing only and to do it well. They may focus on helping you communicate to other people in a narrowly defined way. They might be widgets, or small applications, that live on other websites. They perform a single task, such as telling you what movies are playing within a certain zip code. Others might be a repository for photographs that you've taken from a mobile phone that can be used elsewhere.

Twitter is the poster child for the one-trick pony social networking website. From its inception, Twitter set out to do one thing and one thing only: to allow individuals using Short Message Service (SMS) or text messaging to communicate with the world broadly via followers and the Twitter search. These conversations are displayed on the Twitter website and viewable by anyone so long as the user who is sending outbound messages has their account's privacy setting configured as "public."

Over time, Facebook has evolved its platform so that the home page of a user's profile displays information in a micro-blogging or Twitter-like fashion. Updates from users' social stream on Facebook are published on the web page much like one would see on Twitter. While many developers have written programs that utilize the Twitter application programming interface (API), these programs don't have a direct impact on the user interface of Twitter. These programs are pulling data from Twitter to create their own user experience outside of the social network itself.

With short messages being the primary functionality provided by Twitter, it is easy to see the differences between Twitter and Facebook. The difference is everything else.

Twitter does not allow users to upload photos. Third-party applications must be used to send messages via a user's Twitter account. These third-party-instigated messages insert links to the user's photographs. When this occurs, the user's photographs reside on a different website, apart from Twitter. Twitter does not allow you to upload videos, but a user can put a link inside a Twitter message that points to their YouTube video or to a video on another video sharing site.

A task performed by a user on Twitter that involves sharing anything more than a message containing more than 140 characters must be done outside the Twitter site. This could be a hyperlink inside a tweet (a message sent or received on Twitter) that points to more content. It could also be created from a third-party application that the user has to install or interact with separately from the Twitter website.

With Facebook, all the user needs to do is upload their photo, post their video, or send the message to another user and all the technology required to fulfill the request is incorporated within the Facebook.com website itself.

Hybrids

Hybrid social media websites tend to focus on one primary piece of functionality but also wrap other social networking features into their platform. In many cases, the site started off as a one-trick pony and evolved into a hybrid due to market pressures, user requests, or other forces.

Flickr provides photo and video sharing capabilities to its users and would be considered by most as a social media website. If you look closely though, you'll see that Flickr provides many of the same types of features that are found in all social networking sites. In fact, the most basic features of a social networking site can be found on Flickr, including the ability to add friends to your network, communicate with different people or groups via messages, join groups, vote on or mark pieces of content as favorites, and more.

YouTube, the world's most popular video sharing site, also provides basic functionality found in any social network. Users can upload their own videos so others can view their creations. As is the case with Flickr, YouTube's functionality extends much further than simply sharing videos with other individuals. YouTube allows users to communicate with others directly and indirectly, join groups of like-minded people, vote on content, and create and manage their profiles.

While these sites include basic social networking features, they are built around specific actions. Namely, Flickr is primarily a photo sharing site. YouTube is built to allow people to share and view videos. Because of this, the community-building aspect of these platforms is lacking. Facebook provides a much richer environment for socializing online than any of these hybrid social media sites. However, these other sites certainly have their place in your overall marketing campaign. We'll discuss those situations throughout the book.

A Quick Summary of the Major Social Networks

If you're in any way the person responsible for social media marketing in your company, you are going to need to understand the difference between the different social media networks. Not all of them serve international markets adequately. Some are particularly good in certain countries. Some are better than others in the key demographics you need to reach your target audience. All of them make changes rapidly to adapt to needs in the marketplace. Table 2.1 provides a handy summary of the important points for each social network.

Social Network	Type	Data	Partner
Facebook	One size fits all	13.8 billion total user minutes in April 2009	Microsoft
MySpace	One size fits all	4.9 billion total user minutes in April 2009	News Corporation
Twitter	One-trick pony	299 million total user minutes in April 2009	n/a
LinkedIn	Hybrid, business professionals	202 million total user minutes in April 2009	n/a
Flickr	Hybrid, photos and video	3.5 billion photos total in May 2009	Yahoo!
YouTube	Hybrid, photos, videos	Delivered 5.5 billion video streams in April 2009	Google
Orkut	One size fits all	65% traffic from Brazil and India	Google
Hi5	One size fits all	Claimed in January 2009 to have 60 million users	n/a
Bebo	One size fits all	Integrated with AIM, the world's #1 instant messaging network	AOL
Windows Live Spaces	One size fits all	Tightly integrated with Live Messenger service and its 330 million users	n/a

Source: comScore, company reports, and press releases

You'll need to supplement this summary with online research to get a feel for how things change. Tech blogs such as Mashable (www.mashable.com) do a great job of reporting monthly usage numbers and demographics for social media usage. You can also visit the web site companion to this book at (www.facebookmarketinganhouraday .com) where we'll keep you up-to-date on the latest happenings in social media.

Below is more information on the leading social media platforms available to consumers today.

Facebook No social network can match Facebook's current momentum or broad international customer adoption. It hosts a range of social applications and has been the market leader in social media since April 2008. While Facebook does not disclose specific financial information, the company earns money from sponsored advertising, self-serve advertising, and virtual gifts. Microsoft took a 1.6 percent stake in Facebook for $240 million in late 2007, and the two companies continue to work together on syndicated advertising opportunities through Microsoft adCenter. A healthy developer ecosystem has been created around Facebook, although the third-party developer craze was lessened somewhat by a series of restrictions placed on developers after early applications propagated too many messages through user profiles and news feeds. More on that in Chapter 8.

MySpace Similar to Facebook, MySpace has an interface for allowing users to update their status, set their "mood," write blog posts, and quickly create a personalized presence on the Internet. One main difference from Facebook, however, is treatment of the MySpace home page once a user logs in. MySpace uses the real estate for sections such as Featured Content, Videos, Music, and Celebrity Updates and for sponsored advertising from its partner, Google. This "half-step" provides MySpace with a number of additional places to insert interesting content and advertising.

Popularity of MySpace has waned since its two-year reign as market leader from 2006 to 2008. Despite the drop-off, eMarketer estimates that MySpace will generate almost $500 million in mostly advertising revenue in 2009. In the future, MySpace is expected to focus on advantages in user creativity, music, and video and compete more aggressively in social gaming. Visit http://pulse2.com/2009/05/30/myspace-ceo-owen-van-natta-talks-about-myspaces-strengths-and-weaknesses/ for an interesting interview with MySpace executives regarding the company's future prospects and competition.

Twitter While Facebook and MySpace quietly satisfy the needs of millions of people, Twitter has gotten all the press lately thanks to use by celebrities such as Oprah Winfrey and Ashton Kutcher. Twitter is a much more limited social network, however. It is simply infrastructure that allows users to share 140-character messages with other Twitter users. A user can follow other Twitter users to get real-time updates from them. Most things shared on Twitter are mundane events in peoples' lives, updates, and so on. Users can also share photos and Web links with other Twitter users via shortened URLs. Despite its simplicity, Twitter has experienced stratospheric growth as the product has gone beyond early adopters and to the mainstream. Facebook and other social networks have begun to adopt "Twitter-like" functionality in their products where possible to combat the perceived threat from this new upstart.

LinkedIn In many ways, LinkedIn ushered forth the modern social networking movement. Launched in May 2003, it has collected resume data and business networks of over 40 million users. It has become the largest and most prominent social network for business in the world. However, the LinkedIn experience is significantly more controlled than that of other social networks. The user interface and all profile data is largely predetermined, as it is in Facebook, but LinkedIn takes it all another step further by strictly regulating applications built on the site by third-party developers, startups, and major corporations. The site is most often used for qualified, surgical introductions to individual business contacts as well as for background checking and research on individuals in the business world.

YouTube YouTube quickly became the world's most popular video sharing and viewing destination in the world after being acquired by Google in 2006. According to comScore, 107.1 million people viewed 6.8 billion videos on YouTube in April 2009, which dwarfed the statistics of all other sources of online video. As on any other social network, users establish profiles on YouTube to upload video, establish their own channels, or tag videos as Favorites. These profiles are now integrated with the Google login and password, so users of iGoogle, Gmail, or Google Docs can get started quickly with YouTube. Companies can also establish a free YouTube channel for how-to videos, commercials, and other types of content.

Flickr Flickr is another specialized social network, focused primarily on sharing photos with friends. The site has all the upload, storage, and album features of digital photo printing companies like Snapfish and Kodak Gallery but includes tags and tag clouds from the blogging world that help users find exactly what they need. Although it is certainly the most fully functional photo sharing social network, many people instead opt to share photos on Facebook or MySpace. Flickr was acquired by Yahoo! in 2005, and its functionality has been gradually integrated with other Yahoo! services since. Flickr introduced video sharing features in 2008 and high-definition video options in 2009. It is expected that Flickr will become an increasingly important part of Yahoo!'s social media strategy in the future.

A number of other social networking sites and platforms have emerged, but many are in decline as a result of the mainstream adoption of Facebook. Sites such as Bebo, Hi5, Orkut, Friendster, Classmates.com, and others are now struggling to compete with Facebook. Usage data for all of these is either flat or declining in the United States and most other markets, although there are exceptions. When planning an international social media campaign, you'll need to consider where you are launching and how you can be most effective with social media in that country. For more information, check out a map of social media usage by country at `www.vincos.it/world-map-of-social-networks/`.

Finally, a series of location-based social networks such as Loopt, Brightkite, Whrrl, foursquare, and Gowalla have emerged over the last several years to help people find friends and connect in person. These applications generally require a web-connected smartphone that can detect a user's location and make that information available to friends and/or nearby merchants. The idea behind these products is that people want to know where their friends are and what they are doing and an application with these features is a better alternative than picking up the phone or setting a status on another social network. It remains to be seen if any of these applications are going to become popular; none of them have a significant enough user base to consider for a broad-reaching social media campaign. Location-based services may, however, bring about the next generation of proximity marketing—the ability for companies to market products and services specifically to nearby consumers. However, such experiments are in their earliest stages at this time. Look for major technology and media companies to align with location-based networks over time as they aligned with social networks.

Seven Truths of Social Networks

While mainstream use of social networks is only a few years old, we already know a lot about how consumers use them. Besides, a few years is a generation in Internet parlance anyway. Here are seven truths of social networks that you can rely upon. If you are going to bookmark one page of this book, bookmark this page because these truths should guide your thinking regardless of what you do with social media:

1. Social media is the preferred way for people in younger demographics to communicate with each other. Nothing else comes close.

2. Social media is based on the concept of friends, but that term today is very loosely applied. Similarly, profiles are loosely defined and can be used in a variety of ways by people, companies, brands, and so on.

3. The more active a consumer is on the Internet, the more likely they participate in multiple social networks. Oftentimes, these people are influencers within a circle of friends and have a tremendous impact on the opinions of others.

4. Once information is shared on a social network, it is out there and can't easily be contained. Everything is out in the open and largely visible for other people to see.

5. Social media is best applied in addition to existing Internet marketing programs and alongside other Web assets. When building a strategy, you must think comprehensively.

6. The rules are still being made. Social media "etiquette" is still relatively immature. Tread carefully.

And the seventh and final truth involves the factors that contribute to social media usage. Everyone on social networks is motivated by some combination of the following human needs:

Love Finding love, keeping up with loved ones, and so forth

Self-expression/emotion Sharing life's details with friends

Sharing opinions/influencing friends Using social media as a platform for influencing opinions, usually about politics, religion, or other things we don't typically debate in person

Showing off Sharing life's successes and/or achievements with others

Fun/escapism/humor Using social media to get a good laugh

Memories and nostalgia Catching up with old friends and sharing old stories

Making money Using social networks primarily to support professional pursuits

As you can probably tell, the motivation for using Facebook varies significantly depending on your customer. Most companies with mature marketing departments spend a lot of time on customer personas to understand who customers are and how they behave. While this can, at times, trap a business into oversimplifying its customer base, this is one case where I think developing personas can be especially effective even for a smaller business.

Let's think of this in practical terms. For instance, single people will typically be far more interested in finding a love interest than a happily married person in their 40s. The happily married person may want to use Facebook to keep up with relatives and loved ones. A grandmother will be more interested in sharing pictures and stories about loved ones than her grandchildren will be. If you are going to create a successful marketing campaign, you're going to have to identify the people you are trying to reach and exactly how you can reach them more effectively. Figure out who your customer(s) are and what their motivation is for using Facebook. That exercise will help you craft a much better campaign for your target market, and it will also inform your ad copy and/or creative. We'll talk more about building the right social media campaign for your target audience later in this chapter.

What You Want: Viral Marketing

Execution of an effective viral marketing concept is the dream of many marketers today. We all dream of taking a great idea, a few hundred bucks, and a camcorder and turning that into an Internet sensation with a huge return on investment. Some people call it viral marketing, others call it word-of-mouth marketing. Whatever you call it, social media is the infrastructure that makes all of it far more possible today than ever before. With the codified relationships in social media and the canvas available for viewing interesting things, it isn't out of the question that you can reach a lot of people as long as you catch lightning in a bottle and create the right thing. One person's experience or recommendation can easily be entertainment for hundreds if not thousands of people. This is a cycle you obviously want working for you, not against you.

We've all seen things spread like wildfire over the Internet—jokes, chain letters, you name it. I remember in particular the dancing baby (www.cnn.com/TECH/9801/19/dancing.baby/index.html) from the early days of the Internet in 1996. We all felt the new technology taking the world by storm, but there was just something about that three-dimensional dancing baby that made us want to send it around to friends through e-mail. Today, most of us don't send jokes and such to friends on e-mail unless the content is really interesting, really funny, or relevant to someone's work or social life. Social media is far less restrictive, and it gives everyone a loudspeaker. Therein lies the opportunity for marketers. Anything you do or say, as well as anything your consumers do or say about you, has the potential to spread uncontrollably. People have the power to comment on your brand, product, or company and get the word out to a great number of people much more efficiently through social networks.

Burger King's Subservient Chicken campaign for the launch of the Tendercrisp Chicken Sandwich in 2004–2005 was an example of an effective, albeit well funded, viral marketing campaign. Burger King launched a commercial with a guy on his couch, directing another person in a chicken suit to act in various ways. It simultaneously launched a website at www.subservientchicken.com with a video of a man in a chicken suit (Figure 2.3). The chicken could be controlled by visitors, who would enter in a text box commands such as sit, fly, lay egg, even "march like a German soldier." The site and marketing effort created significant buzz. People hit the site repeatedly to figure out what commands they could give to the chicken. *Adweek* later reported that the site received over 14 million unique visitors through March 2005. Why? The campaign was creative, fun, and innovative yet it required visitors to participate and discover new things. Most importantly, it resulted in a successful launch of the Tendercrisp Chicken Sandwich, increased store traffic, and increased revenue for Burger King.

Figure 2.3 Subservient Chicken does the YMCA

Negative publicity can also spread like wildfire. United Airlines had a public relations disaster on their hands with the "United Breaks Guitars" video of July 2009. A disgruntled musician whose guitar was broken on a flight posted a video on YouTube (www.youtube.com/watch?v=5YGc4zOqozo) that got over 3 million views in the first two weeks. It was terrible publicity for United Airlines but great for the musician. On a smaller scale, you'll often see that disgruntled customers are willing to share negative experiences they've had with companies on the blogosphere, Twitter, and Facebook. Empowered customers, especially active users of social media, know the power of complaining in public, and they're starting to use social media to get what they want.

None of this is exactly new. We have been exposed to new ideas and new business opportunities for years. Our grandmothers attended Tupperware parties. We've all seen the pink Cadillacs from Mary Kay. Maybe you attended a college swarming with Amway representatives. Perhaps your first experience with multilevel marketing was Burke's "Confederated Products" pitch over dinner in the movie *Go*. While these pitches can, at times, be uncomfortable, multilevel marketing companies have done a fantastic job over the years of preaching their marketing message in an efficient manner. Now I'm not suggesting that you should turn your company into a multilevel marketing business, nor am I saying that you should annoy social media users into becoming evangelists for your company or product. But I do think that we have a lot of history that we can reference when considering how to be effective on social media.

What is new today is that all the interpersonal relationships are exposed online. We can keep up with friends, new products, companies, and brands in real time. We can share the experiences we have, good and bad, more efficiently than before. More of our lives than ever before —our choices, our problems, our successes—are recorded, communicated, and shared. In that sense, it challenges all of us as marketers to use social networks as a channel for customer engagement and for being more understanding, more human, and arguably more subtle.

Other Opportunities in Social Networking

Aside from viral marketing campaigns, social media affords you other opportunities to engage with customers. Some of these are regarded as traditional marketing functions while others may be in a different part of your company managed by other people. This is why later we'll discuss organizational dynamics and why it's to your long-term career benefit to become a social media evangelist inside your company. But for now, what types of things can your company and/or brand manage more effectively with social media?

Complaints It's becoming more and more common for people to use their loudspeaker to complain about bad customer service and/or bad experiences with products and services. You can't stop people from saying whatever they'd like, but you can aggressively work to remedy the situation to turn the unsatisfied customer into a satisfied one.

Praise It's rare for your customers to praise you, but in the case of especially good service or experiences, it does occasionally happen. This is a great opportunity for you to reinforce your attention to detail and customer service, as long as you tell people the good things about what you are marketing.

Lead generation/business development Social media is "the great democratizer"—that is, people are far more accessible than they were 10 years ago. They are blogging, commenting on different social networks, and making their thoughts and feelings known. As a salesperson or business developer, you have access to all the information you need on sales and business development targets. This is one of my favorite applications of social media.

Recommendations While Amazon.com was one of the first pioneers in this area, it has become common for companies to adopt their own recommendation strategy for products and services. Think *Consumer Reports* but in the form of individual testimonials. Some companies are more active than others in "managing" feedback.

Outbound communications/updates/mailing lists Skeptics say that social media is just a modern day mailing list. That would be true except for the fact that social media provides ample opportunity for people to share and comment on things they receive. It raises the bar for effective marketing communications. If you want people to talk about you positively in social media, you have to say something pretty compelling.

Fan clubs Your most passionate supporters will likely be willing to identify with your brand. In the past, clubs have been created to allow marketers to communicate regularly with fans. Now, using social media, costs are reduced to the amount of money it takes to produce your content. It's time to get creative.

> Don't be ashamed to reach out to businesspeople on Twitter and the blogosphere. Social media is a perfect icebreaker for conversations with prospective clients, customers, or partners. Just be sure to start a conversation, and don't sell until you've established some common ground.

Some of these things may be better executed inside existing social networks. Some may require you to add social features to existing websites. Others may require recalibration of your team to respond and engage with customers proactively. You'll have to consider all of these things when putting together a comprehensive social media campaign that gets people to act. Let's take some time to go through the universe of social networking as it stands today so you have a better grasp on the possibilities.

Campaign Ideas

Now that you have an idea of the basics of the different social networks, it's time to consider how you can use these services to improve your business. Opportunities are not just in the marketing arena. Social media technologies help people with similar interests or behaviors find and meet each other and share problems and solutions. You can use social media to improve efficiency in any customer or internal corporate communication. While these technologies are applicable to a variety of areas of your business, you are likely to make the biggest and most immediate impact by launching something in the marketing arena.

The key to success with social media marketing is mapping your business goals to the social networks that can make you most successful. How do you assess this? Ask yourself a few key questions when putting the plan together:

- Are there enough people in your target demographic on the social network?
- Is it common for people on the social network to say good things about your company or brand?

- Are there other ways for people on the social network to approve of your company or brand?

- Does your product fit the needs of your target demographic?

- Can you turn positives or negatives about your product into a viral marketing success?

But perhaps the most important question in any major corporation is about risk. Is your company willing to take a chance on social media marketing? I'm not talking necessarily about dollars and cents or coping with success. Is your company a cultural fit for the experimentation necessary to make social media work? For reasons outlined before in this book, social media is both hot and new. Facebook, Twitter, and other social media properties have been covered extensively in business magazines and other publications. Management at your company may see this as a huge opportunity or a potential for embarrassing failure. Like other examples on the Web, those who experiment ultimately win.

What types of things can you do with social media from a marketing perspective? I like to think of any new social media marketing project in terms of the sales funnel. After all, as marketers we are making sales easier, right? You'll need to figure out where your priorities lie in the sales funnel. Identify what is broken and fix it.

Prospecting How do we find people with a stated or latent need? How do we introduce them to our product or service for the first time? Or if they've heard of us already, how do we remind them about how great we are?

Customer list building They are as good as gold—lists of qualified customers who want to hear from us. Where can we find more people willing to listen to things we have to say? Can we get clever with social media to expand our reach?

Communicating with qualified customers Now that we have customers, how does social media make it easier for us to reinforce our message with them regularly? Are you able to produce the types of content that work best in social media?

Lead generation and e-commerce Do our efforts reinforce the sales process either by generating leads or by facilitating e-commerce purchases? If this is our main priority, are we able to measure the outcome and ROI (return on investment), and have we elegantly integrated it in a way that doesn't anger our customers?

Customer relationship management Social media affords opportunities to make your company or brand considerably more personable than the old ways of communicating via an 800 customer service phone line and postal mail. It's also a "Pandora's Box" of complaints that people are probably sharing via social media today.

Where Facebook Isn't Quite Enough: China

While Facebook enjoys being the largest social network in the United States, such is not the case throughout the rest of the world. The most glaring geographic example of Facebook not being "the only" place to be in social networking is in China.

If your company or organization is interested in doing business internationally, your marketing efforts must follow. You must also be keenly aware of what is happening in other countries.

Take, for instance, an April 2009 report on TechCrunch.com on the top social networks in China: (www.techcrunch.com/2009/04/05/chinese-social-networks-virtually-out-earn-Facebook-and-myspace-a-market-analysis/).

The study reveals that the top social networking sites in the United States, like Facebook, MySpace, LinkedIn, Twitter, don't even register in the top 10 social networking sites in the world's most populous country. This is particularly important when you consider that there are more Chinese people on the Internet than there are Americans. You could put together the best marketing campaign the world has ever seen, but if it runs only on Facebook, you won't make a dent in Chinese mindshare.

The following map shows the most popular social network by country. You can visit www.vincos.it/world-map-of-social-networks to see this map as it changes over time.

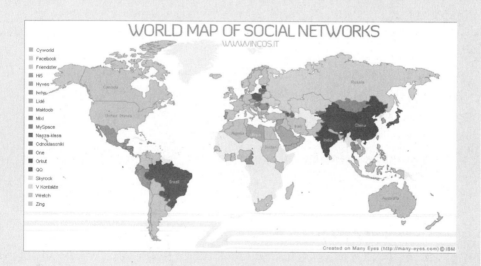

Most of these things require good social media campaign execution, but in all likelihood doing some of them well will also require cooperation from colleagues who manage your website, e-mail mailing lists, advertising budgets, or customer service department. This probably isn't a big deal for those of you in smaller companies. But in larger companies, each of these is often run separately by managers with different interests and goals for their teams. I've seen it happen too many times already—the lucky person who manages social media for their company is often the "object of everyone's affection," meaning that they will take a lot of negative feedback even in the best of circumstances. Only you will know if you should upset the apple cart or move things forward incrementally as you go.

Social media is the ultimate cross-functional discipline for a company. While it is most closely identified with marketing, it is truly more of a shift in information flow. If harnessed appropriately, social media can become a competitive differentiator for your business. If not, it will attract enemies and fail. You need to take charge of the situation to ensure that you get the most out of Facebook and other social media properties for your business. In the next chapter, we'll discuss exactly how you can do that. Let's now turn our attention to the basics of how Facebook works, from setup to friending and news feeds.

Facebook Basics

In the following sections, we'll go over some of the basic features of Facebook, including setting up an account, accumulating "friends," and the News Feed.

Account Setup

The entire setup process at www.facebook.com is designed to be as simple and intuitive as possible for the user. With more than 400 million accounts, you get a lot of data about streamlining the process and making things as easy as possible. On the home page, Facebook asks users for the basic information necessary to create an account/profile: first name, last name, e-mail address, password, gender, and full date of birth. (Note: we recommend once your profile is set up, you then go in and edit your personal information to only show your month and day of birth in your profile for security purposes.)

For the sake of creating examples in this book, we'll use this as an opportunity to create an account for Frank W. Furter (Figure 2.4).

After the user creates a profile, Facebook walks them through a process that is designed to make their experience richer and more interesting. First, the user is prompted to enter their e-mail login credentials. This allows Facebook to scan the user's Inbox to see if any friends already have a Facebook account. This is mostly self-serving for Facebook; it is a way to help people invite new people to Facebook more than it is a tool to help a user immediately find friends already on the social network.

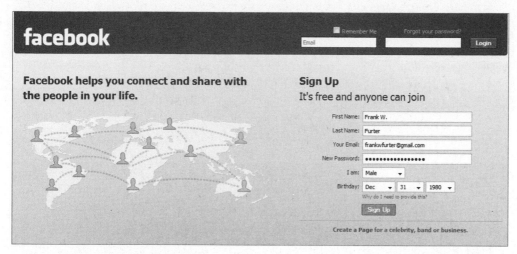

Figure 2.4 Facebook home page and account setup

Second, the user is asked to enter information on schools they attended or the company where they work. It's handy for a few reasons: Most of our personal connections are made in either school or the workplace. For Facebook purposes, it's especially handy because it is used as a way to help people find old friends or colleagues. And remember, one key to Facebook's success is the ability of people to discover something interesting or new there every day. So for Frank W. Furter, I'm going to enter my high school, Northwest Rankin, and the year I graduated, 1992. But here's where it gets interesting. After I enter my information, Facebook presents me with a list of people from my graduating class! I can now choose friends from the list and make them part of my "circle" on Facebook. We'll talk more about what that means later. You wrap up by adding a profile picture or importing one from a web cam.

That's it. It took about 5 minutes to go through the process of establishing a Facebook account and profile. The rest of the profile includes ways to enter additional information and expose it only to certain types of Facebook users. We'll go into more detail on that later too. For now, what are the main takeaways for a marketer?

- It's a simple process that takes only a few minutes. Just about anyone with basic computer literacy can become a Facebook user.

- Everything in the setup process is geared to helping users find friends on Facebook and build their network.

- An extraordinary amount of personal information is collected in the setup process, but it really is just the beginning. Users can provide a lot more information about themselves through Facebook after the profile is created. (And, keep in mind, you can choose how much or how little your Facebook friends can read about you via Facebook's granular privacy settings.)

- It's also stunningly easy to set up a fake profile. With simplicity and ease of use comes the ability for people to misrepresent themselves. Now there are some cases where this is valid, not to mention maybe even the right thing to do even though it is against Facebook's Terms of Use to maintain multiple accounts. More on that later. The takeaway here is to remember that it is very easy for people to set up a Facebook profile with any persona they would like.

Friending

The News Feed is an aggregate of your friends' activity you'll see every time you log in. Facebook uses algorithms to choose what they deem as most popular. Profiles, friends, and the News Feed are the key components to understanding how Facebook works and how information is shared across Facebook users. Friends are people who have the right to see information about you as well as anything you post.

You can probably tell how much someone uses Facebook by the number of friends they have. It isn't because Facebook is a tool for popular or outgoing people. But the more friends you have, the more active you'll be on Facebook and the more time you'll spend. It's a cycle that Facebook has perfected. Today, Facebook is the most popular destination on the Internet measured by time spent on the site. Eighty-seven million Americans spent an average of 4 hours and 39 minutes on Facebook in June 2009 according to Nielsen Online (`http://mashable.com/2009/07/14/facebook-ultimate-time-waster/`).

Building an active network of friends is the key to becoming someone who uses Facebook every day. But why exactly is that the case? What interactions does Facebook simplify or make more convenient?

Keeping up with old friends and acquaintances passively There is no more efficient way to keep up with people who aren't in your life on a regular basis. Facebook gives you the opportunity to know what is happening with old friends and acquaintances without having to call them, send a letter or e-mail message, or chat on an instant messaging service. This can be one tremendous benefit, especially if you are a social butterfly and are on good terms with a lot of people.

Learning things you didn't know about friends Profile data, status updates, and vocal support for other people, groups, or entities on Facebook can tell you a lot about people. Sometimes you find out good things and commonalities. Sometimes you learn things that result in disappointment. Either way, some people just really like knowing as much as they can about the people around them. Facebook makes it easy to communicate and snoop around to see what friends are saying and doing,

Commenting on friends' opinions, shared links, and random thoughts Facebook gives users the opportunity to share links, status updates, and random thoughts with friends. More importantly, any friend can comment on things that are exposed by another friend on Facebook. These are conversations that, in the physical world, often take place over lunch, a happy hour, or dinner with friends. While users can't necessarily have a good deep conversation on Facebook as they can in person, they can interact with basic off-the-cuff reactions to things they read and see.

Socializing through photos, events, playing games, and social applications Sometimes the basic features of Facebook don't allow for specific types of social interactions that people would like to engage in with their friends. Third-party applications have filled the void in many of these cases, while Facebook has also built additional features into the platform to make these social interactions possible.

None of these kinds of interactions, viewed on their own, are particularly significant. But collectively, they represent the value proposition of Facebook for an individual user. Nowhere else on the Internet can a person find more old friends and former colleagues in one convenient place. Friend someone, and they are in your circle. In the end, you'll be able to keep up with that friend as much as you'd like. If you're as busy as I am, you probably need this to appropriately manage your social life and prioritize your time.

The News Feed

The News Feed has emerged as probably the most important part of Facebook. It's the first thing users see upon login—a running list of the latest updates across the user's unique social graph. But it includes far more than updates from friends. The News Feed also includes updates from fan pages and third-party applications installed by the user. Items in the News Feed can include status updates, photos, events, and links to other sites or articles on the Internet. Friends or other fans can comment on any of these things or choose to "Like" them, so it is possible to see how people you don't even know react to updates.

So why is the News Feed so critically important to mastering Facebook? We spoke earlier in this chapter about Facebook becoming a "social" operating system of sorts. Traditionally, we've used operating systems to help us start our work day, write a paper, build a financial model, or pursue some other productive activity. But as computers and social networking get more intertwined in our lives, it is possible that we'll start our day not with work, but rather with casual social interaction with friends on

Facebook. The jumping-off point for us won't be the traditional "desktop" but rather the Internet browser running Facebook.

This is especially possible as the News Feed becomes more and more useful. Today it contains primarily updates on friends, but it could very easily become a filter through which we get content that interests us from all over the Web, from companies, businesses, or brands that interest us as well as from our friends and business colleagues. As it includes more and more information, it becomes more and more useful, especially if controls for filtering content get better over time. As you can tell from the screen shot of my News Feed in Figure 2.5, there is a lot here that can keep someone busy!

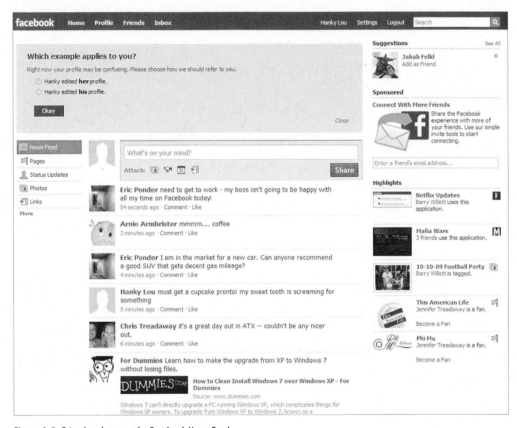

Figure 2.5 Friend updates on the Facebook News Feed

A significant and increasing number of people are beginning to use Facebook in this manner, especially in younger demographic groups. That's why being in the News Feed is so important. Breaking into the News Feed is currently the easiest and most important consideration for brands and companies looking to establish a presence and identity on Facebook. Your biggest fans, not to mention future customers, are on Facebook every day. If you aren't in the consciousness of prospective customers on Facebook, odds are your competitors are or will be. The one thing all of them see is the News Feed.

We are currently in a period of time when a lot of companies and brands have recognized that they need to have a presence on Facebook. Most of the time, this is in the form of a fan page, Facebook's preferred type of landing page/presence for companies, organizations, and nonprofits. More and more, brands engage with customers on another form of media (TV/radio commercial, e-mail campaign, Twitter, etc.) and ask them to become a fan. I've always found the nomenclature a little clunky when it comes to some brands or products. It makes more sense to me if you're talking about Willie Nelson, my favorite college football team, or Reese's Peanut Butter Cups. But that said, a lot of people are scrambling to establish a minimal presence not knowing entirely where things are headed.

Today, the News Feed is both an important and underutilized part of Facebook. When I consult businesses on how to use Facebook, I make sure they say something every day just to remind fans and supporters of their company or brand. This "something" has to be useful; you shouldn't be selling your products every time you say something on a social network. We'll have more on tactics and best practices when we discuss fan pages in more detail in Chapter 5.

Develop a Facebook Strategy and Measure Success

3

We've set the stage of the social media landscape and introduced the critically important concepts of the News Feed, profiles, and friends on Facebook. Now we'll use these concepts to develop a strategy to get you started. Chapters 4–7 will walk you through executing the strategy—but execution means nothing without a good plan to get started.

Chapter Contents

Defining Your Facebook Presence

It seems like a relatively simple concept, but a lot of companies struggle with determining what their presence on Facebook and other social media will be. Should you lead with brand? Product? Information on your business? Newsletter content? What will resonate with customers in a meaningful way that will compel them to listen to you and share your wisdom with their friends? If you are struggling with this, you aren't alone. It isn't easy to translate your assets into a social media success story.

When helping clients with their social media problems, we've had the most success starting off by thinking about the exact reasons a consumer interacts with the company. What is the value proposition of your company or product? What does the product provide that competitive products don't provide? Do you spend more time marketing the actual benefits of your product, or do you market a lifestyle to which people aspire? Facebook won't cure problems with a product or brand, but it will give an opportunity to reach out in new and interesting ways that, to some extent, reinforce what people already think. Therefore, it's pretty important to think through your most successful customer campaigns and find commonalities across them. If you are trying to establish a campaign that highlights differences between your products and your competitors' products, you should probably undergo the same exercise for them as well. It sounds almost elementary, but you really need to think critically about your business, where you fit in, what you have (or should have) learned from past campaigns, and how you can sell your vision in the context of social media.

Understanding Who Your Customers Are

Empathy with target customers is another key part of the brainstorming process. What do they want from you and your company? More important, what *don't* they want from you? Product stewards (product managers, marketing managers, evangelists, executives, and so on) like you put their lives into improving products, marketing efforts, sales performance, and so on. But as such, you can also be too close to empathize with customers who get marketing messages at every turn—most of which are annoying, intrusive, or flat-out offensive. They come in commercials, Internet advertising, product placement, email, social media…you name it. Good Facebook campaigns will enhance a customer's life in a meaningful way.

Those of you in larger companies have probably spent a fair amount of time or resources thinking through customer segmentation and personas. Personas are a way to humanize a customer segment by making some generalized assumptions about how individuals in certain segments live, what they do, how they think, and so on. The sample personas in "Sample Personas for Acme Foods" illustrate an example of personas for a fictional frozen food company.

Personas are great for kick starting the creative process. Although they can sometimes be a crutch used to oversimplify thinking, they can be very helpful in thinking about customer engagement.

Featured Case: Sample Personas for Acme Foods

In this fictional example, Acme Foods is looking to understand different segments of its market by creating personas that reflect the reasons customers are interested in their products. Here are a few examples.

Debbie is a 41-year-old housewife in Cedar Rapids, Iowa. She is married, has three children under the age of eight, and cares for her aging mother who is being treated for lung cancer. Her husband travels for business three days per week. She is responsible for all the household chores, cooking, and meal planning, so she doesn't have much time for the Internet, although she is a regular e-mail user. Her family eats at home six days per week. Her children are overweight, so she is increasingly concerned about nutrition and portion control.

Brock is a 22-year-old college graduate in Palo Alto, California. He is single, and he just entered the workforce after graduating with honors from Stanford University. He just got a lease on his first apartment, and now he is learning to cook and prepare meals on his own. The only problem is that he is now busier than he has ever been. He buys food at the grocery store mostly based on convenience. His refrigerator is empty, but his freezer is full. He keeps up with friends on Facebook, and he watches more YouTube than live television.

Annie is a 66-year-old retiree currently living in Savannah, Georgia. She enjoys playing golf, spending time at the beach, catching up with old friends, and visiting with her 11 grandchildren. Her husband is now diabetic, so they don't enjoy dining out as much as they did years ago. Annie has never enjoyed cooking—she looks for shortcuts in the kitchen wherever she can find them. The retirement community provides packaged meals three times a week. She now frequents the computer center to learn how to use the Internet.

Jill is a 31-year-old attorney in Bristol, Connecticut. Now that she's settled into her career, she's taken up cooking as a hobby. She likes using fresh ingredients whenever possible, but she always has backup ingredients in her freezer just to be safe. She has read about the health benefits of frozen foods, but she remains a skeptic. She aspires to open a restaurant later in life. She just found Facebook, but she's afraid of sharing personal data on the Internet.

Mapping Customer Needs to Effective Tactics

Some tactics will resonate well with certain personas, and others obviously won't. This is an important consideration—social media and Facebook campaigns can't be expected to (and likely won't) solve your problems across all customer segments. Pick and choose opportunities, and make sure you are reaching those customers in friendly, helpful ways that map to your brand or product. Some tactics will work, but others could offend your customers. Don't be so close to your social media effort that you fail to see when your tactics actually bother the customer. Facebook and social media are interesting, innovative ways to reach out to your customers, but poor execution can certainly backfire on you. Think customers first and your business second, and you'll probably be more successful.

How does this work in practicality? Let's think through a few examples. A local home builder wants to take better advantage of social media. So, start by asking the primary and critical question, "What do customers of the home builder want?" They want the best house they can get per their prioritized purchasing criteria: size, neighborhood, convenience to work/play/children/family, price, and so on. How will they find this house? Good question. There are a lot of ways people can find houses. Maybe they hear about houses from a friend, perhaps they drive by properties in a certain neighborhood and find what they want, perhaps they find a great deal in the newspaper, or maybe a friendly real estate agent has suggested properties for them. No matter what, it's fragmented and oftentimes difficult to find a great deal. So, the customer's main motivations in this case are convenience, knowledge, time savings, and assistance with a very important purchasing decision.

Keep the home builder in the back of your mind, and now think about a different example—a popular local restaurant that has a unique local flair. What do customers of this restaurant want? We'd venture to say they occasionally want a great meal at a great price. But the restaurant is more to local customers than just another place to eat. It's a lifestyle, a part of the fabric of that city that makes it a special place to live. It's a brand of the people, and the association with it speaks volumes. So, the customer's main motivation to engage with this restaurant is one of affiliation, personality, and appreciation for local business.

These are two totally different cases where customers are motivated differently and where appropriate and effective Facebook marketing tactics would differ. Customers for houses want totally different things than people showing support for a unique local business. And perhaps more important, people make a one-time decision to purchase a home, whereas they may eat at the same restaurant 30 times a year. So, the characteristics of the business—transaction cost, transaction frequency, local differentiation, and brand affinity—all have a significant impact on the tactics that would make sense. You'll see this in more detail as we walk you through the different marketing elements that Facebook provides.

 When in doubt about your customer, keep asking questions. Whether you're in the brainstorming process or in the middle of a focus group, it doesn't hurt to keep asking questions until you get answers that clarify the motivations of others.

Close-Up of a Successful Social Media Campaign

We've discussed the differences in the various social networks, and we've covered some considerations for determining what your customers really want through segmentation and personas. Now it's time to map those needs to things that you can effectively deliver in Facebook and social media.

We'll now take a moment to focus on marketing strategies by highlighting some of the key features of the Facebook fan page. We'll use the example of the Threadless site/fan page, which has more than 100,000 fans (http://facebook.com/threadless). Threadless.com releases new graphic T-shirts weekly that are designed, submitted, and rated by their own community. Since Threadless is so dependent upon its customers/ community for its product and for the content created around its products, it's easy to understand why Threadless views Facebook as a critical element in its overall marketing strategy.

Threadless provides several examples of the components of a successful Facebook marketing plan:

Step 1: Defining the audience As with any successful marketing campaign, it's critical that you accurately define the audience on which you're focusing your efforts. Threadless is obviously focused on tech-savvy kids and young adults. However, it's not as though Threadless had to start from scratch with this first component of its Facebook campaign strategy. The company's product planning and management already took this into account. The audience was already defined as part of the product planning and management process. The only thing most companies will have to do here is translate their audience definitions to the appropriate content on the Facebook platform. The content on the Threadless fan page demonstrates that the company has at least considered how customers in their target market will use Facebook and respond to a fan page.

Step 2: Determining the goals and objectives Your next step is to determine what the goals and objectives are for your Facebook presence. Is it simply a means to enhance customer service, or do you expect to see an increase in sales? Do you expect to see a direct correlation between your activities on Facebook and conversions on your e-commerce website? Knowing what your goals are is only half the challenge here. It's also important to have a grasp on how to measure your efforts. Make sure that you know what "success" looks like. Put metrics into place that allow you to gauge success or failure on Facebook as relates to your efforts.

One way Threadless is using Facebook is as a direct marketing channel. However, they haven't lost sight of what the platform's original intent was: socializing and communication between friends. But as you review its profile, you'll find several elements that have strong calls to action with the clear intention being a conversion or purchase. In this situation, it would be easy for Threadless to use a basic website analytics application such as Google Analytics to track referrals from Facebook to its primary e-commerce website. Threadless can then follow the user's breadcrumb to derive the percentage of conversions that originate from Facebook.com. Reviewing the following source code shows that there's a high likelihood that it's doing just that:

```
<script type="text/javascript">
var gaJsHost = (("https:" == document.location.protocol) ? "https://
ssl." : "http://www.");

document.write(unescape("%3Cscript src='" + gaJsHost + "google-
analytics.com/ga.js' type='text/javascript'%3E%3C/script%3E"));
</script>
<script type="text/javascript">
try {
var pageTracker = _gat._getTracker("UA-3478547-1");
pageTracker._trackPageview();
} catch(err) {}</script>
<script type="text/javascript">
pageTracker._trackEvent('sale_homepage', 'ab_test', 'A'); </script>
```

Not only do you see that Threadless is using Google Analytics as its website tracking tool, but Threadless has defined a `sale_homepage` page on this landing page for the site.

Step 3: Setting configuration options Facebook provides more settings and configuration options than any other major social network in use today. It is critical that you understand what these settings do and the flexibility Facebook gives you. For instance, which tab will be your default landing page? The default landing page is the first page that a user sees when coming to your Facebook fan page. How many people do you want to give administrative access to for editing your page? Will you allow customers and users to leave comments and posts on your Wall? In this case, Threadless accepts the risks inherent to allowing people to post commentary to its Wall and allows visitors to share thoughts on the different T-shirt designs that they post on the Threadless fan page. This brings us to our next point: is your page compelling? We'll talk more about fan page settings in Chapter 5, "Month 2: Establish an Effective Corporate Presence with Pages and Groups."

Step 4: Creating a compelling page After people find your fan page, your marketing strategy has achieved only part of what it should. Threadless encourages interaction by encouraging people to comment on the designs of its newest T-shirts and by allowing them to post pictures and videos wearing Threadless merchandise. Threadless posts information about sales that they currently have going on and markets contests that they are running. This provides the user with a great combination of social interaction with other people who have similar interests and provides Threadless with a vehicle where they can directly market to a captive audience.

Facebook allows most applications to run as tabs on the top of the fan pages. Threadless takes advantage of this feature by providing a rich user experience and extra value for users through event postings and discussion boards. On the Events tab, users find postings of events that are of interest to consumers of Threadless T-shirts. In the discussion board area, people discuss issues that they have with customer service, pop culture, getting designs featured, and a myriad of other topics that may or may not directly involve the Threadless brand directly. As it turns out, the majority of discussion threads do have some relationship to Threadless and its products. The benefit for the brand? Threadless is nurturing its own audience within the virtual walls of its Facebook fan page. It has created a destination point that allows people to come in, feel comfortable, and socialize. All the while, more than 100,000 Facebook users are being exposed to the Threadless brand, which keeps it "top of mind" in the consumer's psyche.

Defining Your Social Media "Product"

One thing that is common across different social media campaigns is the fact that each has a fairly well-defined set of rules by which they operate. The social media presence is, in effect, an interactive online "product." The medium is a combination of Facebook, Twitter, other social media destinations, and the Web. All of it is consumed by a computer or cellular device. Customers, fans, and followers are found for the "product" through a variety of means, such as viral marketing, Internet marketing, email marketing, social network marketing, and word-of-mouth marketing. There is an implicit contract between the company and the customer that the "product" will perform as expected and that the company won't violate the terms under which the customer was first attracted to the product. Your thinking should assume that your social media presence is a product of its own that needs care, maintenance, and performance metrics that will help guide decision making. This social media "product" enhances a consumer's experience with the product or service you are trying to sell or the brand you are trying to manage.

Different situations in business require different tactics. Some tactics are off-limits to you as a marketer of a certain kind of product, while others are fair game. You shouldn't get too critical of yourself or of your company, nor should you significantly change what your product, service, or brand represents to the marketplace. Translate what you do to the social media context and experiment on the edges. The "Quick-Start Guide for Social Media" sidebar should kick start your creativity and guide your thinking as you brainstorm project ideas.

Quick-Start Guide for Social Media

Maybe you are approaching social media for the first time, maybe you have inherited a failed project, or maybe you are resurrecting some old ideas. Whatever the case, sometimes you need quick answers to help you see opportunities and make quick decisions.

Get good answers for the following 10 questions before you decide how to engage. We highly recommend this exercise before getting started regardless of whether you will run your first project in-house or with the help of a consultant.

1. What is most recognizable about your brand? This can be a person, a place, a logo, a jingle, and so on.

2. Does your brand have a spokesperson or character who "is" what you are trying to sell? If not, are you open to creating one?

3. What is the goal of your project? Sales/e-commerce? Improved image in your market? Better customer service and satisfaction?

4. What specific metrics will you use to measure success?

5. When discussing the opportunity in social media with executives at your company, do they view social media as an opportunity, a risk, or an unknown?

6. Does your company or brand have official policies for blogging, employee activity on social media, and outreach to customers? Is it centralized or decentralized?

7. What types of content do you have that would be interesting to share with social media users?

8. Are you willing to share interesting content from third-party sources on the Web with your customers?

9. Creating your campaign, maintaining it, tracking metrics, and making adjustments will take time and expertise. Do you have interested people in your company who are willing and able to do this work?

10. What is your backup plan in case the social media project fails or doesn't meet the goals of your organization? Who can you call for an objective third-party opinion if you have a problem?

Specific Applications of Facebook Marketing

Facebook offers several options and features for marketing your product or company. While we're discussing developing your social media product on Facebook, it is helpful to take a look at how some other brands, companies, and organizations have utilized these features.

Advertising

When Charlene Li was an analyst at Forrester Research, she produced a series of case studies where she showcased the differences between traditional marketing and social media marketing. The key take-away from the series of case studies was that marketing on Facebook requires communication, not advertising. Now, advertising of any kind requires some method of interruption. This can come in the form of a commercial interrupting a television show or radio program, a billboard interrupting the landscape on your commute home, a large decal on the floor in the grocery store interrupting your shopping experience, or any other myriad of creative techniques advertisers have devised to turn your attention from the content or task at hand toward a message from a client who wants your attention.

One of the challenges with advertising on Facebook when the platform first introduced ads was the relatively low response rates from users. Although Facebook's pay-per-click model of advertising offers competitive rates as compared to similar platforms on Google, Yahoo, Microsoft Advertising, and others, Facebook users have been consistently obstinate when it comes to responding to advertising on its profile pages. As an advertiser/marketer, Facebook offered a unique challenge. It has an extremely large, desirable audience that refused to click ads.

To be sure, there are plenty of options for you as a marketer to consider when it comes to purchasing advertising on Facebook. For instance, as with most sites, you can purchase standard IAB (Interactive Advertising Bureau) ad units across the Facebook.com domain. Depending upon advertisement, you can expect a click-through rate of anywhere between 4 percent and 26 percent, according to Forester Research. That's a huge range, but even on the low end the news feeds deliver impressive results.

Companies and organizations also have the option of creating Facebook Ads. Facebook Ads (previously called Facebook Flyers) are nothing more than self-serve advertisements (`www.facebook.com/advertising/`). Advertising with Facebook Ads allows users to make their own custom-designed ads on Facebook at low prices. Users have the option of creating Facebook Ads on either a cost-per-click (CPC) or cost-per-thousand (CPM) model.

These are just a few of the advertising options available on Facebook. To be sure, all of these options should be considered when developing your Facebook marketing plan.

Engagement Ads

Keep in mind the entire Facebook platform has been developed to encourage and facilitate communications. Enter the Facebook Engagement Ad. Dell Computers uses Engagement Ads to provide users with the ability to engage with its "Social Media for Small Business" ads in the same way the users interact with other content on Facebook.

Through video-enabled Engagement Ads, Dell allows members to leave comments on the ads that then show up with their friends' news feeds or sign up as a "fan" of a Dell product or marketing channel via Facebook's "pages" feature. Additionally, if a brand signs up for it, an Engagement Ad can be used as a vehicle to allow Facebook users to send a brand-related virtual gift to a friend.

3M used many of the features of Facebook pages in its marketing strategy to launch the Scotch Shoe, a tape dispenser designed to look like a Mary Jane shoe.

Although many in the company were excited about the launch of this new product, targeted at a female market, budget constraints put traditional media out of reach and made promoting the product a challenge. Although many in the organization were skeptical, the 3M marketing team chose Facebook and the channel to launch this unique new product.

"We have the sales and market share, but with a product like tape, it is difficult to get your consumers passionate about your product," said Brian Stephens, who handles e-marketing for 3M Canada's consumer and office division. Nonetheless, 3M had to create product awareness and generate buzz for this new product to sell.

3M chose to market the Scotch Shoe on Facebook for a few different reasons. Facebook is Canada's most popular social networking platform. Along with more than 350 million users worldwide, Facebook is home to more than 12 million active Canadian users. In Canada alone, Facebook boasts more than 7.5 billion impressions per month.

Marketing on Facebook is free. Of course, there are costs involved with ad creation, copywriting, design, marketing, planning, execution, campaign and community maintenance, and more. But creating a business fan page costs nothing on Facebook. When you are on a budget, it's hard to beat free.

3M created a Facebook fan page. This gave its customers and fans a targeted destination for free, which allowed 3M to not worry about designing and developing a new product page on the 3M website, saving scarce financial resources for better use elsewhere. On the fan page, 3M provided fans with all the relevant information about the product, such as images and videos, store listings, and product availability. The Facebook page also allowed 3M to survey, post discussions to facilitate dialogue, develop and nurture relationships with community influencers, and collect feedback about the product.

3M produced and promoted contests to drive traffic to its fan page. One contest incentivized users to become fans by offering a gift card for a shoe store. Another contest awarded the winner a free Scotch Shoe. In both cases, the contests were directly targeted to the product's key demographic. This, in turn, encouraged interaction and engagement on the fan page. To enter the contests, users were required to enter commentary and feedback about the Scotch Shoe on the fan page, thereby dramatically accelerating the amount of exposure the fan page received via the social media ecosystems of the product's fans. Remember, any time a user entered a comment on the fan page for the Scotch Shoe, that comment was exposed to every person who followed that user via their news feed, which shows up on the home page of every single person who is Facebook friends with the Scotch Shoe's fan page member. (See: `http://www.facebook.com/ScotchTapeCanada`.)

3M launched three different Engagement Ads during this campaign. As part of the marketing strategy, 3M closely monitored the performance of its Engagement Ads and adjusted the rotation and targeting on a regular basis. The result? The Scotch Shoe sold out almost immediately in every store that stocked the product. The Scotch Shoe Facebook page has more than 21,000 fans and thousands of wall comments. According to MarketingProfs, the Engagement Ads created for the campaign delivered more than 1.5 million impressions and 300,000 clicks. (Source: `http://www.marketingprofs.com/casestudy/137`.)

3M didn't have big marketing dollars to execute this campaign. Scotch certainly isn't one of the sexier brands like Apple, BMW, or Nike, but it was still able to run a successful Facebook marketing campaign and hold contests that engaged its customers without giving away prizes that would have otherwise been cost prohibitive. The 3M marketing team used Facebook as an effective, low-cost platform to successfully launch a product and create new relationships with its customers.

Your Facebook To-Do List

Now turn your attention to execution. What are the specific tasks required to establish and maintain a successful presence on social networks? Figure 3.1 shows the basic workflow for social network marketing.

Figure 3.1 Social media workflow

The first thing you may notice is that the decision to create a campaign kicks off a work process that is iterative. Welcome to the Web! At each stage of the process, you really should have the next step in the back of your mind. It's rare that one of these steps takes a significant amount of effort, but the aggregate can get time-consuming, especially if you are running or managing multiple campaigns or if you are taking advantage of several social networks at the same time. Let's go through what each part of the social media workflow really means.

Set Up Campaign

The entire workflow starts with a concept—an idea that will drive the execution of the work along with the tone of the project. So, it's safe to say that when you are getting started, you are squarely in creativity mode. As you define your "product," what will the experience be for an end user? Can you do something special that will inspire your audience? Take the Subservient Chicken example from Chapter 2, "What Is Facebook?" What does Burger King have to do with a man in a chicken suit taking orders from an Internet user? Not a lot, unless you want your brand to be fun and lighthearted.

Of all parts of the process, this is the one best suited for outsourcing to creative agencies. Creative professionals can really help by contributing unconventional ideas that may resonate unexpectedly well with your customer base. If you are going to go this route, *don't* interfere with the creative process, but *do* make sure you task the agency to come up with a variety of ideas for you to consider. Nobody succeeds every time out—baseball players, quarterbacks in football, or creatives—so don't look for one great idea but, rather, a few concepts that can drive your final decision. And remember that *you* are the one making the decision. At the end of the day, you are the customer. You need to be able to execute on the idea you choose, and that idea has to fit what you intuitively know about the brand or product that you manage on a regular basis.

Procure Content

Content is the lynchpin to successful social media. With all the noise out there, you need to have an interesting or useful voice, and you have to communicate regularly enough to stay relevant. This can be in the form of articles, essays, status updates, podcasts, videos, music, and so on. Fortunately, norms on the Internet have evolved in such a way that you don't have to create your own unique content every time you want to say something. So much content is available on the Internet that you can sometimes just point to content produced by others. Alternatively, you can use existing content that you've created for other reasons. You can commission new content for use on social media. There are a lot of strategic considerations here that we'll cover later in this book. For now, understand that you'll need to find, repurpose, or create new content (pictures, video, podcasts, status updates, blog posts, and so on) if you're going to effectively engage with customers via social media.

Update Content

Having the content certainly isn't enough. You need to make sure you use the content effectively. And since social media is truly interactive, you're going to get both direct and indirect comments and feedback. How will you keep content updated and respond to feedback? Who will manage this process? These questions certainly need to be addressed well in advance of launching your Facebook campaign. You need at least an understanding that guides the social media presence—the hierarchy of people who are allowed to make updates, what they are/are not allowed to say, scenarios they are not allowed to address, and so on. Without understanding across your organization, you are implicitly creating a situation that turns the social media effort into a political minefield. This is particularly important given that social media is at the intersection of sales, marketing, business development, customer service, and customer satisfaction.

Track Metrics

Someone, somewhere in the process, needs to update the daily metrics that are created as a result of your activity. Some of this already happens when metrics are generated for activity on your website. In all likelihood, your team is already using one of a number of statistics or web analytics vendors (Omniture, Coremetrics, Webtrends, or even Google Analytics). These products track unique users, page views, and other important data that tells the tale about how your websites are used. The use of social networks similarly creates a rich data set that tells you how customers receive your social media presence and campaigns. Some of it is readily available by just scanning a fan page, a group, or a profile. Other data can be found in Facebook Insights. One thing is certain—critical data is probably located in a number of places. You need to pull appropriate data into a spreadsheet or database so you can analyze it appropriately. We'll look more closely at the importance of tracking metrics in several places in this book and in detail in Chapter 9, "The Analytics of Facebook."

Analyze and Revise

After your social media presence has run for a period of time, you'll have a rich set of data that can tell you whether your effort is succeeding. Success may be an absolute goal such as 2,500 Facebook fans or an additional 5,000 unique visitors for a website during a month, or it may be a trending goal like 10 incremental fans per day after 90 days. Progress against these goals will need to be judged based on all the relevant data. For instance, maybe you are getting a lot of traffic to your Facebook presence, but it mostly comes from paid advertising, when you need something a little more "viral." So, you've achieved your goals, but you've done so in a way that isn't sustainable and won't make your boss happy.

Revise: Set Up Campaign, Take Two

Once you determine whether you can improve or whether you've maxed out the benefits of your efforts, you'll know what you need to change. Changes can come in the form of increased/decreased advertising, demand generation from e-mail marketing or other sources, more/less regular communication, better coordination with other web properties, or a different type of messaging altogether. Revisions are OK and a natural part of the process. Rarely does a social media presence launch without any revisions. You should expect to go through a few rounds of the entire process before you figure out the sweet spot where customers respond to your efforts.

It takes a special person to know how to do all of these things well, especially considering that success relies upon both creativity and proficiency with data analysis. Usually people are *either* right-brained or left-brained, not both! It's an important dynamic to understand—these projects are generally best run by people who naturally complement each other.

Diversity of Opinion and Strengths

Most successful marketing projects are well executed across several criteria. The campaign meets customer needs or wants and is true to the core values of the business. The value proposition of the product or service is communicated effectively. The design of the campaign is well done, and the brand elements are elegantly integrated. Communication with customers is effective and fits the needs of the campaign. Numbers are captured to reflect the success of the campaign, and your colleagues instinctively know how and when to act to make modifications.

What we've described is, in simple terms, a successful marketing campaign. Yet few people have skills across all these areas to be a one-man or one-woman marketing machine. Why? It takes a variety of different skills, and they rarely appear in a single person. Some of it is education—for example, you don't typically expect educated engineers to be the most fun at a cocktail party. Similarly, you'd never want a born salesperson to brand your company. By tapping into a variety of people with different strengths, you'll do two things. You'll get some overlap of responsibility so no one person can take down your marketing campaign. You'll also get a diversity of opinion that can make the entire project run more smoothly.

Now that you know the basic requirements for a Facebook marketing campaign, it's time to make your plan consumable in your organization and get started.

Month 1: Create the Plan and Get Started

4

Now that we've gone through all the basic background information you need, it's time to get started on a project. Getting your colleagues comfortable with social media and all it entails—the good and the bad—is a key factor for organizational buy-in and ultimately success. Remember, these projects involve a lot of trial and error. Your company and your management team have to be comfortable with that dynamic if you are going to have the flexibility you need to find a successful social media marketing strategy for your organization.

Chapter Contents

Week 1: Lay the Groundwork

Early in any project, you really should be in fact-finding mode more than anything else. You should research what other people have done and look for examples of companies that execute well. Read everything you can about successful and failed campaigns. Remember that there are a lot of examples of both out there. You can find them by just searching to see what popular brands and your competitors are doing. The best and worst cases tend to get covered in the blogosphere. Week 1 is all about doing due diligence without even getting into the details of what Facebook or other social media services can do for you. Find out what your colleagues think and what people in the industry are saying about customer engagement via social media.

Monday: Set Project Goals

At the highest level, what are you trying to achieve with the project? We talked about a few of these opportunities earlier in the book—additional sales, increased revenue, lower marketing/customer engagement costs, improved customer service, collecting feedback quicker, and so on. Most of the time, you and your management team will want all of them, but you'll really need one or two. It's better to be selective about your goals and nail them than it is try to solve every problem for every constituent in your business. Table 4.1 presents some of the types of things you can do with a social media campaign, how you would measure it, and examples.

▶ **Table 4.1** Examples of Opportunities in Social Media

Goal	Metrics	Example
Increased sales	Incremental revenue	Social media campaign launched specifically to sell/market products; URLs set up to identify social media as channel that found the customer
Improved customer service	Increased number of service queries handled, faster response time	Facebook fan page and Twitter account established for customers to ask questions of your business
Save money on marketing or advertising	Lower $/touch vs. other marketing options	Facebook advertising campaign run to compare costs with traditional marketing efforts
Earn more blogger, journalist, or analyst attention	Number of blog posts mentioning the organization or product Number of articles written Number of analyst mentions	Informal engagement 1:1 with people active in social media (Facebook, Twitter, and so on) to inform them of a new product, service, or event

Then there is always the concept of *buzz*, which is the amorphous term used to broadly describe a palpable increase in the positive responses to a product or company in social media. You know that you're getting good buzz when you find that people are saying a lot about you and you haven't really done anything to force it. We find that people use the term when they like what they see but don't quite understand why there is a positive response from customers or pundits in the marketplace. This isn't a criticism—you may conduct a campaign that doesn't immediately result in significant increases in your metrics only to find that, for whatever reason, there is considerably more buzz several weeks or months after the fact. Social media is a handy and relatively inexpensive way to introduce a concept to people well in advance of a product launch or a major marketing push. Buzz is the indirect benefit of those efforts.

Overall, if your company has been active on Facebook and social media, your company is probably more sophisticated at setting goals and measuring success. The bar to achieve success may be pretty high. If it's your first project, the goal may just be as simple as learning what to do and what to expect in the future. Learning is a perfectly reasonable goal, especially if you keep your costs low and your tolerance high.

When working with clients, we often ask them to visualize the 15-minute presentation they are giving to superiors to update them on the status of the project. How will that meeting go? What numbers will support your success? What specific results will help them understand that the project has been a success based on your strategy, your recommendations, and your effort? You know your management chain better than anyone else—it's best to think through their expectations at the beginning of a project so you can guide it to success.

Tuesday: Analyze Stakeholder Needs

Ideally, you'd take a full day here to interview key stakeholders to understand their perspectives. But if you're short on time, you may be able to learn just as much by putting together a questionnaire that your colleagues can answer easily via e-mail. Make a list of all the people who may be impacted even peripherally by your work on Facebook and social media. I'd be as inclusive as you can when compiling your list: people in your management chain, colleagues who work on different products, people in organizations that support the marketing or sales effort, and so on. The last thing you need is to be blindsided by influential colleagues who think they were not adequately consulted. These can be your harshest critics.

Start by putting a list of questions together. You want to understand how they view you, your project, your organization, your product, and the nature of the work. Some relevant questions to ask include the following:

- What does the person think of social media?
- Is the person an active Facebook or Twitter user?
- What are some of the company's best campaigns for dealing directly with customers?
- What opportunities does the company have to improve its customer engagement?
- What should your company be doing on social networks?
- What would social media success mean to them?

Then there are questions you probably don't want to ask directly but can impact the landscape of your project:

- If the person is an influencer on marketing decisions, does the person think that it is a waste of time?

- How will this project increase their workload? If so, are they aware of it, and are they prepared to deal with it?

- Does the person truly want to see the project succeed? Will the person be difficult when you need help advancing your project?

- Will you get the benefit of the doubt from this person in executive or management reviews?

You're doing a few things with the stakeholder analysis. First, you are comparing your assumptions on project goals/priorities to the perception of your colleagues. You may find that the goals you have set for the project are significantly different from the goals that other people have for the project. This is your opportunity to confront the differences and make a course correction if necessary. Second, you want to learn who your friends are within your company. Let's face it—all companies are in some ways political. Some people have authority; others either want it or think they deserve it. It's the nature of business today. You're probably aware of the political minefield in which you work, but it's better to extend the olive branch to as many people as you can as early as you can. You don't want to find out that certain people in your company have a political aversion to your work at the time when your success or failure is being judged. We generally advise middle managers to do what they can at this stage to build consensus around the project. It's a great way to give yourself enough time to learn as you go and get the benefit of the doubt should anything go sideways.

Wednesday: Analyze Customer Needs

Your work earlier this week to determine project goals and the motivations driving or influencing the project inside your company should begin to give you some ideas about campaigns. Now it's time to take all of that to the very people you rely upon to turn your idea into a marketing success. Granted, as a marketer, you should always be engaging with your customers to learn about their needs. But translating that to social media success can be a bit tricky. You'll need direct feedback from relatively disinterested customers in your target demographics to further understand the opportunities and limitations.

The best way to do this doesn't generally involve a lot of money. Do things that are relatively simple and almost immediately actionable. Find people you already know in your target demographics, and give them a cup of coffee or ice cream in exchange for a 30-minute chat. It's essentially your own focus group. If you'd rather have a larger set of opinions, create a survey on SurveyMonkey or a similar service. It's easy to get paralyzed by not having resources to conduct a professional, statistically valid study, and sometimes there are good reasons to conduct such things. But this probably isn't one of those places. As we've mentioned in this book, the Web is the land of experimentation. Users will vote with their presence, and you'll see the results in the number of fans or followers you have, page views, unique users, comments, and so on. Your strategy should be to act on imperfect or incomplete data early in the project and be more reliant on mountains of data as the project matures.

When you get access to your subjects, you're going to have to ask them a lot of questions:

- What do they do on social networks?
- How much time do they spend on Facebook? How often do they log into Facebook? And what do they do once they get there?
- What annoys them about Facebook?
- Are they a Facebook fan or Twitter follower of companies? If so, which ones?
- Have friends shared recommendations on social media? If so, which ones stand out and why?
- What types of content, information, and so on, from the company would you be willing to share with your friends?

There are many more that are applicable to your specific situation. Before sitting down, come up with another three to five questions that can help validate ideas from you or your colleagues. Try not to let your own perceptions of the project or of feedback you've received get in the way of your learning. Be humble, and listen as best you can. Also leave some time for free-form feedback or suggestions. Oftentimes, some of the best ideas don't originate with your company but rather with your customers.

We should mention one other cautionary note here. It's really easy to take customer feedback and run with it full speed. After all, when we hear something from a customer, it's valid and "straight from the horse's mouth," right? Although that is true for the most part, you can't always trust that verbatim feedback to represent what customers really want. You have to map feedback to promises you can keep, both profitably and sustainably.

> It's dangerous to listen too closely to what customers say they want. Remember the old Henry Ford quote: "If I'd asked my customers what they wanted, they'd have said 'a faster horse.'" Customers may not be aware of how technology can help them in new and innovative ways. It's your role to translate their feedback into new and interesting offerings that they'll love.

Thursday: Determine Work Roles

By now you've set your goals, and you've gotten feedback from internal stakeholders and customers. It's time to think through the operational mechanics that will make your Facebook marketing project sing. Regardless of the size of your business, there are a wide range of roles and responsibilities associated with any project. Branding, messaging, design/creative, e-commerce, product management, website management, IT, and others all may have some role in the success or failure of your project. In small businesses, these roles may be filled by one or two people. But in corporations, you can have entire teams that work on one element of what you need. Like it or not, these people won't necessarily have the same priorities you have. So, you have to get them on your side.

The chart in the following sidebar illustrates how the role of social media champion is really suited for people who are well regarded inside their company. You'll regularly need to get the cooperation of your colleagues to do things they aren't necessarily resourced or equipped to do, often times on short notice. The job is one part visionary, one part marketer, one part politician. Do what you can to give people as much time as you can to help you. You have probably heard the quote "Failure to plan on your part does not constitute an emergency on my part." If you limit your emergencies to times when it's truly warranted, you'll gain the respect of your colleagues, and you'll probably get what you need more regularly.

Featured Case: Necessary Skill Sets

The size of your company will probably dictate the extent to which you have to court colleagues in other functional areas of your business. Social media projects are by definition cross-functional. To do things the right way, you're going to have to become the conductor who keeps the orchestra playing a harmonious tune.

What functions map to different parts of your organization? Here's an example from a recent client engagement. We dealt primarily with the manager of the social media project, but she had to deal with a variety of colleagues across her company:

Branding: Use of logos and brand assets

Design: Creation of new/modified image assets

Product management: Sign-off on the way the product was used

E-commerce: Coordination of the project with other online campaigns, e-mail marketing promotions, and so on

Website management: Campaigns on the Web that pointed to Facebook, and vice versa

For each of the roles mentioned above, do what you can to have a point person available to take requests, feedback, and so on. You really don't want the responsibilities to be ambiguous either—talk through the requirements, what people will need to do, and what the deadlines will likely be. You have to know who will do what, when, and what the rules of engagement will be. If you are in a larger corporation, your work will likely be handed to a junior member of the team. But don't let that fool you: you'll have to keep that person and their manager happy to get their undying cooperation and love. Earlier in this book, we mentioned that you're truly building a social media product when you create a Facebook campaign. You're the product manager here, so you'll have to manage relationships as much as you'll have to manage the end product.

Friday: Set or Review Social Media Policy

As you navigate the political waters of your organization, you'll undoubtedly face questions about the organization's official policies regarding the execution of social media products. We're talking as much about who does what as who can edit Facebook on behalf of the company, who can comment on success or failure, who can access statistics and summary reports, and who is in the room for executive reviews.

If you are in a large corporation, odds are that you may already have some loose guidelines for blogging set forth by public relations people. This can be a good start—because such guidelines tend to reflect a company's treatment of risk, customer advocacy, and interaction. Put another way, some companies simply put more trust in their employees to make judgment calls that may ultimately reflect on the business. Others prefer a more centralized communications structure that closely manages company positioning. Smaller companies tend to have less complex rules about customer engagement for a few reasons. They tend to be scrappier and more action-oriented. In our experience, this has a lot to do with the fact that larger companies are generally more risk-averse because they are "under the microscope" more than their smaller brethren.

What you really want to do here is make sure your team is on the same page across blogs *and* social media. Although we're not huge fans of "makework," (that is, unproductive work done primarily for the sake of satisfying process) an e-mail or document that summarizes the basics can be very helpful to keep you from having arguments or misunderstandings as your campaign evolves. Here are a few questions to consider when putting together your company's policy on social media:

- What are the official social media accounts for the company?
- Who manages them?
- How often will you post updates from the different accounts?
- What types of content will be shared from the different social media destinations?
- Will the social media account engage in conversation with users?
- When posting news and updates, which accounts have priority?
- What are the loose rules for how the Web, blogs, and social media interact?

Now, you know your organization a lot better than we do. Some companies manage their brand and outbound communications very closely, while others have a more decentralized approach. Think Proctor & Gamble on one hand and Southwest Airlines on the other. It really comes down to philosophy for a lot of businesses. Where your company or organization stands will drive a lot of other factors:

- Whether you will need a stated policy for information shared via social media
- Whether you will communicate with customers directly via social media
- Whether the Facebook presence is managed in-house, by a trusted vendor or consultant, or by a combination of both
- The degree to which updates to the Facebook presence must be approved in advance due to fear of offending parts of the customer base—either accidentally or on purpose
- Whether you should promote your product, your brand, or your company

We have worked with organizations that first spend a lot of time on an "official social media policy" that drives what they can and can't do. And we've worked with others that simply shoot from the hip and worry about problems as they come along. If you don't have such a policy, spend your hour today to create a basic framework that establishes some rules. Think of a few difficult situations you may encounter—a difficult customer, a question you don't want to answer, verbal abuse, and so on—and think about the most appropriate response that fits your company's culture. Make your Facebook marketing project fit the cultural norms of your organization, lest your misunderstanding cost you professionally.

Week 2: Draft and Present the Plan

You've spent the last week gathering information from your colleagues, customers, and management. By now you should know your limitations for the project, and you should begin to see some specific opportunities. You must put your thoughts into a coherent package that can help you start the project.

We've alluded to this several times in the book, but we can't overstate that success relies on your ability to set up a structure by which you can experiment. No two projects are alike—what works for your brand may not work for someone else's, and vice versa. The problem is that you won't know going into your project if your approach will be naturally viral, if it will require demand generation via advertising, if your lighthearted approach works with consumers, or if you need to deliver "just the facts." You may have a hunch of how things will work, but you need freedom to learn and react to customer feedback.

Featured Case: Bad Reactions to Social Media Policy from the Sports World

Sometimes, the reaction to an organization's social media policy can take on a life of its own. Take, for example, the case of ESPN in August 2009. ESPN released a social media policy that is by all accounts pretty fair. ESPN reporters are, in fact, as much representatives of the network as they are individuals—and their social media policy was set accordingly. But one commentator, NBA analyst Ric Bucher, sent a message via Twitter that said ESPN had "prohibited [employees and commentators from] Tweeting unless it serves ESPN." The result was a PR nightmare for the "total sports network," and it sent its PR team into quick action the same day. Nonetheless, the blogosphere lit up with a number of critical posts suggesting that the network doesn't care about fans and wants to control the sports industry. Check out http://mashable.com/2009/08/04/espn-social-media for the full text of the policy along with ESPN's official response.

Also in the sports world, the Southeastern Conference of college athletics in the United States released a similarly restrictive social media policy later in August 2009. According to the policy, ticketed fans can't "produce or disseminate (or aid in producing or disseminating) any material or information about the Event, including, but not limited to, any account, description, picture, video, audio, reproduction or other information concerning the Event."

Uproar against this policy ultimately led to its revision 11 days after the policy was released.

What is the reason for all the wrangling over social media in the sports world? Two words: money and control. The only problem is that attendees and consumers today are the same people who insist on sharing their experiences with friends through social media. The consumer is an active participant in social media culture. Keep that in mind as you craft your own social media policy for your employees and your customers moving forward.

Monday: Research Best Practices and Success Stories

Although Facebook is relatively young as a platform, in 2010 and beyond you have the advantage of hindsight. A lot of companies have gone before you to create a Facebook presence. Some have failed; others have enjoyed wild success. Some companies have done very well by letting their communities manage themselves. Before you put pen to paper, you'll want to know more about what has been done in the past. You have to know as much as you can, because these stories oftentimes reach the newsstands, the popular business periodicals, and the blogosphere. You'll get a lot more credibility in your company if you are the expert and not a colleague who just keeps up with business news.

A variety of sources keep up with innovations in Facebook and social media marketing. Some of our favorites are listed here. You'll want to look for sources that can keep you up-to-date on the latest creative uses of Facebook or social media. We cover some of these in this book and on our blog, but you'll want to keep up with a few sources so you can bring the world's best work to your specific situation.

Facebook Marketing: An Hour a Day: www.facebookmarketinganhouraday.com

Mashable: www.mashable.com

AllFacebook: www.allfacebook.com

Inside Facebook: www.insidefacebook.com

Social Media Examiner: http://socialmediaexaminer.com

Government 2.0: www.govloop.com, http://radar.oreilly.com/markd

Enterprise 2.0: www.web-strategist.com

It's handy to read blogs from practitioners in your field. Ironically, Facebook isn't the easiest way to get familiar with content from bloggers and other industry pundits who you did not know previously. Industry magazines, business magazines, trade shows, Twitter, and search engines are good ways to help you discover some of these people. Once you start digging, you'll find that a lot of experts are grappling with the same issues you face every day. Most are relatively open with their experience and their advice—and they share it at low cost or free on the Internet and on their blogs. Thank God for the Web!

Tuesday: Assess the Social Media Activity of Competitors

Before launching your own presence, you really should know exactly what your competitors are doing on Facebook and other social media sites. If you're going to comprehensively analyze your competitors' activities, consider staying on top of the following:

Features Keep track of all the elements of the competitors' presence that appear to be run or officially sponsored by them. You need to know whether they are maintaining a profile, Facebook fan pages, Twitter accounts, blogs, or other social media accounts. Since social media sites typically rank high on search engines, you shouldn't have any trouble finding these sites with a search engine.

Commitment Monitor the quantity and quality of social media updates. Is the competitor truly committed to social media for customer outreach, or does it appear to be more of an experiment? Objectively speaking, would you consider their effort a competitive differentiator, or is it just the bare minimum necessary for a company these days?

Popularity Keep track of the number of customers who appear to be communicating with your competitor. This can be a simple metric such as the number of fans/followers/friends/participants they've attracted, or you can dig deeper to see how much "conversation" they have with their customers via social media. This is good to give yourself a benchmark for performance—either as a stated goal or as a personal goal.

PR/coverage Analyze how much your competitor's social media work is discussed through articles, in popular periodicals, by bloggers, and so on. It's been said that there is no such thing as bad publicity. We guess that depends on your risk tolerance. A good campaign or strategy can get a lot of people saying good things about a company. When looking for this, be sure to discern between a competitor's own employees talking about the social media effort and seemingly disinterested third parties doing so. It's far too easy to appear anonymous on the Web—sophisticated competitors will plant moles around the Web to say good things about themselves to make it all more impactful.

A chart that summarizes all this data is a helpful and important resource that you can use to both benchmark yourself and monitor the playing field in the future. If you've effectively gathered the data, you've built the scorecard as it relates to your competitors. Now, your management may not hold you to that high a standard or your competitors may not be executing well, so the numbers are largely irrelevant. But as long as you know where your competitors are, you'll be much more informed when setting goals and positioning your progress. Spend a little time to put this chart together with as many hard metrics as you can find. Leave the subjectivity to perhaps only your assessment of PR. You'll need a snapshot at the beginning of your project and the commitment to update it regularly. Add your performance to the chart to be honest about how you stack up.

Wednesday: Assign Metrics

As you're finalizing your proposal, you need to spend some time thinking about score-keeping. How will your superiors know with confidence that you are successful? This comes down to a few things—what numbers you'll share with them, how often you'll share updates, and how you'll manage expectations.

It always starts with the sophistication of the people ultimately responsible for the effort and what they expect to see. Ideally you spent time last week talking with them in detail. Getting everyone on the same page is important—so it's probably a good idea to go back to the most influential stakeholders to get feedback on your plan. Give them an opportunity to own part of the project through suggestion or advice, and they'll be easier on you when times are tough.

Choosing metrics for your scorecard is one part art, one part science. You certainly want to fill it with numbers that you know you can affect, but your management chain will likely want to tie the scorecard to meaningful business metrics: return on investment, low customer acquisition cost, number of fans/subscribers, how you do relative to your competitors, and so on. A good scorecard will have elements of both that will easily demonstrate a few things: maintenance, capturing opportunity, efficient advertising spend, competitive environment, and customer interaction. Figure 4.1 shows a range of popular metrics and how easy or difficult they are to affect today.

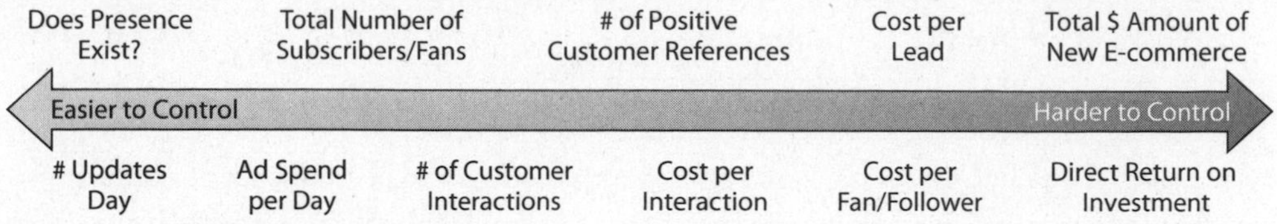

Figure 4.1 The continuum of social metrics

Table 4.2 shows an effective scorecard for a simple Facebook marketing campaign that utilizes Facebook fan pages and Facebook advertising. The first two metrics are entirely based on effort and measure simply whether the project manager did their job. The third metric, number of fans added, is a measure of the overall effectiveness of the effort as measured by incremental fans. Advertising spend tells you whether the manager stayed within budget. The number of customer interactions per week is a measure of how engaging the effort is and whether there is sufficient follow-up with customers. Advertising cost per fan is a customer acquisition cost metric that determines whether the ad spend is effective. This is an admittedly simplistic measure—we'll talk in Chapter 6 about isolating the exact impact of advertising dollars. Finally, the ratio of total number of fans to a competitor's total number of fans tells you how you compare to other companies in your market.

▶ **Table 4.2** Example of a Basic Facebook Marketing Scorecard

Metric	Last Week	Goal	This Week	Goal
Daily updates of scorecard/metrics	Yes	Yes	Yes	Yes
Number of updates or posts/day	0.7	1.0	1.1	1.0
Number of Facebook fans added	77	80	106	90
Advertising spend	$37.28	$40.00	$39.15	$40.00
Number of customer interactions per week	13	25	19	30
Advertising cost per fan	$0.484	$0.50	$0.369	$0.44
Ratio of our total number of fans to competitor's total number of fans	1.03:1	1:0:1	1.07:1	1.05:1

You should know two additional things about metrics and your scorecard. First, you and your management team should consider all of this to be somewhat fluid, especially early in the process. As you work on the project, you may determine that some metrics matter more to you and others matter less. This is a learning experience for many people who take on such projects for the first time—it's OK to make a mistake or course-correct as you learn.

Second, the spirit of the scorecard isn't that you necessarily get locked in to doing things just because they're on a scorecard but rather that you get in the habit of recording and analyzing relevant data about your efforts. These projects generate mountains of discrete pieces of data, and you can use this data to help drive decision making as long as you commit to recording it regularly. It can be tedious, but it's very worthwhile. Some data is available to you long-term, but Facebook discards other types of data such that you can't go back to get it if you forget to record it. Use spreadsheets to record progress and analyze data, and collect as much of that data as you can, even if you don't think it will be immediately helpful. You never know what you'll want to use later.

Thursday: Set Reporting Strategy

Now you'll turn your attention to the how and when of reporting metrics to your superiors. The funny thing about Internet marketing is that even in 2010 a lot of managers aren't experienced enough to know the ins and outs of reportage. As a result, every statistic that you report could turn into a potential black hole of debate that may be totally unproductive. This may also make people question your work or how you are analyzing progress.

Getting out in front of these issues is key to managing perceptions, and education is the way to do it. Take the time to educate people on what key metrics mean—it will go a long way to improving your internal credibility. It also shows people that you have nothing to hide, which will come in handy especially if you do have some metrics that you need more time to improve. At the end of the day, you want people to understand that you can measure your progress, you can be self-critical, and you know how to fix problems that emerge.

When establishing the reporting cadence, think through the ongoing reporting need and the frequency of management reviews. You will probably need to share updates with some of your colleagues on an ongoing basis so they are always in the loop. This is most efficiently handled on a weekly basis, although we have seen cases where a small team gets daily updates on progress. Management reviews should be scheduled monthly at the most—otherwise, you won't have time to see the outcome of inevitable changes or corrections to your strategy and tactics. The frequency and depth of your reporting will be driven by management requirements and how critical the project is in your company.

If you communicate proactively and openly, you're doing everything you can to manage expectations and reactions to your work. We see people run into problems in their company all the time when they hoard information or don't ensure that management understands the goals, the measurement, and the process of establishing a healthy social media campaign. Deal with issues directly as they occur, and be open to feedback. Distrust is created when people don't communicate—you have a leadership role to play as the manager of the social media project.

Friday: Present the Plan

You've spent most of the last two weeks gathering information, negotiating with stakeholders, and preparing a plan to help your company take better advantage of Facebook and social media. Now it's time to sell it. We've talked at length about the value of metrics and the importance of communication to get cooperation from your colleagues. Here are a few other potential potholes that you should consider as you summarize your thoughts:

Management/mitigation of unintended consequences Good executives at major corporations are trained to mitigate risk wherever possible. You'll need to show that you've thought through all the potential negative situations that may arise from your effort and that you have a plan for dealing with problems and unintended negative consequences.

Organizational fit Are you the right person in the company to run the project? Would this cause a political problem in your company that will create problems for the management team? Have you reached across organizational lines proactively to make the project run as smoothly as possible? Will the project be at odds with other major initiatives inside the company? You don't want to compete with your colleagues unless there are good reasons to do so.

Fit with corporate culture/norms Are the things you are proposing a fit for the way the company communicates with customers, partners, and so on? If so, is that a good thing? Management may have a different perspective on this than the rank and file. Be sure to understand how superiors see the opportunity in advance of your presentation.

Future commitment Will this project cause the company to take on a future financial or head count liability that it currently does not have? Do you have a handle on the costs associated with the effort and how that may change over time? Could backing out of such a commitment cause customers significant consternation and create negative perceptions about the company or brand?

If they are balanced and fair, your superiors will likely ask you for a good balance of metrics that you can control and stretch goals that will make you really work. That's OK. Remember, you are trying to learn what will work and what has worked on Facebook. ROI is certainly the toughest metric to guarantee today—more on that in Chapter 10, "Organizational Considerations," when we talk about what managers and executives should demand of employees who run social media projects.

One Final Point for the Day of Your Presentation

Be sure to keep your cool when you pitch your ideas. Not all of your ideas are going to necessarily work. That's OK. React calmly and professionally to feedback. It's the best way to make people confident that you can take feedback and you can do the job!

Week 3: Establish a Presence with the Facebook Profile and Friends

Congratulations! Now that you have a plan and you've taken feedback from the firing line of your management team, it's time to execute! You're probably already very familiar with the basics of Facebook, but you may never have looked at all the opportunities from a business perspective. We did a quick walk-through of the basics of the Facebook profile and friending in Chapter 2, "What Is Facebook?"—now we'll talk about these features with an eye toward marketing opportunities. We'll avoid feature walk-throughs as much as possible here, to focus on how different elements of Facebook help you create a campaign that your customers will appreciate.

Monday/Tuesday: Learn About Data in the Facebook Profile and Security Settings

As we've discussed previously, everything about your identity is summarized in the Facebook profile. There, you have the ability to say as much or as little as you want about yourself. Table 4.3 summarizes the personal information users may expose about themselves. It is a ridiculously rich set of data, most of which is accessible to marketers for better targeting through Facebook advertising, which we will cover in detail in Chapter 6, "Month 3: Creating a Following with Facebook Ads."

▶ **Table 4.3** Facebook User Information

Category	Data Listed
Basic Information	Gender
	Birth date
	Hometown
	Neighborhood
	Family Members
	Relationship Status
	"Interested In"
	"Looking For"
	Political Views
	Religious Views
Personal Information	Activities
	Interests
	Favorite Music
	Favorite TV Shows
	Favorite Movies
	Favorite Books
	Favorite Quotations
	About Me

Continues

Category	Data Listed
Contact Information	E-mail
	Instant Messenger Screen Names
	Mobile Phone Number
	Land Phone
	Address
	City/Town
	Neighborhood
	Zip
	Website
Education and Work	College/University
	Graduation Year
	Concentration/Major
	Degree Attained
	High School
	Employer
	Position
	Job Description
	City/Town
	Dates Worked
Groups	Facebook groups to which the user belongs
Pages	Facebook pages for which the user is a fan

The downside to collecting all this information is that it may make a user nervous. Think about it—if the Facebook profile is totally filled out, it contains quite a bit of personal information that is often used in sensitive situations such as when you've forgotten your password for a credit card or when old friends you haven't seen in years want to reconnect. It's perfect for criminals who may want to steal someone's identity or use profile data to impersonate that person or act maliciously on behalf of that person.

Facebook established a rich set of data privacy controls with privacy settings for limiting exposure of certain types of information to certain people on Facebook—friends, friends of friends, people in certain networks, nobody at all, and so on. All of this was done to make users more comfortable when adding life's personal details into the social network. Figure 4.2 shows the available privacy options. Users can also customize the privacy they want on a user-by-user basis if they are particularly concerned about certain individuals. Facebook truly has done a remarkable job of simplifying a user's management of their own personal data.

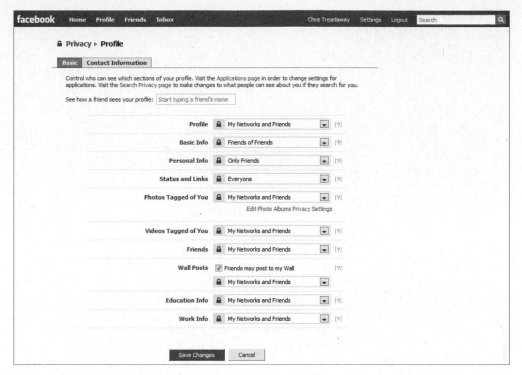

Figure 4.2 Facebook privacy settings

All of it means a few things for marketers:

- You simply won't be able to access some people who are more careful with the data they share on Facebook.
- However, most Facebook users, by virtue of adding self-identifying data to their profiles, are by default exposing themselves to marketing offers.
- Facebook has an unbelievably rich set of demographic and behavioral data on its users, and that data will likely play a major role in the future of Facebook advertising and marketing on the platform.

In the sense that Facebook can gather accurate and up-to-date demographic targeting data from users, Facebook has only a few rivals (Google, Yahoo, Twitter, maybe Microsoft, and a few others).

Wednesday: Decide How You'll Use Your Facebook Profile

If you already have a Facebook profile, you'll need to decide whether you want that profile to do "double duty" as your own personal profile *and* the profile that serves as the administrator account for the corporate presence (a fan page, group, and so on). If you do choose to have your personal profile be the Admin for the company fan page, we strongly recommend adding one or more additional Admins to share the "load" of accessing and managing the company fan page. Even though Facebook insists on connecting a personal profile to a fan page, they are still treated as two entirely separate entities and no one would ever know you are the Admin. Having said that, if you wanted to post content on the company fan page as yourself, you would not be able to do so without first being removed as an Admin. It can get complex, and many marketers on Facebook have come up with creative workarounds, including setting up "dummy accounts," which technically is against Facebook's Terms of Use.

Alternatively, you may want to set up a Business Account for your company to be the Admin of the fan page. A Business Account provides extremely limited access to Facebook's main features; however, it can be the best solution to avoid having your personal profile tied into the company fan page. Don't worry so much about data flow, getting on News Feeds, posting pictures, and so on right now because those are not unique benefits to the Facebook profile. This is really about whether you want to use the Facebook profile to include a personal touch complete with personal details and relationships that develop over time with real people. Facebook allows users to have up to 5,000 friends on their personal profile. You may end up being friends with a wide range of people, including your own immediate and extended family members, real personal friends, colleagues, prospective customers, industry experts, media contacts, and more. Make sure that your choices regarding the Facebook profile fit what you need to achieve and, if applicable, the brand assets you already have and the commitments you are willing to make in the future.

Machiavellian types may be thinking by now, "Facebook exposes so much data, I can use it to learn about people I work with or those I want to target." Customers, partners, or other types of business contacts often share a lot of information about themselves through Facebook. If they've friended you directly, you can see most of this information. Similarly, data is available if you've worked at the same place in the past and you both are on the same company network.

There are also more circuitous ways to get access to content people share on Facebook. If they've posted a picture on one of your friend's profiles, depending on how the two parties have their privacy settings configured, you could go through all the pictures in that particular photo album. If they've posted a status update, you can find it using Facebook's Status Update search, which was developed as a means to compete with Twitter's search (`http://search.twitter.com`). Despite the wealth of privacy and security settings in Facebook, there are still a number of workarounds like this that allow unintended people to see personal profile data. A great salesperson can use little things found in the Facebook profile to better empathize with a sales target and ultimately win them over. Facebook provides the vehicle by which people share a lot of information that can be used as business intelligence for a business advantage.

Similarly, you can also use the Facebook profile to create whatever persona you want. There are thousands upon thousands of organizations to follow, groups to join, and links to post. Everything you do, say, and associate with paints a picture of who you are—and those little things can certainly impact how business contacts perceive you. If you have friended customers, partners, or other types of business contacts, your Facebook presence can be used to keep them up-to-date just like you do for friends. Similarly, you can share articles, photos, or other types of content that you think may influence them in some way. In essence, you can deliberately manage how your Facebook community at large perceives you. By being mindful and strategic about what you share, you may find yourself making friends with very key contacts and deepening your relationship with these individuals. It's really up to you to determine just how aggressively you'd like to use your own Facebook profile to talk about your business or market yourself to prospective customers. We do recommend making use of Friend Lists to manage a) how you filter your own News Feed and b) who gets to see which posts via your privacy settings.

Thursday: Set Up Your Profile and Make Friends for a Consumer Campaign

We briefly discussed friending in Chapter 2 to make you familiar with the basics of how people interact on Facebook. Now we'll talk about it as it relates to a consumer campaign. You really have two options when it comes to creating a Facebook profile to support a consumer campaign. You may want an actual person to be the focal point of a campaign to personalize your organization and to give the appearance of human- ity and being approachable. If so, you'll have a fairly loose policy about friending, and you'll want to watch activity on the Wall to ensure that people don't abuse the privilege of communicating directly with you.

One such example of this that took place in social media was the rise of Robert Scoble. Scoble was an early blogger and technical evangelist employed by Microsoft to showcase the company, its products, and its people. His blog, Scobleizer (www.scobleizer .com), became a tremendous hit and a "must read" for anyone wanting to keep up with startups and new Internet technologies. But just over three years after taking the job at Microsoft, Robert Scoble announced he was leaving the company to join a startup. The face of Microsoft's technical evangelism efforts was all of a sudden gone.

On one hand, Scoble's efforts worked really well to personalize Microsoft and soften the software giant's image. On the other hand, it also exposed a real weakness in allowing a single person to have such an influential role. When a single person has such a significant impact as the face of an organization, it can be devastating when that person leaves. The person can take with them the brand that has been created and the audience that follows religiously.

The second option you have is to establish a fictional character for a cam- paign. A fictional character on Facebook appears and acts just like a real person who can travel, update their status, share pictures, comment on current events, and so on. Similarly, that character can "friend" individual Facebook users and also accept friend requests. When a user becomes a friend of another Facebook user, a notification appears on the News Feed of each person's friends. It's a quick and viral way for people to find out that a new friend from a previous social context has joined Facebook.

Actions taken by the fictional character will appear on friends' News Feeds, where they can be acted upon, commented on, shared, or "liked." When friends of your fictional character do any of these things, a notification will appear on their profile and the News Feed of their friends. It doesn't take a lot of imagination to realize that this can be one heck of a viral benefit to you. What product manager at McDonald's wouldn't want the ability to establish the Hamburglar as a living character on Facebook with thousands of fans eager to hear about how he's going to get his next McDonald's hamburger? Sadly, this is exactly what Facebook is trying to avoid by restricting the presence of fictional characters on the News Feed. We're a big proponent of testing the limits—what's the worst that can happen? Facebook will shut you down? Well, it actually happened, as described in the "The Hard-Knock Life of Dummies Man" case study.

Featured Case: The Hard-Knock Life of Dummies Man

In the summer of 2007, Ellen Gerstein, marketing director for Wiley Publishing, had a great idea for marketing the *For Dummies* books. She thought she'd create a Facebook profile for "Dummies Man" to make the brand and *For Dummies* books more personal. She was totally unprepared for what happened next—Facebook shut down the Dummies Man account not long after its launch. Here's a quick Q&A with Ellen, where she shares her experience:

Q: *So, what exactly happened when you tried to create a profile for Dummies Man?*

A: The idea to create a profile for Dummies Man came about when I was working with Joe Laurino, our summer intern, on some Facebook marketing ideas. I casually mentioned that it would be fun for Dummies Man to have a Facebook persona. Joe ran with the idea and created a profile for him based on his likes (helping people learn new things), dislikes (idiots), and so on. He also added a bunch of information about our publications in there as a way to showcase some new books. It seemed really fun, and we got a lot of people at work curious and interested in Facebook as a result.

Q: *What were you trying to achieve with a Dummies Man profile that you couldn't achieve with a Facebook page?*

A: The idea was to make Dummies Man accessible to readers in a way that only social media allows you to do. You can connect with him, share book ideas with him, even throw sheep at him! We wanted to take this to readers in a very personal way that we had not tried before.

Q: *Did you ever get a chance to make your case directly to people at Facebook regarding the profile?*

A: One day, I tried to log into the account and was denied. After a fair amount of legwork, it showed that the profile was suspended because the person who set up the account (me) was not using her real name. I tried reaching out to a few contacts at Facebook but was directed to write to the automated customer service e-mail addresses on the site.

Although I may have felt this wasn't fair, I totally acknowledge that this was within Facebook's right as laid out in its terms of service agreement. It's their sandbox, and if I don't like how they are playing, my recourse is to pick up my pail and shovel and go home. I understand that. What did anger me was that Dummies Man was singled out, while others having profiles not under their real names were not shut down. Not to pick on him, as I am a fan, but the example I brought to the attention of Facebook was that of Fake Steve Jobs. How can you say that "Fake Steve Jobs" is someone's real name? How was he (Dan Lyons) allowed to keep that account and not Dummies Man? I wasn't trying to bring down Fake Steve Jobs but rather to make the case that we both had a place on Facebook.

Q: *In retrospect, do you think that all of this proved to help your company? Or was it harmful?*

A: I think both the benefits and the damage were minimal. We got some play in the blogosphere about it and were able get a bit more press out of it when Robert Scoble's profile was removed from the site (`http://scobleizer.com/2008/01/03/ive-been-kicked-off-of-facebook`). I think it showed most of all that Wiley cared enough about social media as a means of connecting with customers that we were trying something new, even if it ended up being something we got our wrists slapped for, however lightly.

Q: *How does it feel to pave the way for other companies to put their fictional characters on Facebook?*

A: I think Facebook has lightened up and made it easier to have that presence, while still maintaining the overall feel they intended to have. As long as you are generally respectful of what Facebook is trying to do, I think it's great to have fictional characters on there. It's what social media was made for!

For more on social media and observations on the publishing industry, check out Ellen's blog at `http://trueconfessions.wordpress.com`.

This isn't always a positive, however—it's just as easy for someone to hijack your brand by creating a phony profile that you *don't* control. Figure 4.3 is an example of the search results for profiles of "The Most Interesting Man in the World," a fictional character that was the face of Dos Equis marketing in 2008–2009. Presumably few of these are not endorsed or managed by our good friends at Dos Equis. Imagine for a moment what a malicious person can do by managing such a profile, friending a large number of people, and saying whatever they want in an effort to propagate messages virally on individuals' News Feeds. This may horrify you, but sadly there isn't a lot you can do about it short of contacting Facebook or any other social network where your fictional character is hijacked. It certainly warrants monitoring at minimum, and fortunately this can be done rather easily by friending rogue accounts to make sure they aren't misusing your character. But you may want to go to the extent of shutting down people who create these accounts entirely. Your company's philosophy on its brands will be a good guide for how you should treat these situations should they emerge.

"Overfriending" means different things to different people. It could be getting too close to perfect strangers. For others, it could be a matter of accepting or sending in the region of more than, say, fifty friend requests a day. Facebook doesn't publish theses limitations but anecdotally we have found sending no more than around twenty outgoing friend requests per day keeps you under the radar. If you're including a personal greeting (which we recommend), try changing up the wording a bit, as Facebook's bots are looking for repetitive, verbatim wording.

Figure 4.3 Search results for Dos Equis

One solution to growing a friend base quicker is to use other marketing mediums to ask people to friend you. There's no limit to how many incoming friend requests you can have. Internet marketer, John Reese, holds the record for reaching the 5,000 friends max in the shortest amount of time: a mere five days. How did he do it? He simply sent a message to his sizeable opt-in e-mail list asking his subscribers to add him as a friend on Facebook. Of course, this brought in a flood of new accounts to Facebook as many of these people did not yet have Facebook accounts. There are pros and cons to asking your existing database to friend you: if, like Reese, you have a sizeable database, you may use up your friend "slots" with people already in your reach. So, you might want to save some of those slots to establish relationships with new people.

Friday: Repurpose a Profile for Business

Alternatively, your interest in Facebook may be to sell products or services on a business-to-business basis, or you may be selling products to consumers that involve a longer sales cycle and require more consultation. That's the realm of business development, where relationships built over a long period of time matter. Business development tends to imply more "strategic sales," in other words, higher touch, more surgical, higher-stakes interactions with people who make big decisions that can impact your success or failure. Social media is a fantastic tool for business development. It breaks down communications barriers that were the rule of the day just 10 years ago. It gives you low risk and potentially helpful excuses for interacting much more casually and much more regularly with prospective partners. It also exposes the social side of our lives, which may be helpful in a sales context. Not only that, but it can help you learn more about the very people you are trying to sell to—their thoughts, concerns, likes/ dislikes, and so on.

First things first, you need to decide whether this is a good opportunity for you and your organization. Will your customers or partners be willing to engage with you on Facebook? How will they view your friend request? Will they be threatened or amused by your occasional comments and activities on the social network? By creating Friend Lists and adjusting your Privacy settings to your liking, using these Friend Lists, (e.g., determining who can and cannot see what content), you can easily control how your business-related posts and personal sharing are propagated. Using your Facebook profile for business development is dangerous because unless you use a duplicate profile for business activities or you carefully sanitize everything you say and do on Facebook, you're going to mix business and pleasure. Some people deal well with that, but others don't. Some individuals have an aversion to mixing business and pleasure; in fact, many people hesitate to get too involved with social networking on a wider scale because they are afraid of having to "live in a glass house." This is perfectly natural; most everyone likes to have an element of privacy to his or her life.

On the one hand, you may choose to have a completely open policy and only share content—both business and personal—that you're totally okay with being found in a Google search, possibly featured on the front page of a mainstream newspaper and/or archived for years. One distinction we've found helpful over the years is to think of your experiences as falling into one of three categories: Professional, Personal, and Private. Since the prevalence and popularity of social media, the line has become rather blurred between our professional and personal lives. Typically, people are interested to know a bit more about you behind your "work self." Sharing about hobbies, travel, family, and interests is actually interesting to most people. However, here's where you get to maintain control: you still may have a private life and simply never share anything online that you don't want out in the open.

Although we tend to favor Twitter over the Facebook personal profile for business development outreach through social media, some people are more willing to become a Facebook friend than others. Just proceed cautiously. Before friending someone, get a sense of whether they'd appreciate it. We wouldn't necessarily be pushy about this— some people draw lines in various parts of their lives, and your intrusion may be seen as inappropriate. If you have a business contact who requests to be your Facebook friend, you're probably in good shape with that particular contact. Before accepting the request, be sure to review your profile critically to ensure you don't have anything there that may be embarrassing to you. You can be sure that a business contact who wants to know about you will check every picture you've posted, pictures where your friends have tagged you, comments on your News Feed, who your friends are, and conversations you've had in the past.

If you've used Facebook's security settings to keep different parts of your life separate, now would be a great time to double-check the settings and public visibility of your profile. If your profile is open to the public, assume the worst—that your business contacts will do due diligence on you before deciding to trust you or do business with you. You may need to make some changes there, so you don't hurt yourself as you try to build your business and earn a customer's trust through a Facebook friendship. Here are a few other steps you can take to ensure your profile is appropriate for business contacts:

Sanitize your profile Go through the effort of reviewing status updates and pictures to ensure you don't share anything that may be embarrassing or potentially offensive to your new professional friends.

Avoid ongoing political, religious, or other controversial commentary These are things that you should truly avoid to keep from offending people, assuming you aren't affiliated with political or religious organizations. You may even choose to not fill out your own Political and/or Religious Views on your Info tab. Some individuals may have strong opposing beliefs and actually choose not to do business with you because of this. On the other hand, it's possible those who resonate with your beliefs would want to do business with you all the more.

Remove controversial groups or Facebook pages from your profile Groups and pages imply a level of support that goes well beyond an occasional comment. Remove anything that will damage your credibility with business development contacts.

Stay vigilant Sometimes your friends can post some things that are off-color or potentially embarrassing. Once you see things like this, be sure to remove them or disassociate them from your profile.

> People share an amazing amount of information on popular social networks. Create a social graph of all your primary targets. Learn everything you can about them from Facebook, Twitter, Flickr, LinkedIn, blogs, and so on. You know that empathy and knowing your customer's needs can help make the difference between a sale and a lost opportunity. Use the social networks to make you smarter.

Week 4: Use Basic Facebook Features to Promote Yourself

Odds are that you are already a Facebook user and you already know the basics of sharing information with friends through your profile. But how should you think of your options in the context of promoting a business? This week, we'll walk you through the different options you have on Facebook and how you can best utilize them.

These features are available to you if you've set up a profile or a fan page for your business, which we will discuss in more detail in Chapter 5, "Month 2: Establish an Effective Corporate Presence with Pages and Groups."

Monday: Post Status Updates

Status updates are in many ways the backbone of the "real-time data" revolution. These are generally short-form messages of a few hundred characters at the most that share one of life's mundane details, an observation, a random fact, or a link to something else on the Internet. Although Facebook and MySpace have both had status updates for a long time, Twitter has popularized them and to some extent taken status updates "mainstream." That said, Facebook status updates can be considerably more impactful in certain situations.

First, let's look at how status updates are presented to other users on Facebook. Status updates, along with other types of notifications on Facebook, appear on the News Feed. As we discussed earlier in this book, the News Feed is the feature that all Facebook users see upon logging in. Because so many status updates are entered by a user's friends, they can quickly appear and disappear in favor of more recent updates from different friends. Figure 4.4 shows the Facebook status updates from some of our friends. Users have some options for seeing status updates as well. They can filter out everything else to see just the updates their friends have shared by clicking the Status Updates link in the upper-left corner of the News Feed screen, as shown in Figure 4.5. Users can also opt to hide status updates from particular friends, which you can also see in Figure 4.5.

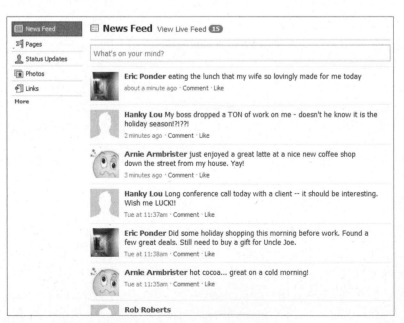

Figure 4.4 Facebook status updates

Figure 4.5 Filtering status updates

To post a status update, you do so in what's called the "Publisher" and you have up to 420 characters, though usually less is more when posting content. There is a Publisher at the very top of your home page where it says "What's on your mind?"—this posts to your personal profile. In addition, there is a Publisher on the Wall tab of your personal profile. (Similarly, your fan page has a Publisher at the top of the Wall tab).

What are the implications for marketers and business developers? For one, anything you post as a status update can be seen by anyone who chooses to be your Facebook friend. In fact, if you have your "Posts by Me" Privacy setting set to "Everyone" then literally anyone who comes to your profile can see your wall and all the content there. So, be careful, be relevant, and be entertaining if that is your goal. Stay out of political or religious rants and observations, strong language, or polarizing statements if you are using Facebook primarily for business purposes. You are likely to offend someone with whom you could do business. It's an unnecessary risk. Also remember that you can be "hidden" from view on a friend's News Feed. Some percentage of people who you have as a friend will not hear from you once they make the decision to hide you. So, your message will not quite go out to as many people as you think. That's yet another reason to proceed with confidence but also with caution.

Tuesday/Wednesday: Share Links, Events, Photos, and Videos

You may have noticed at the top of Figure 4.4 that there are icons beneath the Publisher box where you enter your status update. These icons allow users to add links, events, photos, videos, and other content to a status update. This feature adds an entirely new dimension to the types of things you can share—not only can you comment on something, but you can embellish that comment with content to make the experience around the status update more engaging.

Take, for example, links in a common scenario we see for clients—a company wants to post a link to a web page from a Facebook profile or fan page. The idea is that they want to share specific web content—news stories, press releases, YouTube videos, blog posts, and so on—with Facebook users. In this case, the status update is truly secondary, although it makes sense to add a comment or something to appropriately frame the shared content and plant a seed in a user's mind about how they should view/feel about the content. As you post your link, Facebook pulls in a series of thumbnails from the web page that can be shared alongside the link. You'll have the option to cycle through a selection of thumbnails and choose the one that best represents what you're posting: "A picture says a thousand words." This is particularly handy if you are sharing content from your own property and if Facebook picks up your brand's image. It's a free impression that is there for all your friends to see.

You can similarly share events with friends using this process. Events are great calls to action and are used to keep people informed about things that are happening. Figure 4.6 is an example of an event.

Think of Facebook events as a supercharged version of Evite. They have all the same features—event details, maps, contact information, photos, and guest management tools—but they allow invitations through the Facebook social graph. These events can be shared among friends, and they can be promoted through the Facebook News Feed. We've seen bands and comedians do a great job at this by publishing their tour stops on Facebook as events. Marketers are increasingly doing the same for trade shows, product launches, and so on.

Photos and videos can also be shared through the Publisher, as well as through specialized apps that Facebook runs for every user. You have two options with photos and videos. You can store them on Facebook, or you can link to libraries or individual photos/videos on third-party sites such as YouTube, Vimeo, Flickr, and others by sharing links to that content. When posting a YouTube link, for example, Facebook actually pulls in the embedded video with the player and users can play the video right in their News Feed or on your Wall without leaving Facebook.

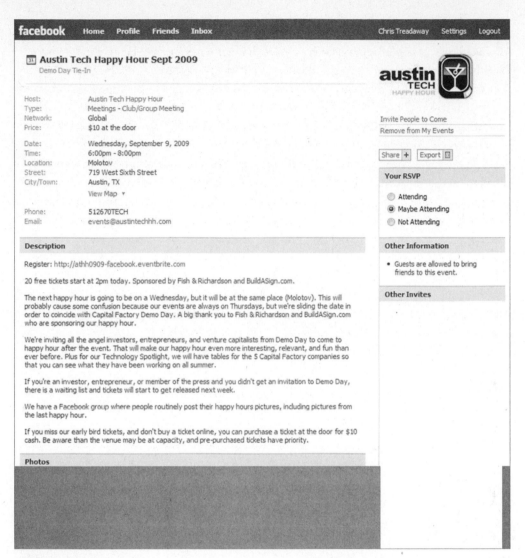

Figure 4.6 Event summary

Thursday: Install Third-Party Apps

Of the tens of thousands of third-party Facebook apps, you may find only a small number of them serve any great use from a marketing standpoint by adding to your personal profile. Many popular apps tend to be light hearted and/or game type apps. Sure, you may meet like-minded individuals or potential customers while playing FarmVille, Bejeweled, or Mafia Wars…but it depends on how you want to invest your social networking time.

We've found the following apps to add value to a personal profile and help you to be perceived with a more rounded presence on Facebook:

- Profile HTML or Extended Info: both these apps allow you to add your own custom HTML. A good use of these apps is to add your own "Follow me (us) on Twitter" badge. Also, adding your own opt-in box to encourage visitors to your profile to subscribe to a free download, for example. (http://apps.facebook.com/profile_html & http://apps.facebook.com/extendedinfo)

- YouTube Badge: great way to display a selection of videos from your own YouTube channel or your favorites. (http://apps.facebook.com/youtubebadge)

- Networked Blogs: import your blog post for extra exposure on Facebook. You could import your blog feed via Facebook's Notes app instead, but Networked Blogs offers a few more extra features. (http://apps.facebook.com/blognetworks/index.php)

- My Flickr: if you have images on Flickr, import them via this app for added exposure. (http://apps.facebook.com/myflickr)

- SlideShare: if you have slides on this site, import them via the app for added valuable content. (http://apps.facebook.com/slideshare)

Friday: Understand Other Aspects of the Facebook Platform

The last day of this week is a good time to become familiar with the other ways Facebook allows users to interact with friends both inside the social network and on the Internet. Here is a quick summary of a few of them—they are listed in order of most commonly used by marketers to least commonly used to date:

Badges Facebook allows users to create small widgets that can be put anywhere on the Internet and summarize basic Facebook profile data—usually a picture, first name, last name, and other basic data of the user's choosing. Badges can be created for both profiles and fan pages and can inform users of a website or an organization's Facebook presence (http://www.facebook.com/facebook-widgets/profilebadges.php). Chapter 5 includes more detail on badges and creatively using the Facebook fan page.

Applications/games Facebook applications are third-party apps that use the Facebook social graph and provide some functionality to users over and above the basic Facebook platform. In certain cases, these applications can propagate messages to the Facebook News Feed, but only after the user agrees. You should run a few Facebook applications to get an idea of how companies use the functionality and get game content to be present on users' News Feeds. We've listed a few recommended apps in the preceding section and will talk more in-depth about applications and branded games in Chapter 8.

Notes This is Facebook's attempt at a simple social blogging platform. Users can type whatever they'd like in a note, tag certain friends because they are part of the story or because they want attention, and share it on Facebook where it can be found on a News Feed and commented upon. If you've used WordPress or TypePad, it won't take you long to realize that Facebook notes are far less sophisticated. But Facebook notes are really more about the Facebook platform and helping people share thoughts from inside Facebook. You can import any RSS feed via the Notes app—most commonly, your blog feed.

Gifts For a long time, Facebook allowed users to buy free or $1 virtual gifts that could be shared with fellow users and appear on their profiles. These gifts are very popular, especially because they commemorate major events such as birthdays, anniversaries, and so on. In August 2009, Facebook announced that the gifts functionality will be opened to third-party developers. This is an opportunity that certainly bears monitoring, because it may open new opportunities for marketers to create viral gifts that may provide a branding benefit.

Marketplace Facebook allows individual users to sell items, services, and so on, to other Facebook users through the Marketplace. It is similar to Craigslist, a modern version of old-fashioned classified ads, or other services that allow people to sell or barter with each other. Marketers may have trouble coming up with scenarios that fit the Marketplace, so we won't spend a lot of time discussing this particular Facebook feature. Marketplace was originally a default feature of Facebook; then in March 2009 Facebook teamed up with Oodle—a classified ads service—and relaunched Marketplace with a much more commercial spin. (`http://apps.facebook.com/marketplace`)

Month 2: Establish Corporate Presence with Pages and Groups

5

Facebook fan pages and groups have evolved from humble beginnings to become effective ways to communicate with consumers. Both were set up by Facebook originally to respond to MySpace, which rose to popularity by being a place for musicians, bands, and comedians to announce tour stops and news. Today, Facebook fan pages and groups are the preferred approach for many marketers to establish a corporate presence on Facebook and ultimately keep consumers informed.

Chapter Contents

Week 1: Learn About Pages and Groups

Pages and groups have always been Facebook's preferred destinations for business, while Facebook has steered individuals toward profiles. When both were first released, the differences between pages and groups were fairly significant, but there was a lot of ambiguity about which was the better option. Many companies on the leading edge of social network marketing had no choice but to create both a fan page and a group to see how consumers would react to both. As time has progressed, Facebook has evolved the page concept into something more akin to "profiles for business." People who create Facebook pages for their business now have very similar functionality to what we outlined in Chapter 4, "Month 1: Creating the Plan and Getting Started," for profiles. Groups, on the other hand, have evolved more into a tool for individual Facebook users to express themselves and to put users into groups for "closed" communications with a subset of friends. Today, most companies opt to create a Facebook fan page while monitoring the activity of groups. Nonetheless, both can be used for marketing purposes, and both can affect consumer perception of your brand, company, or campaign.

Monday: Observe a Successful Facebook Fan Page

The best way to learn the elements of an effective fan page presence for your organization is by observing the work of others. Very little is new or novel—and Facebook contains a wealth of examples of good fan pages that you can review to give you ideas of what would work in your specific situation and with your target customers.

One such example of a successful Facebook fan page is Raising Cane's page, a popular chicken fingers restaurant headquartered in Plano, Texas. Check out its fan page in Figure 5.1.

You may notice that the first thing you see is the Wall for Raising Cane's fan page. It contains official announcements from the company, images, links that have been posted, and comments from fans. Notice how many comments and positive interactions this particular company has with its customers! Raising Cane's has posted something every day, and their customers are responding. In this particular case, the restaurant appears to closely manage posts on the Wall—customers are not writing things directly on their Wall. You may want to allow this in your particular situation.

Here are a few other things you should notice about this fan page:

- The company has been pretty successful for a regional fast food chain—it has more than 44,000 fans!

- There is an option for you to become a fan at the very top of the screen next to the name of the page.

- Raising Cane's is aggressively using photos, with 18 albums (see Figure 5.2 for examples).

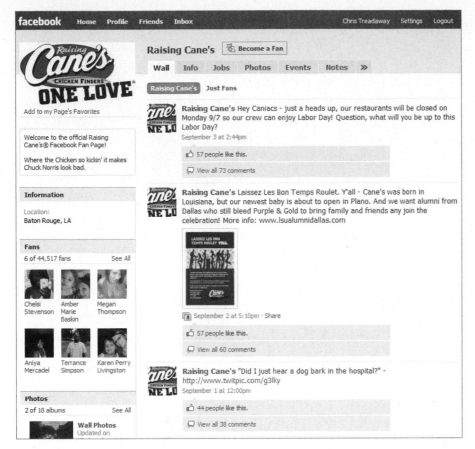

Figure 5.1 Raising Cane's fan page

Opening Pandora's Box

It's funny how something seemingly innocent like comments on your website or fan page can cut both ways. On one hand, it's a good way to get people talking about your product or service—and it can be a feature that helps drive traffic to you. On the other hand, if it isn't closely watched, it could turn nasty.

What are some things that you should consider when opening your site or fan page to user submissions and comments?

- Is your organization comfortable with the concept? Culturally, is your organization willing to deal with the good and the bad? Your organization may want to tightly control messaging or user feedback. If so, user comments and posts can be more damaging than an environment where broadcasting customer feedback isn't seen as a risk.

Continues

Opening Pandora's Box *(Continued)*

- Does your organization have experience with user-submitted content? If you are blogging aggressively or if you already have comments on another web property, others have probably faced difficulties and learned how to deal with problems.

- Will you really interact with customers, or will the feature give you a business benefit? Inherent in this process is the creation of a community of people who have a common interest—your product or your organization. If you can creatively use this as an outlet for calls to action or for better exposure, it may be a good option. If you're doing it just to "fit in" with the crowd, you're probably not motivated by the right things.

- Are you afraid of giving your customers a loudspeaker? Although this could be a great way to communicate with customers, it is also a great way for people to publicly air grievances. If your customers are more polite, it may work very well. But by doing this, you may be giving your customers a reason to get other people in the community upset at your organization.

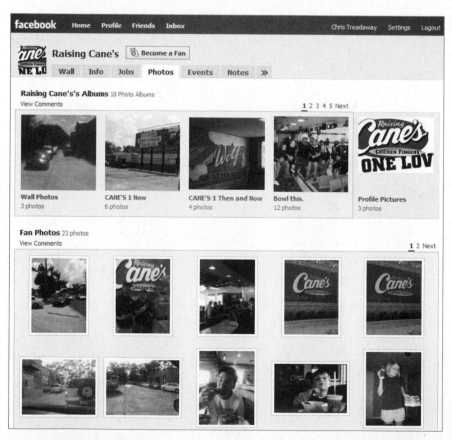

Figure 5.2 Raising Cane's Photos page

- Raising Cane's regularly runs contests and playfully announces winners on their wall (see Figure 5.3).
- The company is also using Facebook to help its human resources department find employees (an app powered by Monster.com; see Figure 5.4).

Figure 5.3 Raising Cane's Contests

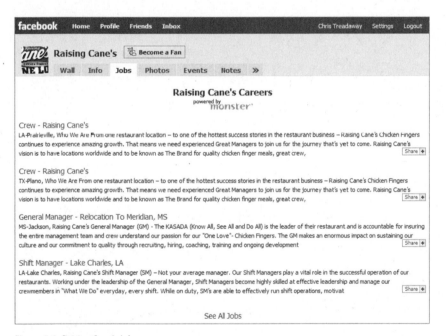

Figure 5.4 Raising Cane's Jobs page

We like the Raising Cane's example because it's pushing the limits of Facebook to help its business in a number of ways. Through the use of the Wall, the company is able to communicate with customers on a regular daily cadence. Therefore, a large number of their fans are getting a daily reminder of Raising Cane's that conveniently appears in the fans' News Feed. More important, this "community of fans" is helping to sell the Cane's concept by commenting and liking various Wall posts. All of it helps in a subtle, almost subconscious way. Presumably, the daily reminder plays a role where people choose to eat when they are hungry and can't come up with a better idea.

But over and above the daily Wall post, the restaurant is using photos, events, and other types of content to reinforce the restaurant and the brand with fun and energy. These things can help turn ordinary people who enjoy an occasional chicken finger basket into supporters who recommend the restaurant to friends and family. Alongside the marketing benefits of daily fan page maintenance, they're sourcing their network of Facebook fans for employees. This helps in a few ways:

- It helps inform passionate fans of the restaurant of available positions, which in turn helps the company source passionate employees.

- It reduces the cost of talent acquisition (if Canes' are indeed able to find qualified candidates).

- It is a simple yet meaningful way to show fans available job opportunities with the company.

One more important point regards Raising Cane's presence on Facebook: conducting a search yields a large number of fan page and group results. Many of the fan pages are clearly created by the company for specific restaurant locations, but there are a few which appear to have been created by fans. Certainly the large number of Raising Cane's groups are mostly user created. In order to clearly distinguish the official Facebook fan page for Raising Cane's, the company included this line in the small info section below their fan page image: "Welcome to the official Raising Cane's Facebook Fan Page!" (Figure 5.1.)

Tuesday: Become a Fan of Successful Fan Pages

So, let's start by reviewing an effective Facebook fan page. Log into Facebook, pick a brand or a company you really like, and enter it in the search box in the upper-right part of the screen. In the search results, click Pages, and click the fan page you'd like to see. Pages with a higher number of fans obviously are doing something better than those with fewer fans, so you should opt for those that have been more successful as you seek examples. (Alternatively, you may wish to browse the index of all Facebook fan pages in their respective categories. Here is the direct link to the directory, which is not easy to find on Facebook: http://www.facebook.com/pages/?browse. Or, two other sources are at http://www.facebakers.com and http://statistics.allfacebook.com/pages).

Conceptually, what features or elements of a Facebook fan page will help your business? If building a good Facebook fan page is one part art and one part science, then how can you emulate success in your own situation? Here are a few ideas:

Interaction Does the fan page encourage people to interact with each other or comment on the things you post or share? What kinds of content seem to work best to encourage interaction?

Soft-selling How far does the fan page administrator go to directly sell products or services? Is the fan page used to influence fans in any way?

Creativity What elements of the fan page are a clever or more interesting extension of the brand that makes it more acceptable or more interesting to the target market?

Informing How is the fan page used to communicate business information to customers? Is it too frequent, or is it used appropriately?

As you investigate success stories, consider becoming a fan of a half dozen or so, and observe how they communicate with you over time. You're looking for your snap reaction when you get a communication from a fan page—are you annoyed or are you happy to hear from them? Little things like this can have a big impact on how your fan page will be received. And how will this differ by demographic group and for your particular situation? Remember, some demographic groups accept a more or less frequent amount of communication from popular brands. Observe and remember to empathize with your customer base. Don't impose your standards on the marketplace—misreading what would or would not be allowed could cost you.

Just as with a profile, Facebook posts activity to fans' News Feeds when changes are made to a fan page. So, you won't just be updated when a new item is posted on the Wall. Changes to the Info tab, new events, new photos, new discussion threads, and so on, will appear in fans' News Feeds. Be sure to also check your fan page Updates section (found via your e-mail Inbox on Facebook—though this may be moved at some point). Fan page admins have the ability to message all fans; however, because these messages go into a separate section of Facebook, fans have to find the updates of their own volition. Nonetheless, it's worthwhile keeping an eye on how other companies/brands use the fan updates. File all this knowledge away for the future when you begin to build your company's Facebook fan page.

Wednesday: Learn the Basics of Facebook Groups

If you were to track how people have used Facebook over time, you would probably find that Facebook groups have been on a steady decline as a marketing tool. Why is that? There are several possible contributing factors:

- All content on fan pages gets indexed by Google (including for live searches), whereas indexed content on groups is limited, if any.

- More activity gets pushed to fans' News Feeds from fan pages than from groups users are a member of.

- Fan pages allow the addition of apps that provide much customization potential—especially with the Static FBML app.

- Fan pages offer the potential for unlimited fans that admins can message en masse via updates. Group membership is also unlimited and there is an advantage insofar as admins can send messages that land right in the Inbox. However, once a group reaches 5,000 members, the ability to send e-mails is no longer available. Facebook has this measure in place for "technical reasons and to prevent spam." (See: http://www.facebook.com/help/?faq=14513)

Fan pages have essentially evolved into company profiles, whereas groups are more for people who share a specific commonality beyond just liking a brand, company, or product. In terms of the psychology behind why Facebook users join Groups in the first place, more often than not it is simply a throwaway gesture to show support and declare something that person feels strongly about. Pages are open to the broad Facebook community, and groups are more subject to "membership" or specific qualifications that administrators require for members to participate.

There are three types of groups available:

- **Open (the default)** Anyone can view the group and content and anyone can join.

- **Closed** Invite-only, though anyone can view and read some content.

- **Secret** Invisible to everyone except members; these types of groups are not findable in a search. You have to be invited to even know it exists. Secret groups are ideal for family members. We've also heard of some companies using secret groups as their intranet (in-house internet).

Groups are an effective opportunity for companies that want to communicate exclusively with premium customers, sales targets, and so on. It's best to think of groups as a means to exclude certain Facebook users rather than including all who show interest as you would with a Facebook fan page. If you have good reasons to exclude or qualify users, choose a group (possibly only if you intend for that group to remain below the 5,000 threshold for sending e-mails). If you want to reach as many people as possible, choose a Facebook fan page. In some situations, you may want to use both a group and a fan page to communicate differently with segments of your audience. For example, consider a hypothetical scenario where a company is promoting a popular consumer product. They may want as many "fans" on their fan page as they can get. But they may also want to invite specific "fanatics" to be part of an exclusive, members-only club—a small, rabid community of sorts—to foster information sharing, product announcements, and special events only open to a select few. This is where groups can be used with great effect.

Facebook groups are general destinations for people with like-minded interests to gather and become members of. Group members can write on the group's Wall, exactly as you can on a profile page, as well as leave topics and posts on the discussion board.

According to Facebook, "The Groups page contains all the information about your groups on Facebook." You can see groups your friends have joined, navigate to your own groups, and create new groups on the Groups page. Additionally, you can search and browse for groups to join from this page.

You can create a group by going to www.facebook.com/grouphome.php and clicking the Create A Group button in the upper-right corner of the page. Follow the instructions on the subsequent pages by adding descriptive information about your group and other information. All groups require a group name, description, and group type. When you are finished, click Create Group, and you're done.

After you have added this information, you will then be able to control settings related to your group's privacy and add a group picture. You can change these settings at any time by clicking Edit Group on the group's main page.

Thursday: Decide Between a Fan Page or a Group

So, how do you decide whether you need a Facebook group or a fan page, or maybe even both? Although at first glance they appear to be similar to one another, fan pages and groups contain some key differences that you need to keep in mind when you are setting them up. In a nutshell, groups are easy to set up but have limited functionality. Pages provide a rich set of features that are not currently available on Facebook groups.

Fan pages allow the same type of interaction as groups but with many more options for customization and personalization. Like Facebook groups, a Facebook fan page has a Wall and can have a discussion board, but it can also have much more, such as Facebook applications, Flash, and HTML code. Because of the flexibility of using HTML code, fan pages can be customized to look similar to a website. Although fan pages often are pages devoted to a popular musician, sports star, actor/actress, or politician, they are quickly becoming much more than that, with pages for marketers, realtors, magazines, and writers, according to Facebook.

Facebook fan pages are for real entities to broadcast great information to fans in an official, public manner. Like profiles, they can be enhanced with applications that help the entity communicate with and engage their fans and that capture new audiences virally through their fans' recommendations to their friends.

A musical artist, business, or brand can create Facebook pages to share information, interact with their fans, and create a highly engaging presence plugged into Facebook's social graph. These pages are distinct presences, separate from users' profiles, and optimized for these presences' needs to communicate, distribute information/content, engage their fans, and capture new audiences virally through their fans' recommendations to their friends. Facebook pages are designed to be a media-rich, valuable presence solution for any artist, business, or brand that can be integrated seamlessly into the user experience with socially relevant applications.

Although the primary differences between pages and groups become evident only after you try them, let's look at what's been created to promote GeekBriefTV:

- GeekBriefTV group
- GeekBriefTV fan page

Why would GeekBriefTV create both a group and a fan page? Probably because of the differences between the two. Fan pages are visible to unregistered people and are indexed by search engines. This makes pages an important element for reputation management and search engine optimization campaigns. Additionally, pages allow for the inclusion of Facebook applications, give you the ability to create event listings, and give you access to user/visitor statistics. These features are not available in Facebook groups.

One advantage of Facebook groups is the feature that allows you to send out "bulk invites." You can easily invite all your friends to join a group. Of course, since any group member can also send bulk invites to his/her friends, this can easily be abused, lending itself to potentially being used for sending spam.

With pages, if you wanted to invite your friends in the same way, you'd need to create Friend Lists first, which are limited to just 20 individuals. This can be an extremely time consuming process. We recommend other creative ways of letting your friends know about your fan page and getting them to join.

For a succinct chart of the differences between pages and groups, check out Figure 5.5:

Key Feature	Facebook Page	Facebook Group
"Ugly" URLs	No	Yes
Hosting a discussion	Yes	Yes
Discussion wall, and discussion forum	Yes	Yes
Extra applications added	Yes	No
Messaging to all members	Yes	Yes
Visitor statistics	Yes ("Page insights")	No
Video and photo public exchange	Yes	Yes
"Related" event creation and invitation	Yes	No
Promotion with social ads	Yes (never tried it)	No

SEARCH ENGINE JOURNAL (www.searchenginejournal.com)

Figure 5.5 Difference between pages and groups

Although there are benefits and drawbacks for both pages and groups, it is up to you to decide which one suits your needs best. If you are looking for guidance, then we recommend the fan page for most situations. Based upon our experience, there is not really any compelling reason to choose a group over a page.

Celebrities, organizations, politicians, and corporate entities are using the Facebook fan page option in most cases today. Nevertheless, group pages remain popular in some cases, we believe, because they are easy to set up and they allow for quick conversation and interaction without the hassle of customization and creating the perfect fan page presence. In addition, often the perception of a group is that it is non-commercial; it's mostly Facebook users that create groups. Whereas fan pages are specifically designed for businesses to build their presence so are inherently more commercial than groups.

Friday: Set Up Your Page or Group

Before we dive into specific instructions on setting up fan pages, it's important to note that Facebook forces users to connect all fan pages to a user's personal profile. Many businesses balk at this and have, in fact, run into challenges because of this enforcement. For example, say a member of staff creates the company fan page whilst logged into their own personal account. This means that person is the primary admin for the fan page, which is fine. But, if they do not assign any other staff members as an admin and leave the company at some point, the Fan Page could end up sitting out there in limbo with no one to administer it if the ex staff member can't be tracked down. This has unfortunately happened to many businesses. The key, therefore, is to give careful thought as to which staff member will be the (initial) primary admin for the company fan page. And then have that person immediately assign at least one additional staff member as an admin.

There is no way for Facebook users to discern who is the admin for a page. In fact, even if you set up a fan page in your own name, e.g., as in the case of a celebrity, speaker, author, etc., Facebook treats your personal profile and your fan page as two totally separate and unique entities. Admins have to become a fan of their own page.

The only other point to make about this aspect of connecting personal profiles to fan pages is the fact Facebook does offer what is called a "Business Profile." If an individual (or company) wanted to have a Facebook fan page but currently does *not* have a personal profile on Facebook, it is possible to create a fan page that is connected to this very limited Business Profile. It's not possible to view and experience a fraction of the features Facebook offers via these Business Profiles, so we don't recommend this approach. (See http://www.facebook.com/help/?faq=12850)

To create your Facebook fan page, first log in with the account you'd like to use to administer your company's presence. You can add more people later to help you administer the page. Once logged in, scroll to the very foot and click on the small link for "Advertising" or, navigate to the Applications button in the lower left of your screen and look for the link for "Ads and Pages." Click Ads And Pages on the Applications tab in the bottom left of the screen. This is the primary interface for both administering Facebook advertising and creating Facebook fan pages. (Facebook really want you to buy ads to promote your Fan Page!) Now, depending on whether you have previously purchased Facebook Ads, the interface will look slightly different. Look for the button that says "Pages" (it has the little orange flag fan page icon) at either the very top or on the top left. Click that link, then look for another button that says "+ Create Page" to create a new Facebook fan page. Alternatively, here is the direct URL to create a page (which you can find on the lower left of any Facebook fan page: http://www.facebook.com/pages/create.php

Figure 5.6 shows the fan page setup process. There are a few interesting things to note here. First, local businesses have a variety of ways to profile themselves on Facebook—25 of them to be precise. So, fan pages are built to be compatible with small businesses that need to promote themselves via social media. Second, there is a further distinction between companies and notable people (artists, bands, famous people) in that both need to manage relationships with fans through a fan page instead of a profile. Finally, there is a loose "certification" process that asks the users to verify that they are authorized to establish the Facebook fan page for the business. If you are indeed that person, don't stress out about signing here with a digital signature. The Facebook cops aren't going to call around your office to verify that you are indeed the company representative. This is mainly a way for Facebook to deal with people who create a malicious fan page. Nothing can keep someone from claiming they are an official representative of your business, but they can be discouraged by the threat that Facebook will shut down their account if it is used to slander a business or a person.

Figure 5.6 Facebook fan page setup

One of your initial challenges will be simply deciding which Fan Page Category best suits your business. There are three primary categories to choose from: 1) Local, 2) Brand, Product, or Organization and 3) Artist, Band, or Public Figure. If you are a bricks and mortar business, we definitely recommend selecting Local, then drilling down to find the most suitable sub-category. The category we suggest most often is Band, Product, or Organization, then the sub-category of "Professional Service." The category you choose determines some of the fields that show up on your fan page. However, there are imminent changes (to the Info Tab and tabs in general), so the choice of category may not be as important in the coming months and years. Certainly, fans do not seem to navigate their way through the directory of categories; rather they find you via the promotion both you and your existing fans are doing.

Now that you've set up your fan page, you'll probably notice that it is relatively empty. Facebook provides the structure for your fan page, but it isn't going to do the work of populating the page with content. That's your job. Generally speaking, in the early days it wasn't a problem to ask users and fans to be patient while you built the site. In fact, you can choose to keep your fan page unpublished until you've added some custom content, apps, etc. If you read Chapters 3 and 4, you should already know where you will source content, what you will post, and at what cadence. If not, you have some catching up to do! In the beginning, you want to focus on getting the basics right—it's much better to learn earlier than later when thousands of people can watch you fail!

The Edit Page link (which is located just under the image you are using for your fan page) provides some features that you'll want to explore. It is really more a collection of settings that govern the use of your fan page. On this screen, you can edit the following:

- Who can/can't become a fan (age, country, and so on)
- Whether or not fans can post directly to the Wall or make comments
- Content that can be shared with mobile phone users
- The default tab that is opened on your fan page when a user visits for the first time on a given day
- Settings for other applications that you run

Your decisions about these settings will determine quite a bit about the user experience for your fan page. They drive who you target, the level of interactivity you have, and the first thing that people see when they view your page. The Wall is the default view, but some companies instead opt to have a different experience altogether. Customized experiences can be created by adding a specialized application that runs on the Boxes tab. So if the Wall doesn't provide the right experience for your customers, you can create whatever view you want with a custom tab and make that the default for your fan page. One caveat—this will require custom code and design if you want it to have a professional look and feel.

Fan pages have similar functionality to profiles in a variety of ways. The Info tab exists for a fan page much like it does for a profile, but it has a more limited set of information geared to businesses. (Facebook will be rolling out changes to tabs in 2010, so you may find the Info tab changes over time.) Included in the list of options is a list of websites. This list is typically used to inform users of other websites, social media accounts, and so on. You can similarly share upcoming events through the Events tab, photos through the Photos tab, blog posts through the Notes tab, links through the Links tab, and videos through the Videos tab. Functionally, fan pages are almost identical to in the features on Facebook profiles. In addition, discussions are available by default to encourage people to interact on your fan page. Third-party applications such as reviews, polls, and others can extend the fan page to include more functions of interest to your business. You'll need to try a few things and see what other page administrators are doing to make their Facebook presence more engaging. Most activities that are edited or shared by an administrator on the Facebook fan page will appear in fans' News Feeds. As you investigate new features and opportunities, test the outcomes with a Facebook profile so you can see how other fans will experience your page.

Now, the Boxes we mentioned are not to be confused with a relatively new Facebook feature called *fan boxes* (Figure 5.7). Fan boxes allow page administrators to publish a summary of the fan page to a widget that can run on websites outside Facebook. It's an ideal situation for companies that have a lot of web traffic to an official company home page, a blog, or a product page. You can show users of these sites that you have a Facebook fan page with the fan box. Why is this important? If you are active and have enough fans, it can communicate that you/your brand is modern, and it can communicate with customers on social media. It makes you more approachable and more personable. Now, on the other hand, it can be detrimental if it appears that you have abandoned your Facebook fan page or if you don't have any fans. So, be sure to add the fan box to your website only after your fan page has matured. This feature is all the more reason to make sure the Facebook fan page has a prominent role in your social media marketing campaign. Fan boxes and other "widgets" to help optimize your Facebook presence can be found at: `http://www.facebook.com/facebook-widgets`.

Figure 5.7 Facebook fan box example

Now turn your attention to Facebook groups. Similar to pages, you can access groups by clicking the Applications tab on the bottom left of your screen. In that menu, you should see Groups as an option. Click that link, and you'll see two columns—groups recently joined by your friends and groups to which you belong. You can also search for groups or create a new one by clicking the Create A New Group button at the top right of the screen. (The direct URL is: `http://www.facebook.com/groups/create.php`).

For demonstration purposes, we'll create a new group—the Facebook Marketing: An Hour a Day Support Group (Figure 5.8). As you can see on this screen, step 1 involves entering some basics about the group. In Figure 5.9, step 2 asks for specific controls you'd like to attach to the group, including who can post what types of content to the group's page. Sound familiar? It should—you can do similar things with groups as you can do with pages.

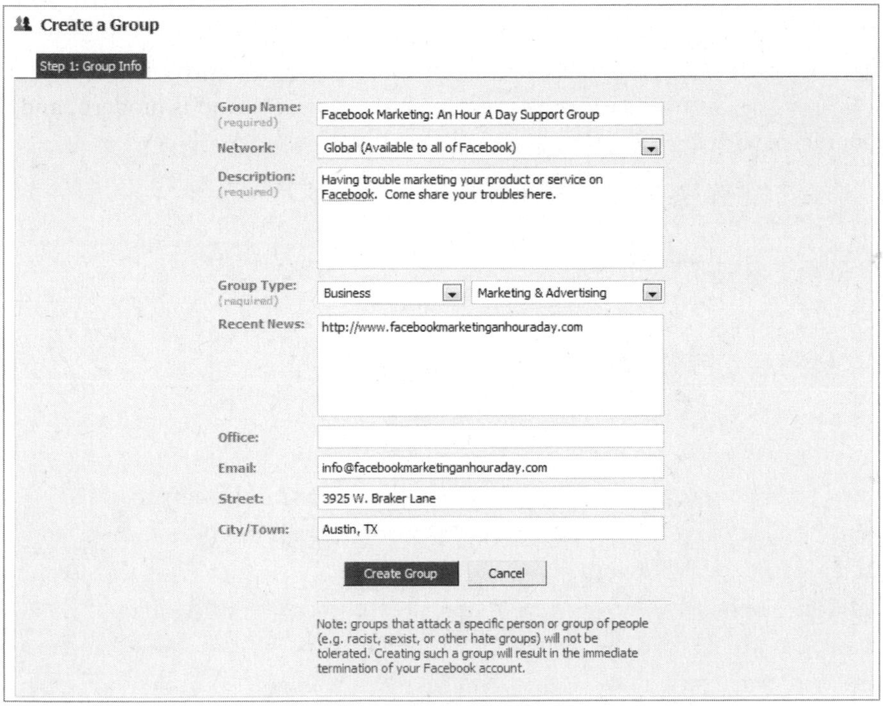

Figure 5.8 Facebook Marketing: An Hour A Day Support Group setup

After the simple two-step process, you're done establishing your first group. You may notice that there are no tabs here, nor is there any way to attach applications to your group. The group experience is largely predetermined by Facebook. You have fewer opportunities to customize a group than you do a page. But there are similarities—you can invite members; send messages to members; promote your group with Facebook advertising; announce events; share links, videos, and photos; and establish a discussion group.

Figure 5.9 Facebook group setup options

Week 2: Determine and Execute Content Strategy

Profiles, groups, and pages are the three ways to establish a presence on Facebook for your company. But these things are lifeless, not to mention pointless, without content that is updated for friends, group members, or fans to consume on a regular basis. We see examples all the time of companies that spend significant time, resources, and money building a fancy website with a great user interface. We'll visit these sites to get good examples for use in our own business or for clients, and we're often blown away by what we see. But for every 10 such sites, we probably visit a second time only two or three times, and we're only rarely a recurring visitor to any site we visit. Why? The answer lies in content, or lack thereof. Content is the lifeblood of any successful web presence, yet companies often don't match time spent on world-class web design with a content strategy that is designed to keep the site live, vibrant, and worth visiting on a regular basis.

Monday: Develop a "Product Strategy" for Content

We've talked a few times in this book about the importance of getting on users' News Feeds every day. The only way to do this without annoying people is by providing new, interesting content at least once a day. So, the Facebook profile, page, or group that you use is merely the container or the infrastructure that holds your presence. The content is the product that users either accept or reject with their continued support.

We've also mentioned the value of mapping your social media presence to your customers' needs. What do they want? What motivates them? Do their needs change at certain times of the year? Why would they recommend your site, product, or social media presence to their friends? What would make them comment and/or interact more with your Facebook presence? You will hit the mark if you think carefully about the needs of your different market segments and then meet those needs with content.

When we think of any new social media presence for a new client, we instinctively think of magazines. Facebook helps every company, brand, or organization become a publisher of their own online, interactive "magazine." You can look at the benefits of this and say, "Sure, I'd love my own interactive magazine!" But it comes with a lot of responsibility. You have to maintain your "magazine." Stop publishing information to it, and you don't have a publication any longer. People will lose interest if you fail to maintain it. Your "magazine" has a perspective on the world—think through the perspective you want to have and don't deviate significantly from it. If you do, your fans may get upset with you. But perhaps most important, give people things they can't or don't get anywhere else. This doesn't necessarily mean that your content has to be extraordinary or unique. Your target markets may just consume information primarily through Facebook—and you could be the one to provide a very simple yet helpful service!

Don't Overadvertise Yourself

The next time you are at a bookstore, pick up a few different types of magazines. Pay attention to how much they advertise themselves. Aside from the necessary insert that falls out of the magazine, you won't find too many "house ads." Remember this when establishing your own presence—people don't need a lot of advertisements for your business when they are already a fan, friend, follower, or member of your group. If you overadvertise, you run the risk of people getting dissatisfied. Focus on the needs of your customer and not the needs of your marketing department.

Tuesday: Talk with Colleagues About the Use/Reuse of Content

The good news is most organizations—large and small—already have mountains of content that would be perfect for sharing through social media. The bad news is that it is likely unorganized or used for entirely different purposes. So, you have a few major problems that you'll need to resolve if you want to use or repurpose content from your colleagues:

Cultural issues You'll need to help your colleagues get comfortable with repurposing content for sharing through Facebook. Some people will be very happy to share information with you, while others will not. Some of the people may want to share information that isn't appropriate for your social media presence—and some information is just simply uninteresting.

Sourcing and sorting the data You'll need access to information/content and need to organize it to build your library. Some of it may already be online, but the real gems may be offline. You need to learn what is available, and you need to organize it so the content you share covers a wide range of topics and doesn't bore your customers.

Operational realities Ensure you can update your social media presence frequently enough to keep your customers happy. This means that you need a person on tap to make sure that everything is updated as necessary.

If your company doesn't produce enough relevant content for your customers or if you can't reuse enough good content for whatever reason, you can always just point to third-party content that reinforces your company's point of view. Just 10 years ago, some people considered this to be a modern form of plagiarism—publishing a link to or summary of an article originally released on another company's website. In today's world of Google, search engine optimization, Twitter, and link building, it's a best practice. It's funny how times and norms change. Few companies are in a position to produce unique content for social media. Most use a hybrid strategy of sourcing their own content and pointing to the best available content on the Web to maintain sites and social media.

As you talk to your colleagues about these issues, you'll get a clear sense of how your organization views the sharing and production of content. From this feedback, you'll be able to create a strategy and some requirements for keeping your Facebook presence fresh and up-to-date. You'll know the language you should use and the amount of third-party content you can rely upon either on an ongoing basis or on slow days.

 Remember that social media makes everyone a publisher of content that reinforces their perspective—be it personal or professional. Individual users have the ability to share content with thousands of people with just the click of a mouse. Take advantage of the fact that everyone is a publisher to get the word out about your campaign.

Wednesday: Set Editorial Policy for Content

Let's review where we are—your social media presence is, in essence, a 21st century form of journalism. You are a publisher of sorts, as are your customers. Success is driven by interactivity, not by an antiquated measurement of how well you "shout." Customers are free to interact with your content and your presence, and their reactions can be seen by hundreds or thousands of people. Facebook gives you some opportunities for controlling the flow of information—you've probably given a lot of thought to how you can use these controls to make Facebook work for your company.

Editorial policy is very important to ensure that the customer experience with your Facebook presence is consistent and valuable. It is the set of rules that govern what you post, how, and when. We're not proposing that you go to the effort of creating an editorial policy for the sake of making work. We think it's a handy way to make sure that everyone associated with your social media presence knows what to do and knows the behaviors that should be avoided. You should have multiple people involved—if for no other reason to mitigate the risk of losing a single person to vacation, illness, and so on.

So, what elements are required for a good editorial policy? The following are a few to consider. Answers to these questions should drive a succinct document that you can circulate to ensure that you don't have mistakes and to help make tough decisions when they arise:

Purpose Why do you have a Facebook presence? Who are you trying to reach?

Types of content What are the primary types of content that you'll share? How will you "mix it up" so consumers can get a variety of experiences (and not just status updates or links)?

Tone/language What is the best way to communicate with your customers? Formal language/informal language? Do you joke around? Are you serious? Informative? Authoritative? Will you use third person or first person, or a mix of both?

Subject matter What will you share? From what sources (internal/third party)? What won't you share? What topics are taboo? Will you change the types of information you release based on circumstances (time of year, the economy, current events)?

Communication Will you engage in a conversation with users through Facebook? Will your presence help people communicate with one another? If it is important to you, how will you use the site to gather customer information?

Organization Can people find what they want easily? If their needs can't be met through your Facebook presence, can they easily be diverted to your other properties (online or offline)?

Frequency How often will you post? Daily? Five times a week? Twice a day? What is an acceptable range for your posts (low and high)?

Advertising Will you advertise your own products/services through your Facebook presence? If so, how? How often? Will you allow third parties to advertise through your Facebook presence?

Clear communication will help everyone on your team succeed. Remember, you don't want to create a massive infrastructure to post to Facebook and monitor social media, but you do want redundancy and consistency. Know who your "editor-in-chief" is, who that person's backup will be, and who will support them.

The editor's job is to provide a product that customers love and one that they'll enthusiastically recommend to others. You also want to be so in tune with customers' needs that you can intuitively drive the future of your Facebook presence by commissioning new types of content, changing editorial policy, and helping solve problems in other areas of your business.

Finally, it's good to have ways to involve other people in your company in the execution of your social media strategy. Fellow employees may have great suggestions for content, campaign execution, creative, and so on. The lessons of "crowdsourcing" have taught us time and time again that great ideas can come from anywhere—you just have to be open to the possibility. If you can create a system to quickly triage suggestions and ideas, you'll probably get a great idea or two you may not have considered. You'll look better when you are able to humble yourself enough to know that you may not have all the answers.

Thursday/Friday: Perform Your Content Audit

If you're going to do a good job posting content, you need an idea of the assets that you have and those you are willing to share via social media. These can be items that have never been shared with customers or content that is already out there for the world to see on your website. It's OK to post content that is already available—many people have been very successful with Facebook by simply exposing fans to existing content that is available elsewhere on the Web. (You're essentially doing your fans a service by aggregating good content for them!)

Start by classifying the types of content that you have based on whether it is already online. You should have enough content nearby that has already been produced for online consumption—it's your lowest-hanging fruit that probably doesn't require much additional work. Make sure, though, that the content is interesting for your customers. It's better to take a little extra time to get the content right.

Keep in mind also that your users may want some variety in the types of content you post. You need different types of things (articles, blog posts, charts, graphs, numbers, third-party articles of interest, videos, podcasts, and so on) to keep things fresh. You'll also need a good mix of product information, commentary that supports your company or brand, events, sales/offers, and so on. Keep your voice consistent but your content fresh and compelling. This audit should ensure that you have a variety of different things to post and that you're able to see how different types of content encourages fans to interact and share with friends more often.

After you have created a list of content for sharing on Facebook, you will likely notice that you have some gems—great content that you know your customers will love. There are two schools of thought about gems. Some people prefer to lead with their best content so the first fans or followers become rabid, enthusiastic evangelists for your brand. Others prefer to hold their best content for later, once a loyal following has been established. There really are no right or wrong answers for this. We usually advise clients to share their best at both times to get the best of all worlds.

Week 3: Add and Experiment with Content

Now it's time to move from ideas to execution—the day-to-day process of keeping your social media presence alive. You have two main options when it's time to publish. You can enter a simple status update, or you can share content. Status updates are good for direct albeit lighthearted interactions with your customer base, while content (in the form of links, photos, videos, imported blog posts, events, etc.) is typically used to share interesting things you want them to see or experience.

Monday: Publish Content to the Wall

Sharing content through Facebook is simple, and the same interface is used for both pages and profiles (Figure 5.10). From either your News Feed screen, your profile, or your fan page, simply click the icon for posting a photo, video, event, or link, and a drop-down box will guide you through completing the process. You can also add a comment to the posted item to add color to the item that you are sharing. To finish, you must click the Share button at the bottom right of the box—it isn't enough to simply attach or upload the item—so be sure to take that last step.

Figure 5.10 Interface for posting content to pages or profiles

As you experiment with posting different types of content, you may notice some subtle differences between the different things you post. Links shared through Facebook are reformatted to include the following:

- Title of the link, pulled from the `<Title>` tag of the web page being referenced
- A brief summary of the link, pulled from the `<Meta "description">` tag of the web page being referenced
- A thumbnail picture that represents the link that is chosen by the poster. (With most all posted links, Facebook pulls in several thumbnails and you can cycle through to select the most appropriate one to post).

This content can also be targeted at specific users, although currently Facebook only allows geographic and language-based targeting. You can edit the title and summary by clicking either and changing the text—but be sure you do this before you click the Share button. Once you click the Share button, you can't edit the post any longer; you can only delete it.

Tuesday: Correct an Erroneous or Embarrassing Post

It's an inevitable reality of publishing to the Web—no matter how careful you are, you are going to make a mistake now and then. Maybe you've posted content to the wrong place. Maybe you said something that you shouldn't have said. In these cases, it's important to stay calm, don't panic, but act fast. If you posted something to your News Feed, you can delete it by going to your profile and hovering over the upper-right corner of your post. A Remove option will appear—click it, and the content will be removed from your profile and the News Feed of your friends. If you posted to your fan page, you can hover over the upper-right corner of your contribution and remove it from there.

You can't stop people from seeing this post in the time it takes you to remove it, but you can minimize the damage of your mistake! In certain cases, it makes sense to acknowledge the mistake and apologize openly to people who associate with you. In other cases, it's just better to let a sleeping dog lie. You'll have to make the judgment call to determine exactly how and if you should address mistakes that you inadvertently publish.

Fortunately, mistakes are not discoverable long-term unless they're so bad that someone took a screen capture of your mistake and has decided to share it somewhere on the Web. Search engines are beginning to catalog data shared via social media for discoverability and to make search engines more accurate. But as of now, there isn't a "Wayback Machine" (www.archive.org) for social media, though there are third party services springing up that back up social media sites—such as SocialSafe.net and Backupify.com—so you never know what's being kept on a backup.

Wednesday: Post Videos and Photos

You can share individual photos, create an album to commemorate photos of a certain theme, or take new photos with your webcam. As with other types of content sharing on Facebook, this process is also very simple—uploading a photo requires you to browse for it on your hard drive and click Share. For an album, you simply give your album a name, a location, and access settings for users or groups of users who may see your pictures. Then you upload the pictures you'd like to put into that album. You can add a description to albums and individual photos; plus you can tag friends who appear in photos. Other options include the ability to select a specific photo for the album cover, reorganizing the order in which photos appear in an album, and posting the album (and/or individual photos) onto your profile using the Share button.

Posting an event is very simple also—just give it a title, a location, and a date/time. You can invite individual friends, friend lists, or other people via e-mail who may not even have a Facebook account. Similar to other types of content, events and photos may be "liked" or commented upon by other Facebook users.

Posting a video is a little more confusing. Facebook gives you two main options for dealing with video—either you can record a video with a webcam or you can upload an existing video from your hard drive. A webcam can be an interesting way to "personalize" your brand or company, but most companies will probably not use this feature for marketing purposes. Most will instead opt to upload a video from a hard drive that has been edited in some way. Figure 5.11 shows some of the options you have for adding details to your videos, such as adding a title and controlling who can view your video. It usually takes some time for Facebook to process your video, so don't expect it to post to your profile or page immediately. After it is uploaded, you may want to "share" your video again from your profile or page. Uploaded videos don't always make it to the News Feed, so it may be helpful to share it again to be safe.

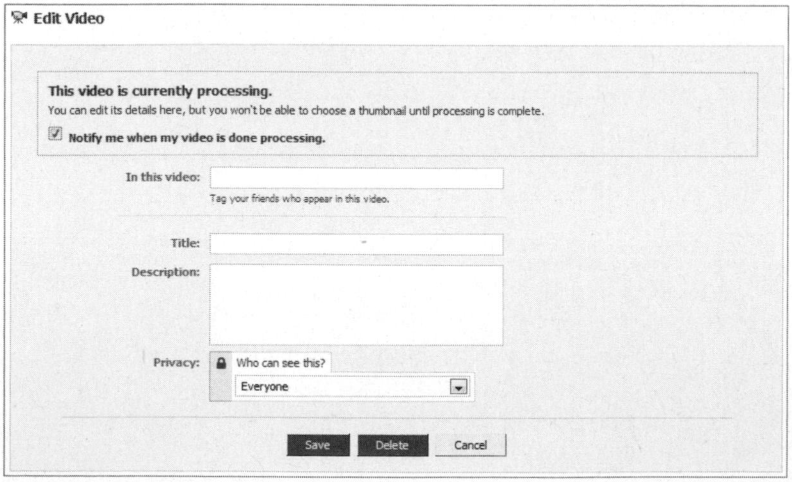

Figure 5.11 Video details

What about YouTube you ask? Well, at this snapshot in time you will need to share YouTube videos as a link. Interestingly enough, YouTube videos that are shared within Facebook can play inside the Facebook profile or fan page. So, a user doesn't have to go outside Facebook to see a video that is shared. How nice of Facebook! YouTube provides significant search engine optimization benefits, so this is an excellent way to optimize your presence and links of different types across popular web properties. People can still "like" or comment on your YouTube videos just as they can "like" or comment on other links you share.

Thursday: Experiment with Content

Experimentation is key throughout any Internet marketing project, but it's particularly interesting early in social media marketing. Why? Because when you start, you have no idea at all exactly how customers will react to you. The beginning is in some ways the scariest part of the project whether you are a marketing manager, a consultant, or just a friend giving free advice. You've sold the benefits of social media, and you've sold people on your abilities. You probably also showed examples of successful companies and how they were able to succeed with social media. If management has agreed to a project, they're probably expecting it to produce.

Don't fret—the answer lies in truly becoming expert in how the little things you do impact performance as measured by fans, friends, and so on. For example, you can learn the following:

- What happens when you post a link/photo/video/note?
- How do customers respond differently to different types of content?
- How often should you post new content?
- How do customers respond to unique content that is unavailable anywhere else on the Web? Is the response different from when you post content that exists on your website? Third-party content?
- Are customers disappointed if you don't post an update frequently enough?

   As measured by the following:

- Increase/decrease in fans/friends/followers/group members
- Sign-ups to a newsletter or other lead generation mechanism
- Number of comments
- Number of "likes"
- Increase in traffic to your website
- Increase in referrals from Facebook.com web pages to your website

Remember that every action you take has a reaction from your customer base. The best practice for capturing this information is to keep a spreadsheet with details on what you post and outcomes over the subsequent 24 hours. Don't rely on memory or anecdotes for this information. If you get into a habit of recording the data for outcomes, you'll have a great resource that you'll use in a variety of ways you can't possibly predict in advance. We'll talk in more detail about creating useful analytics for monitoring and measurement in Chapter 9, "The Analytics of Facebook."

Rising Tides Raise All Boats

As your numbers grow, you'll probably notice more and more interaction on your properties. This is a great thing—congratulations! But remember that with increased numbers, you should expect increased interaction. Hold yourself to higher standards as you generate a larger following.

Friday: Fill Your Presence with Content and People

All week, you should have been gradually adding content to your presence according to the editorial policy and cadence that you set previously. A Facebook presence that is not maintained on a regular basis runs the risk of losing supporters. Sure, it's difficult to maintain something that is so public, but it's key to your success.

You're really looking to fill the presence with content so you don't have white space in the Wall and other places where people will be viewing your presence and making judgments about your organization. The minimum bar here is to fill available space with information and to do so often enough to communicate that you've made a commitment to the presence and that it is valuable. In most cases, you'll need to answer the basic organization profiling questions on the Info tab, and you'll need at least half a dozen pieces of content, status updates, videos, links, and so on, on your Wall.

After you've achieved the minimum bar, you're ready to tell more people about your Facebook presence. This would be an appropriate time to invite people—employees, partners, friends, family, and so on. Just as with content, you'll need supporters for your presence to communicate to other people visiting for the first time that you are relevant and interesting. The more people you have willing to associate with your organization, the more it appears to be a seemingly unbiased third-party endorsement to strangers and other people who you'll also need to be successful.

Week 4: Monitor and Modify the Plan

At this point, your project should be in full swing. You've picked the means of interacting with your customers (page, profile, and/or group), and you've started posting content to fill out your presence. You have an editorial understanding, you have a voice, and you are committed to posting content on a regular basis to keep your customers happy and informed. Although you are only a week or two into the campaign, the only things you haven't done are Facebook advertising and detailed reporting/

analytics—things that are more appropriate later in the campaign. Some parts of the project are proving to be easy, but others unfortunately are not—this is the time to fill gaps in your operational plan.

Monday/Tuesday: Reassess Your Progress

In Chapter 3, we discussed the discrete tactical tasks necessary to effectively produce your Facebook presence. In Chapter 4, we talked about a few things to consider when assessing your competitors. You've learned a lot about what it takes to get the job done and the challenges you face. So, let's now make sure you can do the job.

Figure 5.12 shows a simplistic view of the cycle of work for any Facebook marketing campaign. While you're always doing a few of these things simultaneously, you start with a theory on the types of content that would be interesting to your customers. You post that content on a reasonable cadence and with editorial policy and voice that fits both your brand and your customer segments. You monitor results and feed a reporting mechanism that will give you time-trending data for later analysis. This analysis feeds revisions to your plan and your approach, and the cycle refreshes. It's rare for this cycle to only go around a few times—you'll iterate repeatedly learning the entire way.

Figure 5.12 Facebook marketing cycle

It's probably too early after a single week to make dramatic changes to your approach—you want enough data to inform decisions. How much data is enough? Typically, a few weeks will smooth out things such as three-day weekends, holidays, vacation schedules, and other types of seasonality that can dramatically impact results. So, let's hold off on data for a few more weeks—we'll cover analytics in detail in Chapter 9. For now, let's focus on the operational issues that you face, for example:

- Are you handling the workload, or are you overwhelmed by the project?
- Are you confident in the choices you've made regarding your social media presence (Facebook, Twitter if appropriate, and elsewhere)?

- Is your effort comparable to or, better yet, better than, your competitors'?

- As a result of your efforts, are customers interacting with you and other fans/friends/followers more?

- Do you have enough interesting content to keep customers engaged, or are you already finding it difficult to source interesting content?

- Do you think you're doing the right things, or do you intuitively believe that you are missing out on some opportunity?

- Do your colleagues support you and support the effort? Are you getting necessary management support?

Be honest with yourself—there is no point in lying to yourself or your superiors. We find a very interesting and effective forcing function is a meeting with a friendly senior colleague to assess progress. Have this "mentor" of sorts give you honest feedback on what you're doing well and what you're doing poorly. But make sure it's a friendly person who won't cause problems! You do need time to iterate and succeed after all.

Wednesday: Get Help Where You Need It

If you are doing a great job and you're on the way to meeting goals, feel free to skim this part of the chapter or even skip ahead. But if any part of this project to be difficult or too time-consuming, it may be an indication that you need help from someone with the expertise or time to manage the process.

We always recommend that companies look internally first to find colleagues who may be able to offer assistance. Oftentimes, companies have a good person or group willing and able to assist right around the corner. Besides, these projects tend to be interesting—so you may get more cooperation than you expect. Keep in mind that if you're the one responsible, you are the primary person to get the job done. This isn't an opportunity or justification for you to get your colleagues to do work for you. But if for whatever reason you can't find help or if it doesn't fit your company's culture to share responsibilities across different groups, you can always get help from people who specialize in Facebook marketing or social media.

Find Experts Who Do What You Can't

If you're fortunate enough to work in a company that can afford to pay for social media expertise, hold firm to a simple rule. Find vendors who do what you can't. Make a list of things in your campaign that you struggle with. Then use that list to find vendors with expertise in those exact areas. You can get the expertise you need as long as you know specifically what you need and you remain in charge throughout the process!

When assessing third parties who can help with your social media project, first know exactly where you need help. Draft a list of goals you want a third party to solve for you. Make sure you're assessing people against the likelihood they'll solve your problems first. Oftentimes consultants will want to do a different part of the project—so you have to stand firm. You should always be open to suggestion, but you should also make sure you hold third parties accountable for the exact surgical help necessary to advance your campaign. The right person to help with the day-to-day maintenance of a social media presence may be different from the right person to help with high-level strategy. Get the right person for the right job.

While doing your due diligence on consultants, consider that the world has spawned a lot of "social media experts." Scrutinize people, and consider a few other things as you make your decision:

Background Has the person, or the principals of the consulting business, had a track record of optimizing new technologies and running successful campaigns?

Fit Is the consultant able to do the things you need them to do? Are they a strategist, someone who can roll up their sleeves and get the job done, or both? Strategy and implementation are two different things—many consultants like to gravitate to the sexy strategy work when you may not even need it, and then you're still left with the need for implementation. Clear communication is key.

Expertise Can the person truly do the job for you? Have they or the company done projects for clients similar to yours? Does the person ask you a wide variety of relevant, fact-finding questions? (The more thorough a third party is in their initial intake process, the more likely they'll do a good job for you, assuming they also have the track record to back this up).

Validation Have third parties validated their or the company's expertise? Are former clients willing to share success stories or references?

Training is critically important. Once set up, a lot of Web 2.0 projects can run on autopilot if someone on staff is able to monitor success and failure. Hold consultants to a high standard that includes training and an exit plan. You don't want to pay a consultant ad infinitum, and you shouldn't have to if you've hired the right person or company.

Thursday/Friday: Produce the First Reports and Analysis on Your Progress

In your company, it may have taken a committee to decide to approve your Facebook marketing project, or it may have taken just a single person. In either event, sharing the things you've learned early in the campaign is a handy tactic to reinforce the decision and to set the right tone for the future. This would be a great time to share initial findings with interested parties.

What constitutes a good report? We've always had success by sharing data on effort and outcomes. What has taken place and what happened as a result—all in the language of numbers. But you can't stop there—a good report will also have some seemingly objective analysis. You're the one writing the report—you'd be remiss to not take the opportunity to offer your interpretation of the numbers and what they mean.

Start slow and try to focus on a single metric or two in the early phases of the project. Figure 5.13 is an example of a good, simple page views graphic provided by Facebook Insights that would be perfect to share early in a campaign. Add a simple commentary to something like this, and you have your first report! Your colleagues are not nearly as expert as you are on Facebook marketing, so reporting will need to reflect important data points that can be both easily understood and easily explained. Over time, you'll have the opportunity to get more complex as people learn alongside you.

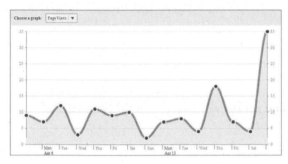

Figure 5.13 Basic early campaign report for fan page

You won't have a lot of time-trending data early in the project, but that's OK. Show what you can, and make sure you manage your colleagues' expectations. Learning often is a huge benefit when companies decide to do social media work in-house. Focus on what your effort has taught you and how it informs future decisions.

Featured Case: *Mad Men* Case Study

For cable channel AMC, August 26, 2008, was a difficult day. Some fans of the show *Mad Men*, a property of AMC, had taken it upon themselves to establish Twitter accounts in the names of the show's characters. Not only that, but they were Twittering in-character and had created an alternate world of "Twittertainment" for fans of the show between episodes. That doesn't seem like such a bad thing, does it?

Well, that wasn't the cause of the difficulty. The day went south not because of the fans' actions but because of how AMC responded. It appears that AMC demonstrated its complete misunderstanding of the benefits of grassroots viral marketing and social marketing channels like Facebook by issuing a Digital Millennium Copyright Act (DMCA) takedown notice to Twitter. AMC claimed copyright ownership over the characters' names and the fan fiction that was being created in "an unauthorized manner" on the microblogging site.

Continues

As expected, Twitter suspended the accounts and began an investigation of them. Twitter really had no option in this case because the act requires that Twitter take the action it did.

Of course, also as expected, it took less than one day for the fans of the show to explode in anger across the Internet on blogs, on Facebook, and of course on Twitter to show their displeasure over the heavy-handed tactics employed by AMC. To be fair to AMC, there is some confusion in the public about what actually happened during this kerfuffle. In several articles, AMC claims that it never sent any DMCA takedown notices to Twitter. At the same time, Twitter isn't talking about what happened or why the accounts were suspended. So, although it is difficult to ascertain what was happening in the background at AMC and at Twitter, what is clear is that a show about advertising had been created by people who didn't understand that the issues faced by the Sterling Cooper agency in the world of Madison Avenue in 1962 was very, very different from the issues a similar agency would have faced in 2008. The issue at hand here is that—say it with us—you no longer control the brand.

According to a piece in *Business Week* on August 26, 2008, Deep Focus, AMC's web marketing agency, stepped up and pointed out to its client that all this fan activity and positive attention toward the show was, how do you say, "good" for the show. NYMag.com put it best: "AMC's Web-marketing group knocked some skulls together at AMC HQ. IT'S FREE ADVERTISING!"

After some backroom discussions about the benefits of fans providing free buzz for the show, AMC's decision makers apparently rescinded the DMCA takedown notice that they claimed they never sent. Twitter restored the accounts, and all was right for fans of the 1960s world of Madison Avenue once again.

Has AMC Changed Its Mind-Set?

Now fast-forward a year later. AMC's current mind-set in regard to social media has completely changed since that cold PR day in August of 2008. Let's be honest, if the end of the story was simply "another big media company doesn't get social media, sticks foot in mouth and head in the rear," then this event wouldn't be in this book. The reason? There are far too many of those stories out there today. Not one of them stands alone any longer. Any time the end of the story is "so-and-so screwed up and went away," there's nothing to learn from that event.

Today, AMC is using online marketing channels like Facebook to promote *Mad Men* and other shows with a successful, comprehensive strategy that covers several social media platforms and drives new, measurable interest in the show daily. Any agency executive at a 1960s Madison Avenue agency would be wise to sit up and take notice.

What's the State of the *Mad Men* Facebook Community?

AMC has created a focused, vibrant community filled with dynamic content that is not only popular with the show's loyal fans but is also entertaining for the casual observer. Building a large following for your Facebook presence requires a network of other platforms, microsites, and offline campaigns, working in conjunction to drive visitors to your fan page.

As you can see on AMC's *Mad Men* landing page (www.amctv.com/originals/madmen), it has a link to its Facebook fan page, its blog, its Twitter profile, and its iPhone app. AMC leverages the traffic its *Mad Men* landing page gets and pushes the audience to its Facebook fan page along with other social platforms.

Many social media campaigns lack this level of integration. They assume their consumers on other social networks will find them on their own. Unfortunately, that is not always the case. AMC understands this and actively courts users to visit one platform from others.

Has the fan base for *Mad Men* been increased? Yes. According to AllFacebook.com, a site that tracks the growth of fan pages on Facebook, The *Mad Men* Facebook fan page is seeing a growth of about 25,000 new fans per month as of October 2009. The fact that the demographic targeted by the marketing team for *Mad Men* aligns well with the demographic that is most active on Facebook has been helpful in this area.

After the Twitter debacle, AMC has learned that connecting all your social platforms with the brand website acting as a hub not only can help introduce consumers to your other marketing channels but can also help grow overall brand awareness.

Has AMC Increased Awareness for the TV Show and Brand?

In a word, "Yes!" In two words, "Absolutely, yes!"

But there's one important thing to remember. As we mentioned previously, this wasn't solely done with Facebook. It's critical that you understand that launching a successful PR campaign online requires the involvement of several different platforms and methodologies. To get to the question of how AMC found success on Facebook for *Mad Men*, it's necessary to look outside of Facebook to see what other things AMC was doing online and offline during this campaign.

It seems that no one questions the stereotype in the show of Madison Avenue executives drinking at all hours of the day or night. Brian Rea, 82, worked at the Little Club in the 1950s, a popular Midtown restaurant. He's quoted in the *New York Times*: "Lunch was a big thing," he said. "They took two and a half hours. We had a lot of agency people come in, from Cunningham & Walsh, BBDO, all having serious lunches with drinks" (www.nytimes.com/2009/08/12/dining/12don.html?_r=1).

Continues

Featured Case: *Mad Men* **Case Study** *(Continued)*

"Cocktails have been a vital element of the show right from the opening scene," says Robert Simonson in the same *New York Times* piece. The first scene in season 1 shows Don Draper sitting in a bar. We learn his drink preference, 'Do this again—old-fashioned, please,' before we know his name or what he does for a living."

When Deep Focus deployed a few microsites in order to support the show and create excitement around the brand, it only made sense that it played to this theme. One of the sites it created was the 1960s Cocktail Guide. It shows fans of the show how to make swanky, hip adult beverages just like the ones that the advertising executives at Sterling Cooper would have had. Now fans can enjoy the show with an authentic Gibson Martini or Manhattan in hand. The fans loved the guide, and so did the traditional press. According to the *New York Times*, blurbs about the microsite were written about on blogs such as the pop-culture RetroModGirl (http:// retromodgirl.blogspot.com/2009/08/madmen-60s-cocktail-guide.html) and the foodie blogs TheKitchn (www.thekitchn.com/thekitchn/the-cocktails-of-mad-menthe-new-york-times-092767) and SlashFood (www.slashfood.com/2009/08/12/mad-men-party-guide).

News aggregation sites (http://showhype.com/story/mad_men_cocktail_guide) promoted the microsite, as did Oprah.com (www.oprah.com/article/food/partyplanning/20090915-mad-men-cocktail-party). There, the pitch to consumers was "Host a cocktail party Betty Draper would be proud of." For each of these scenarios, the blog post or article links to the AMC landing page for *Mad Men* or to its own social media profiles on Facebook, Twitter, and YouTube.

How Does AMC Use Facebook to Drive Attention So It Can Sell Ads During the Show?

Coffee brand Eight O'Clock is the main sponsor of AMC's social media efforts for *Mad Men*. However, let's look at how AMC partners Eight O'Clock Coffee with *Mad Men*'s social media public relations.

The most popular social media campaign at the beginning of season 3 for *Mad Men* was the "Mad Men Yourself" avatar-making site. The site was created by Deep Focus, sponsored by Eight O'Clock Coffee, and promoted on the *Mad Men* fan page and Twitter. The site allows fans to create stylized avatars for use with any of their social media sites. Not only has the site been a huge hit with fans of the show, but the art created by the site has become a very popular meme on Twitter. In late September 2009, a quick search finds all types of positive conversations encouraging peers and friends to the site.

Essentially, the excitement driven by the 1960s hip icons created an army of *Mad Men* evangelists—directing fans and nonfans alike to the Eight O'Clock sponsored site to get their own version of customized 1960s icons for their MySpace, LinkedIn, Twitter, and Facebook profiles.

As of this writing, we are not aware of any additional brand integration with the coffee maker and the show. It would be interesting to see further crossover. For instance, why not have Sterling Cooper, the advertising agency featured in the show, take on Eight O'Clock Coffee as a client in the storyline? Perhaps a simple campaign of product placement would suffice. Why are the characters in the show not walking around the office with paper coffee cups emblazoned with the Eight O'Clock Coffee logo on them?

In any event, you can see how an initial misfire has been turned around, creating a complete social media ecosystem where AMC utilizes Facebook, Twitter, and other social media platforms not only to enhance the brand but as a integral part of the advertising model used to support the show and network.

Month 3: Create Demand with Facebook Ads

6

Facebook advertising is one of the best deals today in Internet marketing; nowhere else can you target users as surgically as you can on Facebook. Better yet, you can do it for a fraction of the cost of the same targeting on other Internet properties and offline outlets. Even so, you should paradoxically temper your expectations. Facebook ads work differently than banner ads or search engine click-through ads. Users respond differently to Facebook ads, and depending on demographics and social norms, some ads work better than others. Success with Facebook advertising requires aggressive monitoring, experimentation, patience, and creativity.

Chapter Contents

Week 1: Learn the Basics of Facebook Advertising

Before we get started with a campaign, we'll review some basic concepts of Internet advertising. All Internet advertising campaigns set out to influence consumer behavior in one way or another. Campaigns range from simple awareness to image building to specific calls to action based on the manager's goals. These goals are determined based on the context of a specific situation within an organization: a company may be looking to improve its image, a nonprofit may be looking to expand its volunteer base, or a government agency may be looking to inform users of a new site that will improve their operating efficiency. Regardless of the intent, Internet advertising, if properly harnessed, can help achieve those goals. For more information on Internet marketing metrics and derivative statistics, please skip ahead to Chapter 9, "The Analytics of Facebook."

Monday: Review Opportunities in Facebook Advertising

Facebook advertising can help with a variety of problems when you decide to hit the accelerator on creating demand for whatever Internet properties you are marketing. Specifically, Facebook advertising is great if you want to do the following:

- Create more traffic or visibility for your Facebook presence
- Test the effectiveness of a change or addition you've made on your Facebook presence and see how effective that change is at converting traffic to something more meaningful (fans, friends, group members, leads, application users, and so on)
- Tap into the Facebook audience to promote an external website or campaign

 If your organization wants to use Facebook advertising in the future for a large campaign, you may want to learn on a lower-priority project. It's better to get a feel for it without pressure to perform—just make sure you measure it and learn from the process!

Whatever your motivation, Facebook advertising can help with any/all of these things if you have the budget to pay for the impressions or clicks and if you have the wherewithal to do the work necessary to effectively monitor your progress. If you have the budget to do the work but you won't have the time to learn how to analyze the data, you are wasting an opportunity to get smarter and become more efficient with your ad spend.

It's a self-serve advertising model, which means that with a little patience and learning you can learn how to turn it from something seemingly esoteric in the beginning to a ship you can steer with remarkable precision. Alternatively, you may want an expert to create an advertising strategy that fits your needs and learn from that process. Either way, you really can turn Facebook into a machine where you put money into one end and get traffic and attention from customers on the other end. That's the goal here.

Tuesday: Choose Success Metrics

Facebook is not unlike any other Internet marketing effort you may undertake. First, you determine your goals for the effort. Make sure you can measure outcomes that will tell whether you've succeeded. If you're lucky, this will only require you to do a lot of manual work to collect the data. If you aren't so fortunate, you'll have to get colleagues to cooperate and provide you with the data you need and at the right reporting cadence.

Here's one example from a recent client engagement. The client wanted to know how an increased emphasis on publishing regular updates to their Facebook fan page with links to their website would impact that website's traffic. We worked with the client to find the right person in the organization to provide data on page views. Two weeks later, we got the data—but it was reported on a monthly basis and not a daily basis as we'd requested. We were told that reports on daily traffic would take a month or longer to produce. For our specific situation, it wasn't a terribly handy or workable solution. Only much later did we actually receive those reports, and then the data was 60 days old!

So, to some degree, the metrics you will use are a negotiation between what would be ideal and what you can actually get. Traditional Internet marketing metrics (page views, unique users, and so on) can be used to measure success and are generally available in a standard web analytics software package, Google Analytics, or a variety of other online sources. Fortunately, Facebook makes a variety of metrics available quite visibly (Facebook fans, group members, and so on) when you run Facebook advertising campaigns.

We'll cover a few measurements that will indicate success for your efforts. Assume for a moment that you are running a Facebook group. You'll add people, lose people, and interact with these people over time. You'll need a measure that tells you that, at the end of the day, you are consistently growing your Facebook group over time. The same goes for profiles, fan pages, and applications. Table 6.1 summarizes the statistics you can measure on Facebook and the derivative metrics that can be measured on an ongoing basis to tell you what is happening. You will measure progress over time—daily, weekly, and/or monthly—to see the impact of your efforts.

Presence	Core Metrics	Derivative Metrics
Profile	# of friends # of Wall posts	Net # of fans/friends added/lost per day # of "likes" per day Ratio of "likes"/Wall posts Ratio of comments/Wall posts
Fan page	# of fans # of "likes" # of comments # of Wall posts	
Group	# of group members	
Applications	# of daily active users # of fans	

In addition, Facebook is improving their insights product to enable page administrators to track impressions and interactions against each post: with this additional set of metrics you'll be able to measure the Click-Through Rate and Engagement Rate for your content appearing in the Facebook News Feed. If a user clicks on one of your posts, that will be counted as Stream CTR. If a user likes or comments on one of your posts, that will be counted in the Stream ETR. (See: http://www.facebook.com/help/?faq=15215 and http://www.allfacebook.com/2010/01/facebook-post-insights)

Get Your Baseline

Before launching a Facebook advertising campaign, find out how your Facebook presence does on its own—without any demand generation. Know how many fans/friends your site attracts before and after advertising to make sure you know exactly what advertising does for you.

Wednesday: Review Data Reporting via Facebook Insights

Facebook takes all the data collection and analysis one step further on fan pages with a specific feature called Facebook Insights. Insights is the most comprehensive set of Internet marketing data that Facebook provides. Insights includes the following:

- A summary of the activity on the fan page over the last week as measured by interactions, "likes," comments, and Wall posts
- The Post Quality metric, which is a measurement of how engaging posts are over the last seven days

- A graph of interactions over time along with data on the demographics of fans who have interacted on the fan page
- A chart of the total number of fans you've had over time, along with demographics details on your fans as a group

Insights is currently only a feature of the fan page—you cannot get similar reports for a profile or a group. Consider this yet another argument for opting for a Facebook fan page for your presence. Figure 6.1 shows a sample Insights dashboard for a client that will remain nameless.

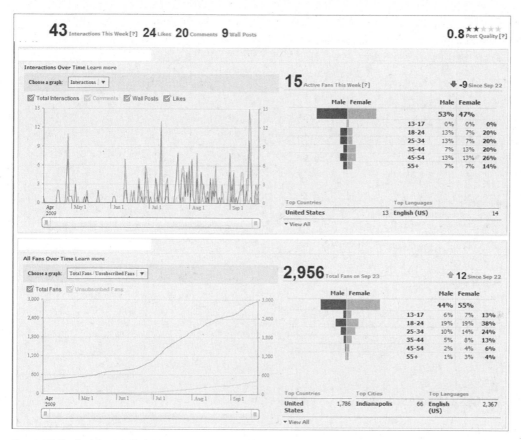

Figure 6.1 Facebook fan page Insights

These metrics are perfect for a simple analysis of your fan page effort. You can learn who your fans are, where they live, the age groups they represent, and the languages they speak. You can learn the same things about your most active and engaged fans—there may be differences between people who just casually follow you and those who regularly interact with you.

In addition to the charts you see, Facebook offers other charts of time-series data to help you analyze your progress. In the Interactions Over Time chart, you can click the drop-down menu to access other metrics:

Interactions Per Post A measure of how engaging your content is after removing the frequency of your posts

Post Quality Relevance of your posts over time

Posts Number of times you and your users (if you've allowed them to post) have put things on your Wall

Discussion Posts Number of posts on your Discussion tab

Reviews Number of times Facebook users have reviewed something on your fan page (if you've enabled this feature)

Mentions Number of times Facebook users have mentioned your fan page in a status update

Of these, interactions and posts metrics will likely be the most active and interesting charts. In the drop-down menu of the All Fans Over Time section, Facebook offers other metrics as well:

Total Fans / Unsubscribed Fans Total number of fans over time, overlaid with the total number of fans who have chosen to hide your posts in their News Feed (unsubscribers).

New / Removed Fans Charts This breaks down the Total Fans chart into the number of people who have become new fans and the number of people who removed themselves from your fan page by date. This is particularly useful to see how/if your actions are annoying your fans.

Top Countries This is a visualization of where your fans reside over time, which is particularly helpful if you run international campaigns.

Demographics This is a visualization of gender and age over time.

Page Views This is the trending data of page views and unique visitors to your fan page over time—note this does not include the number of times your updates appear on fans' News Feeds.

Unsubscribes/Resubscribes This is the number of people who unsubscribe from your fan page by day—another way to tell whether your actions are annoying fans.

Media Consumption This is the number of views of specific content that you upload to Facebook—audio, video, and photo. Note this does not count YouTube videos or links to other external media that you may reference on your fan page.

So, in this gaggle of statistics, what is critically important? In most cases, you can get keen insight by keeping track of a few things. The number of posts per day tells you whether you are hitting your operational goals. The number of comments/"likes" per post tells you whether your content is interesting or relevant. The number of fans/friends per day tells you whether your overall presence and brand is of interest to Facebook users. If you cover these things, you'll have a good picture of what is happening.

Discussions, reviews, and mentions are very specific and oftentimes don't occur enough for you to draw important conclusions, especially if you don't prioritize them as part of your campaign. Page Views is a nice metric, but since it doesn't include the number of times people see your posts on their fan pages, it is mostly irrelevant. It is pretty rare today for people to spend a lot of time on different pages within a fan page. Demographic information is more typically used for a snapshot in time unless you do specific advertising or other demand generation in particular countries. If you do that, you'll want an indication that your campaign targeting is successful. More on that in a bit.

Thursday/Friday: Create Your First Ad

You can get started with advertising on Facebook by going to http://www.facebook.com/advertising. Facebook also occasionally displays a Create An Ad link in the upper-right corner of fan pages that you administer with a "Get More Fans" green button. There is also an Advertising link on the footer of most all web pages on Facebook. Any of these options will get you started.

The first time you visit Ads and Pages, you'll see a screen similar to Figure 6.2. If you've already run an ad on Facebook, the first screen you will see in Ads and Pages is a summary of results of ads you've already run (see Figure 6.3). You'll need to click Create An Ad to put a new advertisement into the system regardless of whether you have already used Facebook advertising.

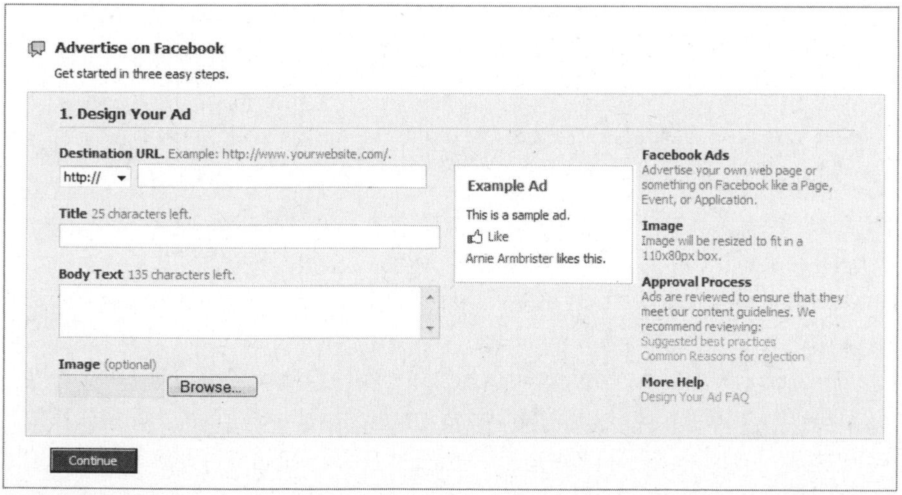

Figure 6.2 Facebook Ads and Pages, first visit

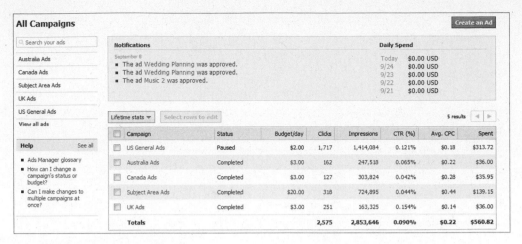

Figure 6.3 Facebook ad manager, results

 If you want to advertise a fan page, group, or application, you will have to become an administrator of it first. Facebook will not allow you to advertise something you don't run.

On the ad entry screen, you will create your first advertisement by adding text to the fields on the left side of the screen. Meanwhile, your ad will update on the right side of the screen—this will show you how your ad will appear to Facebook users. You have 25 characters for your title and only 135 characters for the body of the advertisement, which are firm limits. Be careful as you write your ad copy because Facebook won't allow you to add more characters once you reach your limit. We have certainly written our fair share of ad copy with partially written words because we weren't careful here!

You may also notice links to suggested best practices, common reasons for rejection, and an FAQ. Take a few moments to review these, especially if you are creating your first advertisement. Facebook has strict rules about the types of ad copy they accept, and they think nothing of rejecting your ad if it doesn't meet the guidelines. When you are finished, definitely add an image to your ad—this can be a logo, an icon, a picture—anything relevant to the advertisement that you think will improve the chances of getting people to click it. Some studies show that the ad picture is the top factor that impacts your click-through rate.

After you've entered your ad copy, you'll have an opportunity to target particular users. Remember Chapter 4, "Month 1: Creating the Plan and Getting Started," when we discussed profile data? Here's where you get to tap into it as an advertiser! Figure 6.4 shows where you enter criteria of Facebook users that you'd like to target for your advertisement. Make the choices you'd like, and Facebook will automatically update the number of people who may see your ad at the bottom of the screen.

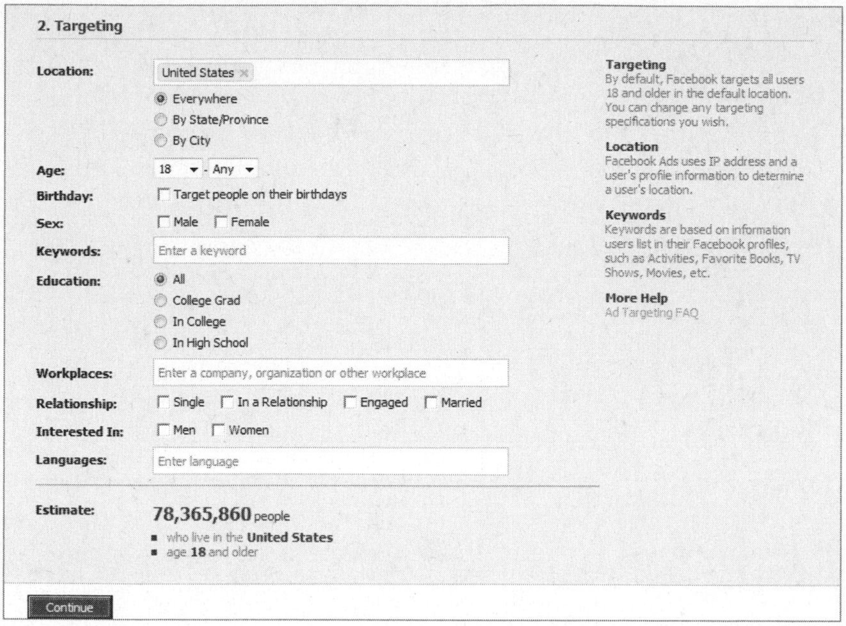

Figure 6.4 Targeting

Think of the possibilities. You can target Facebook users in a variety of ways, including the following:

- People older than 65 in New York state
- Engaged women between the ages of 30 and 34 in Spain
- Male college graduates in Chicago
- Single people on their birthdays
- Employees of companies you want to target for business purposes

The possibilities are truly endless. In addition, Facebook will soon be launching the ability to target users in real-time. This is a huge development and good news for marketers.

The final step in the self-serve process is to define your campaign and set what you are willing to spend on advertisements. Figure 6.5 shows you the options you have in this final step.

Three things are most critical here:

- Set your daily budget. This is very important so your costs don't spiral out of control. Early in a project we like to set the daily budget lower than we've budgeted so we can learn and get an idea of what will happen.
- Schedule your ad campaign. This is necessary if you have a date at which the ad is no longer relevant or if the offer isn't available any longer. If the ads can run

indefinitely, and if you plan to monitor your campaign regularly, there isn't any reason to set a drop-dead date.

- **Pay for impressions or clicks.** Facebook gives you two options—impression-based advertising or click-through advertising. Based on the options you've chosen for targeting, Facebook will also estimate the cost and the number of impressions or clicks that you are likely to receive on a given day.

3. Campaigns and Pricing

Account Currency
US Dollars (USD)

Campaign Name
My Ads

Daily Budget What is the most you want to spend per day? (min 1.00 USD)
50.00

Schedule. When do you want to start running your ad?
- ○ Run my ad continuously starting today
- ○ Run my ad only during specified dates

- ○ Pay for Impressions (CPM)
- ● Pay for Clicks (CPC)

Max Bid (USD). How much are you willing to pay per click? (min 0.01 USD)
0.52   Suggested Bid: 0.46 - 0.59 USD

Estimate: **97** clicks per day

[Create]

Campaigns
Ads in the same campaign share a daily budget and schedule.

Max Bid
You will never pay more than your max bid, but you may pay less. The higher your bid, the more likely it is your ad will get shown. All amounts are in USD ($).

Suggested Bid
This is the approximate range of what other advertisers are bidding for your target demographic.

More Help
CPC vs. CPM
Ad Campaigns and Pricing FAQ

Figure 6.5 Campaign types and pricing

After you've paid for the ad, your ad is sent to Facebook for final approval. Facebook personnel will review your ad to make sure it meets their guidelines before "lighting it up" on Facebook. This process can take as little as a few minutes or as long as a few days depending on their queue and whether you've run a similar ad in the past. Either way, Facebook will notify you of its decision via e-mail. If your ad is accepted, it will start running almost immediately. If your ad does not meet Facebook's standards, you will get a rejection e-mail asking you to resubmit the ad. Facebook typically doesn't give you the exact reason why your ad was rejected, so if you're doing this regularly, you may ultimately become both a detective and an expert in Facebook advertising guidelines!

 When you get started, it's important to collect statistics on what is happening. So, get a few ads running as soon as you can and leave them alone. Once you get a week of data on your ads, you'll be in a better position to experiment and make changes.

Impressions or Clicks? Which Is Better for You?

Are you having trouble deciding between impression-based advertising and click-through advertising? The answer lies in what you're trying to achieve.

Impression-based advertising guarantees you a certain number of *impressions*, or placements on the screen. When you bid 50 cents for an impression-based advertising campaign, you are agreeing to pay 50 cents for 1,000 impressions. This is known as the CPM, or cost per mil (thousand). Because you only pay for the impressions, any clicks you get out of the deal are free.

Click-through advertising guarantees that the only time you pay for advertising is when a user clicks your ad. So, if you bid 50 cents per click, your 50 cents is spent the first time someone clicks your ad—regardless of whether it is the first impression for your ad or the millionth. This is typically the best way to guarantee that a certain number of people will act upon your offer every day.

Sometimes, you'll find that you can get better deals on your intended type of advertising by using the other. For instance, you may want 50 clicks per day, but that will cost you 50 cents each for a total of $25 per day. You may find that you can get roughly 50 clicks per day by budgeting for only $15 in impression-based advertising. The same goes for impressions. You may want 30,000 impressions, but the cheapest way to do it may be by bidding 50 cents each for clicks. The effectiveness of your ad copy and your experimentation will determine what is best for your particular situation if you want to save a little money by managing it closely.

Week 2: Build the Dashboard and Collect Data

By now, you should have at least one ad approved by Facebook and running for your customers to see. This week, you'll monitor the campaign, analyze results, make changes, create more ads for existing campaigns, and establish new campaigns. Why go to all this effort? At a minimum, you'll want to make sure you aren't just blowing your money. But if you're going to spend money on advertising, it also makes sense to make that spend as efficient as possible. Those of you who report to more demanding executives who want proof of at least something resembling a return on investment are particularly under pressure to show how dollars move the needle. Remember also that you're experimenting with a variety of approaches designed to reach customers as effectively as you can. This takes a little care and feeding—your campaign won't optimize itself just because you took out a half hour to create a single ad!

Monday: Know What Data Can Tell You

To truly understand the impact of your marketing approach, you need intelligence on what happens with your web properties before, during, and after an advertising campaign. The standard cocktail of Internet marketing metrics apply: page views, unique users, fans/followers/friends, conversations, and so on (see Chapter 9 for a refresher). The metrics you choose are really up to you—and the right answer depends entirely on your specific business situation. Facebook Insights may also have given you some ideas of new metrics to consider. No matter what, you're trying to understand the impact of your marketing efforts:

Marketing reach If you increase advertising spend by $X, you'll get Y more fans/page views/interactions/new customers.

Investment Every new fan costs you $X and generates $Y in lifetime revenue, for a lifetime return on investment of $Z.

Comparison Interactions on Facebook cost $X, which compares to $Y on Google, $Z through traditional print advertising, and $A on Yahoo!

Targeting Reaching fans in <insert country> costs $X on Facebook, compared to $Y on Google, $Z through traditional print advertising, and $A on Yahoo!

Competitive If you don't get 5,000 fans on Facebook as inexpensively as possible, your competitor will crush you.

Although different businesses have different pressures, just about all businesses today are looking for ways to do things as inexpensively and effectively as possible. Fortunately, you can set up your campaigns to understand the economics of Facebook advertising and optimize your campaigns to make the most of whatever resources you have.

Tuesday: Make Final Decisions About Your Data Reporting Cadence

First things first—you need to create the tool or dashboard that you will use to analyze campaigns. We think there is no better tool for Internet marketing analysis than Microsoft Excel. Sure, Facebook has its Insights, and you can get some data through Google Analytics or advanced statistical packages. But there is a lot of value in collecting molecular data in a spreadsheet, which you can later roll up into whatever view you need to inform yourself and your management team.

Last week, you decided the statistics that you'll track, and you probably also now know exactly what it will take for you to get the numbers you need. Make sure you collect the core metrics on a regular yet consistent basis—either daily, weekly, biweekly, or monthly. Otherwise, you'll analyze one set of data against a slightly different period of time than another, and it will make your analyses inaccurate. Consistency is critical so you're always comparing like data day-to-day.

Daily data collection is generally the safest and most revealing way to go. By choosing daily reporting, you are collecting data in its most useful molecular form. You can go back to any day in the past and see exactly what happened, but only if you've committed to recording data in a spreadsheet or other format that you can save to your hard drive. Otherwise, you are leaving it up to Facebook, Google, or any other service to save data for you.

You can also roll up data over a period of time—say a week, a month, and so on—and analyze how your campaign improved or maxed out at various stages of the project. Most important, you can analyze it on any vector you choose—be it the net number of fans you've added, total cost of your campaign, cost per fan, click-through cost, or any other metric you'd like to see.

Now there is one downside of choosing a daily reporting—like it or not, someone is on weekend duty! If you've missed a day, it may not be a big deal, though. If you're collecting data on the net number of fans you have each day, you can make some educated guesses for days you aren't able to get in front of your computer. Daily advertising data can be pulled into your dashboard in a variety of ways well beyond the day after. But don't make a common practice of this because it will poison your data over time and make assessments about how your properties do on different days of the week useless.

Wednesday: Set Up and Populate the Dashboard

For the sake of examples in this book, we'll show how to set up a dashboard of daily data for a hypothetical Facebook marketing and advertising campaign. We'll also assume a fairly common scenario—tracking the performance of a Facebook fan page alongside followers of a corporate Twitter account. Now if you refer to Table 6.1, you'll see that we should record at least one of a number of metrics: number of fans, number of "likes," or number of comments. Let's keep this one simple and record the number of fans this particular page has every day. We'll do the same thing with the Twitter follower count. We'll also add a column to track the number of new fans/followers we have added each day—this number is generated by subtracting yesterday's number for each from today's number. Figure 6.6 is the beginning of our dashboard.

	FB Fans	FB Fans/Day	Twitter Followers	Twitter/Day
27-Apr	516	5	449	1
28-Apr	517	1	453	4
29-Apr	522	5	461	8
30-Apr	523	1	460	-1
1-May	533	10	470	10
2-May	534	1	477	7
3-May	538	4	479	2
4-May	544	6	482	3
5-May	547	3	488	6
6-May	549	2	491	3
7-May	557	8	492	1
8-May	559	2	492	0
9-May	561	2	494	2
10-May	565	4	498	4
11-May	568	3	503	5
12-May	573	5	511	8
13-May	577	4	513	2

Figure 6.6 Basic dashboard

As you populate your dashboard, you may notice that Facebook records your data in a variety of ways. Some metrics are recorded automatically and are accessible for a long time via Facebook Insights or other parts of the platform. Others, such as the number of "likes" you create, are recorded only when you intervene and count them manually. Yet both sets of numbers are helpful at different times and perhaps might be useful later when you want to analyze your performance over time and compare the data to other situations. So today, and probably for the next few days, you'll need to get into the habit of collecting data that you think may very well be overkill. That's OK—you will want the record of what has happened later. For now, just make sure you populate the dashboard religiously at a consistent time of day as often as you can.

Thursday: Understand Moving Averages

Now let's review a concept that we'll use quite a bit—moving averages. *Moving averages* are a daily average of a consistent backward-looking period of time (7 days, 14 days, 28 days, and so on). They're calculated every day and then charted to give a longer-term perspective on what is happening. They're also good for reducing "spikes" in data that happen for understandable reasons (like weekends) and for reasons you'll never totally understand. Moving averages help clear up data that might ordinarily distract you from noticing the general trend of the impact of your marketing efforts.

Moving averages have a significant role to play in the dashboard and in reporting. We'll go through that later in this chapter. But for now, we'll add moving averages to our basic dashboard—we'll simply add two columns next to the FB Fans/Day column, and label them 7 DMA and 28 DMA for a one-week and four-week moving average calculation. To do this, you'll need to average the current day and the previous six days to get your 7-day moving average. The same goes for the 28 DMA column; you'll average the present day along with the 27 previous days of data. This is all very easy to do in Microsoft Excel or other spreadsheet application. If you don't have enough data yet, hold off until you do. Otherwise, you won't have a full 7- or 28-day moving average, and it will skew your data. Take Figure 6.7, for example.

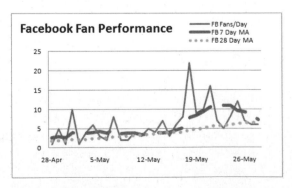

Figure 6.7 Moving averages chart

This is a chart of the number of Facebook Fans we have attracted for a 28-day period—a common chart we like sharing with clients. Notice that the solid line is all over the map; that is the daily outcomes. If we determined success or failure by daily performance, we'd have some violent ups and downs—some really good and really bad days! Moving averages are much more insightful when looking at long-term trends to see whether your tactics are working. The value of 7- and 28-day moving averages is to share progress on both short-term and longer-term perspectives. If you've done this properly, your dashboard will look much like Figure 6.8.

A	E	F	G	H	I	J	K	L
	FB Fans	FB Fans/Day	FB 7DMA	FB 28DMA	Twitter Followers	Twitter/Day	Twitter 7DMA	Twitter 28DMA
30-Apr	523	1	2.7	1.92	460	-1	2.0	4.64
1-May	533	10	4.0	2.23	470	10	3.3	4.85
2-May	534	1	3.6	2.19	477	7	4.1	4.93
3-May	538	4	3.9	2.25	479	2	4.4	4.82
4-May	544	6	4.0	2.46	482	3	4.7	4.79
5-May	547	3	4.3	2.57	488	6	5.0	4.93
6-May	549	2	3.9	2.64	491	3	4.3	4.96
7-May	557	8	4.9	2.93	492	1	4.6	4.64
8-May	559	2	3.7	3.00	492	0	3.1	4.25
9-May	561	2	3.9	3.07	494	2	2.4	4.07
10-May	565	4	3.9	3.21	498	4	2.7	4.04
11-May	568	3	3.4	3.32	503	5	3.0	4.07
12-May	573	5	3.7	3.50	511	8	3.3	4.21
13-May	577	4	4.0	3.64	513	2	3.1	4.07
14-May	584	7	3.9	3.89	511	-2	2.7	3.89
15-May	587	3	4.0	4.00	519	8	3.9	3.82
16-May	593	6	4.6	4.11	522	3	4.0	3.71
17-May	601	8	5.1	4.04	525	3	3.9	3.54
18-May	623	22	7.9	4.68	528	3	3.6	3.43
19-May	632	9	8.4	4.79	530	2	2.7	3.39
20-May	642	10	9.3	5.04	545	15	4.6	3.68
21-May	658	16	10.6	5.50	550	5	5.6	3.71
22-May	665	7	11.1	5.71	555	5	5.1	3.86
23-May	670	5	11.0	5.75	557	2	5.0	3.89
24-May	678	8	11.0	5.96	559	2	4.9	3.96
25-May	690	12	9.6	6.21	562	3	4.9	4.04
26-May	697	7	9.3	6.43	563	1	4.7	3.93
27-May	703	6	8.7	6.46	570	7	3.6	3.89
28-May	709	6	7.3	6.64	571	1	3.0	3.96

Figure 6.8 Dashboard with moving averages

One final note on the dashboard: we're simply tracking outcomes because most marketing managers want to be able to understand and communicate improvements to the most important metrics. Your specific situation may require you to add columns in your dashboard to track activity—how well you are doing your job to keep the presence fresh and how well customers respond with direct feedback ("likes," comments, and so on). The more data you have, the better—you can always ignore or hide certain columns in your dashboard when that data isn't necessary.

Want to really impress colleagues with the depth of your analysis of daily data? After you've updated your spreadsheet for six to eight weeks or more, add a column in your spreadsheet with corresponding days of the week for each date. Then sum and average all the totals for each day of the week to see what days do well and which days don't. When you show your colleagues data that proves your Facebook presence does best on Tuesdays and worst on Fridays, you'll get that much more credibility for being on top of things.

Friday: Make a Backup of Your Dashboard

Once the dashboard is established, it really does become your best friend—whatever you do, don't lose this file. It will contain all the data you need to create the insights you need to provide your colleagues on an ongoing basis, and it will answer basic questions. Where have we been? Is this working? What happened when I made a change? How does advertising impact our ability to attract new fans? Data from the dashboard can inform even the most routine decisions. Be sure to back up this file regularly—ideally you'd be running it from a secure online/offline storage service like Microsoft Live Mesh, or you'd keep the spreadsheet in Google Docs. You don't want a catastrophic computer hardware failure to annihilate your dashboard and all the metrics you've so painstakingly recorded. In the example in Figure 6.8, you should record all your key metrics and extend your moving average numbers to keep them up-to-date. As circumstances warrant, you can use this spreadsheet to create charts showing your progress or how different tactics have made you more or less successful.

Week 3: Refine Your Campaign Using A/B and Multivariate Testing

Now that you have a functional albeit basic dashboard and you know how to create an ad on Facebook, it's time for you to send your campaign into high gear. What do we mean by this? Running multiple ads and campaigns makes a lot more sense when you have the infrastructure in place to see how you've done and how you can improve. And that's what you've built with your dashboard—a simple system for you to test cause and effect. At the end of the day, you're looking to turn your efforts into a system where your every action can produce a somewhat predictable reaction.

Monday: Learn the Basics of A/B and Multivariate Testing

In its simplest form, *A/B testing* is understanding the impacts of doing things two different ways. We'll go through it in a little more detail here, assuming you are marketing a Facebook fan page. For example:

- What is the average number of net new fans on days you posted content? What is the average number of net new fans on days you didn't post new content?
- What is the average number of net new fans you get on days you post content about international politics? Other types of content?
- What is the cost per click on advertising run in the United States vs. the United Kingdom vs. Canada?

Notice that in each case, there is an either/or. You're evaluating two or more things but leaving every other variable consistent across all the things you test.

Answers to the previous questions are critical to optimizing a campaign, but only as long as you have enough activity to pass the "red-face" test of statistical validity. In other words, if you rely on a few days of feedback, you may just choose days when people are particularly or unfriendly to your cause. Running things for a longer period of time will turn your hunches into knowledge. The bar is not true statistical validity but more of a feeling that you've run things for long enough, with different characteristics, and with enough eyeballs that you feel like you could defend the thought process to even the most demanding people in your organization.

Take the first example mentioned, for instance—if you never post content on Saturday, you are likely affecting what should be a totally objective outcome had you posted content every day of the week. If Facebook traffic turns out to be 25 percent lower on Saturdays than other days of the week, a 15 percent lower fan conversion rate may actually indicate success because you're doing better than Facebook does! Without randomness and context for your assertions, you can actually draw the wrong conclusions and make bad decisions for your organization.

Sometimes you don't want to test just two potential outcomes. Maybe you want to see how three or more different things can impact outcomes on a website. This is called *multivariate testing*. Here are a few anecdotal examples of multivariate testing as it relates to Facebook advertising:

- Jane is a product manager running an impression-based Facebook advertising campaign across four English-speaking countries: the United States, Canada, Australia, and the United Kingdom. These ads target groups and pages that are updated infrequently. Which ads generate the lowest cost per click?
- Tom wants to see how both ad copy and geography impact performance of his nonprofit's click-through marketing campaign. Which combination of ad copy and geography does the best job of getting people to sign up for his newsletter?
- Jennifer has three different sets of images that she can use for her Facebook advertising campaigns, but she doesn't know whether one set is best. She'll set up the same ad copy across three different versions of ad copy. Which set gives her the lowest cost per new fan?

Multivariate testing is a great option when you have a number of different criteria you'd like to test but no earthly idea of how individual elements impact performance metrics. It's good for a scattershot approach to give the marketer a quick idea of what works. The marketer can then drill deeper by isolating specific criteria with A/B tests to optimize an advertising campaign.

Tuesday: Understand the Basics of Great Ad Copy

Turn your attention now to best practices for creating great ad copy. As we've mentioned, Facebook Ads and Pages gives you 25 characters for a title for your ad and

135 characters for the body. Ads appear on the right side of users' News Feed, profile, events, groups, fan pages and other major pages on Facebook, and they refresh upon every new click made within Facebook—including when a user clicks on the tabs on a profile, group or fan page. If you are advertising a Facebook fan page, the title will be the name of your page, and you won't be able to edit it. If you are advertising an application, a group, or a website, you will be able to edit the title.

All told, you have 160 characters to make your case to users that they should pay attention to you, along with the opportunity to present an image. Images that you upload will be resized to 110×80 pixels, and this will be presented to you on the right side of the screen after you choose the image you want. Be sure to take a look to ensure your image looks good at that size.

When it comes to effective ad copy, you need to do a few things:

- Be clear. Tell people exactly why your offer is compelling and why they should care.
- Be human. Your ad appears alongside ads from other companies. Speak to people as a person and not as a company or large organization.
- Appeal to segments of your market. Facebook ads can be created to reach very specific market segments. Use this to your advantage to see what works best.
- Don't oversell. Overpromising is a great way to make people angry about the fact that they've clicked your ad. Make it a positive experience.
- Try different things. Customers can view your company or brand in a variety of different ways. Use different approaches to engage.
- Include a "call to action." Don't leave it to a customer to interpret what they should do if they like your ad. Tell them what they need to do next.

Facebook doesn't just run every ad you place. They have a set of guidelines that you must follow for your ad to be approved. We won't cover them in detail here, but you can check them out at www.facebook.com/ads/mistakes.php. You can also refer to Facebook's best practices at www.facebook.com/ads/best_practices.php.

We'll now show you an example of two different sets of ad copy for a local restaurant. The real name of the restaurant will be withheld to protect the innocent. Both of the following ads sent Facebook users of all ages near the restaurant to a reservations page on the Joe's Bar and Grill website:

Advertisement #1

Joe's Bar and Grill
Joe's serves the area's best steaks, seafood, and other local favorites. Make a reservation today.

Advertisement #2

> ### Eat at Joe's
> Nothing is the spirit of the
> Pacific Northwest quite like
> Joe's Bar and Grill. Come
> in today!

Let's break down these two ads. The first has a more formal flair, talks about the food, and suggests a call to action for people to make a reservation. The second is a little less formal but has a weaker call to action. Conventional wisdom says that Ad #1 would be better. Which ad do you think did better?

This is a bit of a trick question. After 10 days of running both ads, it turned out that the second ad did better than the first. Owners of the restaurant speculated that customers did not respond well to formality. But at the same time, the first ad had a few good elements. The call to action was a lot stronger, and the owner liked that it mentioned the types of food someone could order at Joe's. So, what did we do to figure out how to best optimize this particular ad?

We scrapped ad #1, declaring it a loser in the A/B test for these two ads. But we decided to compare ad #2 to two additional new ads to create an A/B/C test across ads #2, #3, and #4:

Advertisement #3

> ### Eat at Joe's
> Enjoy the Pacific Northwest's
> finest steaks and seafood.
> Make a reservation today.

Advertisement #4

> ### Eat at Joe's
> Nothing is the spirit of the
> Pacific Northwest quite like
> Joe's Bar and Grill. Make a
> reservation today.

In ad #3, we refer to the types of food that are served at Joe's, but we went with the casual title. We also changed the call to action. In ad #4, we kept the same call to action, but the remainder of the ad features the same ad copy as ad #2. So, we ran three different ads about the same restaurant in an attempt to isolate the exact words and phrases that optimize Joe's advertising campaign. We don't suppose anything; rather, we use the data that comes back after the ads run for long enough to feel confident in the outcome. This is typically a week or more if we have that much time to let things run and see what happens.

So, which ad do you think was the best? It turns out that advertisement #4 was the right combination of casual language and a useful call to action, but the results were close. We actually ran both advertisements #3 and #4, but we budgeted more money for #4. Joe was happy, and he increased traffic in his restaurant significantly through this advertising approach—but only after running a few tests to see how his customers responded to ads that appeared to be similar on first glance.

As you can see, slight variations in ad copy can play a very significant role in the outcome of a Facebook advertising campaign. You'd be amazed at how a single word can dramatically increase or decrease performance. Now this matters differently for impression-based advertising than click-through campaigns. You are rewarded for creating great ad copy for impression-based or CPM ads, because your clicks are truly free. In the case of click-through ads, your clicks aren't free, but your impressions are. Bad or very specific ad copy targeting certain people can work in your favor because you can get a lot of free impressions when your ads don't compel people to click as often as they could.

Wednesday: Create Ad Variations

Earlier in this chapter, we covered the basics of creating your first ad, so for the purposes of this day, we'll assume you have already created your first ad. Now it's time to create some variations on that first ad that you will later use to compare against each other for effectiveness. The good news is that Facebook knows this is a common scenario for marketers. So, there is a Copy An Existing Ad option in the Ads and Pages application that streamlines most of the process. Just get into the Ads and Pages application, and click the green Create An Ad button. It is accessible via the drop-down menu at the top of the screen.

Choose the ad you'd like to copy, and Facebook will import the settings from that ad into the screen for you—the destination URL, ad title/copy, targeting options, and bid will all be preserved for you. All you need to do is get into the self-serve settings and change whatever you'd like. Your old ad will serve as the control group, and the new ad will be the test, which is not unlike the scientific method. You just want to know which one performs best for the metric you'd like to optimize. Ideally you will run them at the same time for a true apples-to-apples comparison. Feel free also to create many variations—the key is to leave a few things consistent across all the ads so you can isolate the drivers of better/worse performance. There is no point in doing this if you don't get smarter.

Thursday: Judge Ad Performance

So, in the previous example, how did we determine that #2 did better than #1 and #4 did better than #2 and #3? It all comes down to the numbers. Let's first take a look at the numbers that Facebook provides you and define what these different numbers mean.

Figure 6.9 is the summary view of five ads that ran within a single sample campaign.

	Ad Name	Status	Bid	Clicks	Impressions	CTR (%)	Avg. CPC	Avg. CPM	Spent
☐ 🔲	General Ad 1	Campaign paused	$0.26	619	566,406	0.109%	$0.20	$0.22	$122.42
☐ 🔲	General Ad 2	Campaign paused	$0.10	111	118,114	0.094%	$0.28	$0.26	$30.86
☐ 🔲	General Ad 3	Campaign paused	$0.26	517	345,445	0.150%	$0.14	$0.21	$74.17
☐ 🔲	General Ad 4 - Men	Campaign paused	$0.10	34	48,937	0.069%	$0.36	$0.25	$12.28
☐ 🔲	General Ad 5 - Women	Campaign paused	$0.27	436	335,182	0.130%	$0.17	$0.22	$73.99
	Totals			1,717	1,414,084	0.121%	$0.18		$313.72

Figure 6.9 Basic Facebook ad statistics

For each individual ad, you see the following numbers:

Ad name This is the descriptive name you've given your ad—be sure to name your ad accurately so you can know what you see at this summary view.

Status This is whether the ad has run for its allotted time, whether it is paused, or whether it is running.

Bid This is the amount of money you are willing to pay for an impression or a click.

Type Whether the ad was a Pay for Impressions (CPM) or Pay for Clicks (CPC).

Clicks This is the total number of clicks that you've received for the time period.

Impressions This is the total number of impressions that you've received for the time period.

CTR (%) This is the click-through rate, calculated as total clicks divided by total impressions. This tells you how frequently people click the ad.

Average CPC This is the effective price of every click, even if you decided to purchase impression-based ads. This is calculated as the total amount you've spent divided by total number of clicks for the time period.

Average CPM This is the effective cost per thousand impressions, even if you chose click-through ads. This is calculated as the total amount you've spent divided by the total number of impressions divided by 1,000.

Total spent This is the overall spend for this particular ad for the time period.

This view is a great way for you to look at how individual ads do relative to one another, but only as long as you look at relative numbers instead of absolute numbers. Absolute numbers like clicks, impressions, and the total amount of money you've spent on advertising really tell only part of the story. In other words, when analyzed by themselves, you don't know whether those numbers are good or bad. For example, you may have put a lower bid in for a particular ad, and it may not have gotten the traffic necessary to generate as many clicks as another ad. Instead, you should look at relative numbers like click-through rate, cost per click, and cost per thousand impressions to see how individual ads truly perform relative to each other.

In Figure 6.9, we ran an impression-based campaign across all the ads (CPM). You may notice that the effective CPM is a bit lower than the amount we bid. Why does this happen? Bids are truly run like an auction on Facebook—this is also how it is done with Google AdWords, Yahoo! Overture, and Microsoft's adCenter. When you set up your ad, Facebook suggests bid amounts that will guarantee that your ad will get enough impressions to meet your daily budget. But if they can't find other advertisers that meet similar criteria to fill the auction, you'll pay less. Oftentimes, we have seen the effective CPM turn out to be 10–25 percent less than the bid amount, which is all the better for the cash-conscious marketer! It's yet another advantage for impression-based advertising on Facebook.

So, refer to Figure 6.9 again to see how we'd analyze the numbers and how that would inform the next round of changes to our advertising approach. Let's start by looking at the relative numbers—CTR%, Average (effective) CPC, and Average (effective) CPM. We started this campaign by creating three ads all targeting the same general demographic—they are appropriately named General Ad #1, General Ad #2, and General Ad #3.

General Ad #3 was the best in terms of click-through rate. So, if you're looking to generate the most clicks you can per impression and thus get the lowest cost per click, you'll want to put more ad budget into this ad. You'll also want to look at the ad copy for that ad and the targeting options you've chosen to make a mental note of the fact that it worked better than any other ad. If you want to delve further, you can create a few similar ads by using the same targeting options but by slightly tweaking the ad copy of General Ad #3 to see whether you can do even better. We generally kill the worst-performing ad when we test three ads against each other; then we tweak the best performing ad to get a variant, and we keep the second best ad. We then run these three against each other for another week or two to gauge effectiveness, and then we repeat one final time.

We'll similarly look at the worst performance from a CTR % perspective. In this case, Ad #4, which targeted men, did the worst. Again, we'll look at ad copy and any further targeting to make a mental note that this ad didn't work well at all relative to the others. It could be because this particular offer doesn't resonate well with men, or it could be the ad copy. At this point, you can shut down the ad altogether, or you can run an alternative ad against the same demographic to see whether something else will work. Some people prefer experimentation even with poorly performing ads, while others are willing to make relatively quick decisions to retire underperforming ads. There is no right/wrong way to do it—either approach will work. At the end of the day, if you repeat the overall process, you will get gradually more efficient with your advertising spend.

Friday: Educate Stakeholders on the Process

Stakeholders likely cannot, and should not, understand the idiosyncrasies of running and optimizing a campaign. That's your job, right? But this is a good opportunity to educate your colleagues, especially as you kick off your first Facebook advertising campaign with ad copy and the beginning of A/B and multivariate testing. This has all the elements that demonstrate well—creativity, a reasoned approach to a difficult problem, a systematic means for collecting relatively unimpeachable feedback from customers, and data as the final arbiter of any dispute. When social media marketing disintegrates into people shouting opinions over each other with no data to support their assertions, everyone is wasting time.

This is probably the right time to sit down with supporters and hecklers alike to show them what you are doing. Think of it as a confidence-building exercise where you can explain things, answer questions, and, more important, educate folks on the fact that metrics and success criteria are indeed being watched carefully and that you're doing everything you can to make it work.

Regardless of what anyone in your company tells you, there is no way of knowing what the right answers are in advance. We remember one particular engagement where the client was convinced that a certain type of image was going to result in a better outcome, because it had always worked that way before. Ads run with these images actually created new fans at a cost of 3.5 times more than ads run without the imagery altogether. The clients didn't believe us until we showed them the statistics! This is the kind of insight you need—and another prime example of why you need to experiment. What you think will work and what actually works can be two entirely different things. Let data be the judge, jury, and executioner.

Week 4: Analyze and Adjust the Campaign

Last week, you spent a lot of time going through the analysis of a particular ad or series of ads. The great news is that you can "uplevel" all of that work, put ads into groups, and analyze everything at a campaign level.

Monday: Perform Basic Analysis of a Campaign

To see the full campaign view, go to the Facebook Ads and Pages application, or if you're still in the individual ads interface, click the Back button on your browser or click the View All Ads link on the left side of the screen. You'll be directed to something that looks like Figure 6.3—the main interface for the Facebook ad manager. That screenshot shows the results of campaigns we created across several scenarios. We used the same ad copy across all five campaigns to compare its effectiveness in the United States, Australia, Canada, and the United Kingdom. We also ran a series of different subject-area ads to see how results would differ from more general ads we ran in different English-speaking countries. What you see in Figure 6.3 are the outcomes after running five ads for each campaign without having made any changes or edits.

Overall, we spent $560.82 on 2,575 clicks for an average click-through cost of 22 cents per click. Although it isn't calculated on this particular screen, we achieved just under a $0.20 effective cost per thousand impressions as well. By dividing your click-through cost by the impression cost and multiplying by 1,000, you can calculate exactly how many impressions it takes on average to generate a single click. In this case, the answer is roughly 1,100. Why is this important? You can do the same analysis for individual campaigns or specific ads and use the metric to gauge effectiveness of your ad copy. Generally speaking, if it takes fewer impressions to generate a click, the ad copy is more effective, and vice versa. If you're particularly obsessive about costs, you can convert ads with better ad copy to impression-based ads and those with worse ad copy to click-throughs as long as the economics makes sense.

If you look at CTR % and effective cost per click, the most effective advertising was in the United Kingdom. Perhaps our brand or our message resonates particularly well there for cultural reasons or our ad copy works particularly well in the United Kingdom. No other experimental campaign did as well. Ads in Australia and Canada had mediocre performance relative to the United States and the United Kingdom. Look at the spend in Australia and the United Kingdom—it was exactly the same, $36, but we got almost 100 additional clicks in the United Kingdom! Now that's performance. Subject-area ads, with the second lowest CTR % and the highest average click-through cost, didn't fare nearly as well as the general ads we ran.

Looking at this simple chart, we'd first conclude that all the advertising is a pretty good deal for this advertiser, which was looking to extend its brand to Facebook. Very few advertising options anywhere give you such granular targeting, and the interactivity social media provides for the low cost of a $0.20 CPM—not e-mail, banner ads, billboards, television, radio, or anything in print. It's unprecedentedly inexpensive to reach people on Facebook today.

We'd also conclude that if we wanted to optimize for efficiency, we'd devote almost all the ad budget to the United Kingdom. Clicks cost only 14 cents each, and one person clicks our ad for every 651 impressions targeting residents of the United Kingdom. That is by far the best overall performance of any of our campaigns. U.S. ads are also a good investment, while those in Canada and Australia need work.

Tuesday: Recalibrate Advertising

How confident can you be in the conclusions you draw from you analysis? It depends on what you are assessing. We like to run ads for at least a week or two to get enough data to draw conclusions. Similarly, it's nice to run a similar amount of impressions across all ads before making comparisons. In the previous case, it's entirely feasible that we hit people in the United Kingdom on a good week and that the numbers will worsen if the ad is run for more time. Conversely, it's possible that the numbers should be even better in the United Kingdom. We don't know for sure, because in this case we got only one-tenth of the number of impressions that we got for the United States. So in this case, you have two options:

- Leave it alone, and compare numbers based on the page views that you have.
- Devote more budget to the United Kingdom, Canada, and Australia to even out the page views.

It isn't perfect—you won't quite have an apples-to-apples comparison with data from other geographies because you're running the ads at different times of the year. So, you're remedying one problem (discrepancy in page views) but creating another (discrepancy in when the ads run). But it is a judgment call that you'll need to make based on your hunch and what colleagues think you should do if they are involved in the decision-making process. Ideally, you would've noticed the discrepancy as you monitored the campaign all along.

In the case of the subject-area specific campaign, we probably have enough data with more than 700,000 impressions to suggest that these probably didn't work. But that isn't to say that some individual ads didn't do remarkably well. In each case, regardless of overall performance of the campaign, it makes a lot of sense to quickly drill down into the campaign to see what ads performed well and which didn't. You may find that the numbers are very poor at the campaign level, but you may have had one spectacular ad that holds the keys to success for that campaign. So, you'd undergo the same recalibration process again to make sure you can indeed draw valid conclusions from the data—pause some ads, increase budgets on other ads, determine whether you have enough information already, and so on.

Wednesday: Review and Spice Up Your Dashboard

The previous examples illustrate yet another reason why you need to monitor your results through a dashboard and not through Facebook's interface. Facebook does a great job of showing you lifetime numbers and results over the past week, but currently it does not give you time-series results to show you when certain tactics and advertising campaigns are no longer optimal for you. It can't be programmed to help you isolate ads or campaigns that don't have sufficient budget or traffic to tell you that the data it provides is valid and comparable to results elsewhere. It also doesn't help you learn which marketing tactics provide you with the second or third-level outcomes you need to be successful. If you use Facebook's tools to assess your progress alone, you'll be doing a lot of guesswork when you can know so much more.

Here are some features of Microsoft Excel that you can use regularly to help visualize data and isolate issues in a Facebook advertising campaign:

Heat maps and conditional formatting Red, yellow, and green tells an analyst very quickly where there are problems and successes.

Standard deviation Knowing the degree to which data spikes tells you whether you need to investigate why certain ads/tactics/days/approaches are succeeding and why others are not.

Charts/graphs These are handy for reporting and further visualization of data.

This is where it is also handy to roll up data by week and month. There you can look for performance specifically to see whether the campaign, advertising, or tactics you're using are getting stale and are in need of some revision. You can also calculate a variety of derivative statistics inside Excel—usually in columns that are not visible to you until you want to view them later. These are also ideal places to use data analysis tools such as heat maps—derivative statistics can be difficult to understand without visuals to show how they compare to one another.

Thursday: Analyze Your Numbers Further with Moving Averages

So, how does all this work in practice? Let's take a look in more detail at how you can use your basic dashboard to assess your own performance. Figure 6.10 is a chart made from the data we captured in our basic spreadsheet on the number of Facebook fans added in a given day.

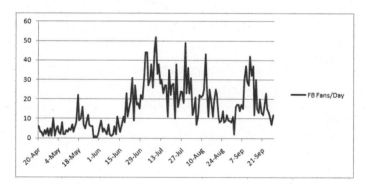

Figure 6.10 Fans per day

Now this chart isn't terribly insightful—it has the basic ups and downs of daily data. The spike at the end of June reflects the creation of an ad campaign. We tripled the ad budget on June 29, and we brought it back down to pre–June 29 levels on July 14. We stopped running ads on August 20 and relaunched them several weeks later. You can see the impacts in Figure 6.10, but overall it's a pretty noisy chart.

Figure 6.11 is an overlay of the seven-day moving average—the average of the previous seven days' worth of activity.

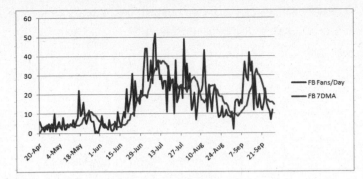

Figure 6.11 Fans per day with seven-day moving average

As we've discussed, this has the impact of smoothing out the outcomes to make the data a little easier to read. You can see peaks relative to the norm for the seven-day moving average on or around May 25, July 13, August 3, August 15, and again on September 17. This is an indication of the overall impact of tactics you undertake—this can be more attentive content posting, interactions with your customers, more effective advertising, new campaigns, or the result of additional advertising budget. So, be sure your dashboard has a record of the things you are doing differently at different points in the timeline. You'll want a good history of what you've done after the fact to better explain how things are changing.

Now let's take a look at the fans per day 28-day moving average in Figure 6.12. This is where the data gets a lot more interesting and provides greater insight into your performance.

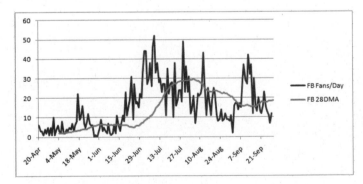

Figure 6.12 Fans per day 28-day moving average

Notice how the 28-day moving average creeps along early in May and early June. That's understandable—we didn't run any advertising in May and early June, but we did slightly increase the regularity with which we posted content. This can easily explain the 28-day moving average increase from approximately 4 per day to 8 per day. We launched advertising for this account in late June, so the 28-day moving average number increased dramatically. Ads ran on and off until early August, when they were shut down for well over a month.

Notice that the 28-day moving average levels off around September 5. No ads were run in the preceding 28-day period. What does this tell us? It gives us an opportunity to measure metrics on our performance in several scenarios. Table 6.2 is another way of reading the numbers.

▶ **Table 6.2** Analysis of Moving Average Chart

Time Period	Approximate Date	Estimated Fans/Day
Before daily content	May 6	3.5
After daily content	June 1	6.5
Advertising campaign	July 27	29
Post-advertising	September 4	16
Incremental fans/day as a result of daily content	3	
Incremental fans/day gained after advertising	9.5	

The net increase as a result of advertising gives us a sense of the lasting benefit of the advertising campaign. But how can an advertising campaign have a continuing impact if no impressions are being displayed to users or if we aren't buying clicks?

There are a few ways this happens. First, it stands to reason that as you have more fans or participants in your Facebook presence, you'll have more chances to impact people. More eyeballs on your content equals more reactions, more feedback, more sharing with friends, and so on. Take a simplistic case of the performance of a fan page with 100 fans compared to one with 10,000 fans. To get a single "like" or a comment, you'd need 1 percent of fans in the first case to respond, whereas you'd need only 0.01 percent of fans in the second case. If the same 1 percent of fans responded in the second case, you'd get a whopping 100 responses to your content.

Sharing has even a bigger impact. Let's say that 1 percent of fans in each case decided to share some of your content with friends—1 vs. 100. Let's also assume that each Facebook fan on average has 75 friends. When 1 percent of fans shares your content with friends, that content appears on 75 News Feeds in the first case but on 7,500 in the second. So, the total impact of your piece of content is 100 of your fans + 75 random Facebook people for a total of 175 News Feed impressions in the first case. In the second case, you have 10,000 fans + 7,500 random people for a total of 17,500 News Feed impressions for a single piece of content.

Now let's further assume that you got 9,000 of the 10,000 fans in the second case directly through Facebook advertising, and you stopped advertising. You still have the benefit of reaching people through content after the advertising campaign has long ended because you don't just lose the fans after the advertising ends.

If you really want to learn as much as you can about how Facebook advertising impacts your success, you may want to consider making frequent changes. Run an ad campaign for a few weeks, and then pull it for a month. Observe what happened before, during, and after the ad campaign. Next, put your ads back on the network after making a few tweaks—ad copy or targeting options, for instance. Raise your ad budget to see how that impacts the seven-day moving averages and then lower it again. If you mix your advertising tactics, you can begin to get a feel for how you can use ad budget to get the results you need.

Another way your advertising campaign can have a major impact well after the fact is in how Facebook presents relevant information to users on the News Feed. Figure 6.13 illustrates the Suggestions section of the upper-right part of the News Feed screen—showing us that one of our friends is a fan of the Redskins Insider Facebook fan page. Facebook finds people and fan pages that friends like and displays them to a user in that Suggestions box. The user can also click the See All link in the Suggestions box to get a list of all the suggested friends and fan pages that Facebook deems relevant. So, if several of a person's friends have become a fan of your fan page, it's altogether possible that you will get a free listing here and occasionally on their News Feed.

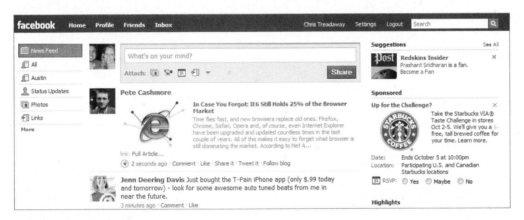

Figure 6.13 Suggestions section

Friday: Review Your Work with Advertising and Start Anew

Facebook advertising is a great way to generate demand for your Facebook presence. Ads are currently the most inexpensive option you have in Internet advertising on a CPM basis. If you can temper your expectations and make your advertisement fit the social context, you can be very successful. Just make sure you track what happens so you have the knowledge and insight you need to make it work the most for you.

So, let's summarize the steps necessary to optimize a campaign:

1. Create multiple ads of similar themes.

2. Organize them into campaigns.

3. Let them run for a week or two while recording daily outcomes.

4. Analyze statistics/outcomes.

5. Retire underperforming ads, and run new A/B tests by creating variations on better ads.

6. Go back to step 3, and repeat until you have optimized your numbers.

If you haven't done some of these things, review that part of this chapter, and progress from there.

With each iteration, you should get smarter, and you should learn new things about your advertising approach. Over time, you should be generating outcomes more cheaply and efficiently. As long as this happens, you should continue to iterate.

But after a month or so of building and optimizing an advertising campaign, you may notice that the campaign isn't doing as well as it used to do. What happened? Just about all Facebook advertising has a bit of a "shelf life"—an amount of time that the combination of your ad copy and the demographics that you target will provide great results. But as people begin to see your ad repeatedly—and some people see it even after having acted upon it—your numbers will naturally drop a bit. That's OK; it's the surest sign that you've captured the available opportunity!

Here you have a few options:

• Continue running the ads because, even though your numbers aren't as good as they used to be, they're still acceptable.

• Run a different ad at the same demographic.

• Run the same ads at different demographics.

The possibilities are truly endless. Just keep in mind that you'll need to track how your ad performs over time, because at a certain point you've maximized the benefits from that specific campaign and it's time to make a decision—make changes, continue, or move on to something else.

Month 4: Advanced Tactics and Campaign Integration

7

Armed with a plan, a corporate presence, a content strategy, and the knowledge you need to run an effective advertising campaign, you can do just about anything you need to do on Facebook. But if you really want to maximize the benefits of Facebook, you'll need to integrate your efforts with other Internet marketing activities as well as your traditional marketing work. By bridging the social, online, and offline worlds, you'll make the biggest impact by reaching customers where they are most comfortable interacting with you.

Chapter Contents

Week 1: Understand Essential Advanced Tactics

Facebook offers a variety of supporting features that can help with the marketing of your Facebook presence. This week, we'll cover those that are helpful regardless of the type or purpose of your campaign. Some offer direct benefits to your presence, some make you more discoverable, and others provide search engine marketing benefits. The specific tactics you use for your situation will be driven by the level to which you want to integrate Facebook into your marketing approach.

Monday: Master Vanity Names/Usernames

The best way for us to define vanity names for you is to remind you of the unintuitive system Facebook used not too long ago to identify pages and profiles. Before vanity names, your profile page or fan page would have a cryptic URL like `www.facebook.com/pages/boynton-beach-FL/The-Crystal-Garden/23410400382`. Who can remember that? As a marketer, you had no opportunity to define the URL that Facebook would use to point to your presence. It was a branding opportunity wasted, not to mention extremely confusing for customers. That is, it was until just after midnight on June 13, 2009. At that point, Facebook opened up the opportunity for people and organizations to create vanity names to help people quickly navigate to their favorite Facebook destinations.

Now think back to the early days of the Internet. Innovative businesses proudly shared their web address with customers on commercials and printed materials. But it wasn't as simple as `facebook.com`. Usually organizations shared their entire URL with users, and oftentimes it was cryptic and far too long to remember. A few years later, people realized that the `http://www.` part of the URL could be assumed and that they could share just the shortened form of their web address. Why is that important in this context? We see the same thing happening with Facebook vanity names now:

`www.facebook.com/Tiger`: Tiger Woods fan page

`www.facebook.com/history`: The History Channel

`www.facebook.com/victoriassecret`: Victoria's Secret

`www.facebook.com/xbox`: Xbox 360

`www.facebook.com/Doritos`: Doritos

The Aftermath of Facebook Vanity Names

So, what happened when Facebook opened vanity names to the public? According to Facebook representatives, 200,000 vanity names were registered in the first three minutes, and more than 1,000,000 vanity names were claimed in the first hour. Several vanity names almost immediately went up on Assetize (`www.assetize.com`) for sale! Quite appropriately, the event was later called "a brand grab"!

Probably the biggest benefit of registering a Facebook presence is search engine optimization—as long as you keep the site alive with fresh content regularly. Sites on Facebook tend to get evaluated very favorably by Google, Yahoo!, and Microsoft's Bing. In fact, your Facebook presence may be one of the top results on the major search engines if you register the right vanity name. In some cases, you may prefer to register a popular or important phrase than a brand name. People will know you by your brand name, but you may also get some search engine benefits by registering the type of business you are in.

Whether or not `facebook.com/<company name>` becomes the way people find companies or brands remains to be seen. But you certainly don't want to have important terms or names taken, or "squatted"—i.e., held by competitors or by people knowing you'll eventually pay a lot of money for your vanity name. If you haven't established a vanity name for your Facebook presence, you should probably drop whatever you are doing right now and do it just to be safe.

All you need is your first 25 fans; then go to `http://facebook.com/username`. Any fan pages that you are an admin for will be displayed, and you'll have an opportunity to see whether the username you want to secure is available first before confirming. Give serious thought before clicking that button because, so far, it is not possible to edit the fan page username you choose.

If you have already secured your username for your personal profile and you've now decided you would prefer to have that vanity URL for your fan page, good news, there is a solution. On your personal profile, go to Settings, then to Account Settings, and then to your username, and click Change. You'll now need to think of an alternative username for your personal profile—perhaps your name plus the word *profile* or another word or middle initial that would make it just marginally different enough from your fan page vanity URL.

Once you've changed your personal profile vanity URL, you're now free to use that username for your fan page at `http://facebook.com/username`.

And for those of you with a valid legal trademark, Facebook offers you some protection. Go directly to `www.facebook.com/help/#/legal/copyright.php`, or contact Facebook through `www.facebook.com/help` for more information.

Tuesday: Send Updates to Fans

When fans join your Facebook fan page, you automatically have permission to e-mail them. However, messages currently do not go to the regular inbox; rather, they go to a section called "Updates" that is viewable as a choice via your inbox. Sending your fans periodic updates is a good practice to keep your fans thinking about your brand and to encourage your fans to come back to engage on your Wall. (Keep in mind, content shared on your Wall helps with your search engine optimization.)

You may find that a weekly update to your fans is plenty. These updates may be the same/similar content to what you send to your regular opt-in e-mail list. Just make sure you change the formatting occasionally and that you use somewhat informal language. Shorter is usually better in terms of how much to say in your updates.

One suggestion for fan updates is to create a discussion thread and then reference that specific thread (each has a unique URL) in the update so your fans can click to go directly to the conversation and contribute.

Plus, you can target your updates as determined by location, gender, and age. This could be of particular use to the likes of speakers, musicians, and entertainers who may be giving a presentation/concert at a specific location and want to notify only the fans in that particular area.

If you're not sure whether your fans are reading your updates, you could always conduct a survey/poll to find out.

Wednesday: Create Custom Tabs on Your Fan Page

In the early days of Facebook, users agreed to run applications that imposed themselves on a Facebook profile. The thought was that users wanted to express themselves not just by sharing information, status updates, links, photos, and so on, but also by running different third-party applications and sharing results with friends.

As time passed, a few things happened. Facebook changed the rules for application developers along with the propagation of applications on Facebook profiles. The News Feed became the first thing that people logged into every day, making profiles a little less important. And finally, Facebook created a sandbox for all the applications to live. That sandbox is known as Facebook Boxes on both personal profiles and fan pages. However in early 2010, Facebook will be removing the Boxes tab, so the only way users will be able to interact with an application on their profile or on fan pages is via tabs. This change is aimed at helping application developers get more visibility and engagement from the users.

Although additional apps and tabs are largely ignored in the context of a user profile, they can play a significant role in the Facebook fan page. Using Facebook's powerful application Static FBML (available at www.facebook.com/apps/application .php?id=4949752878), you can create entirely customized content for your fans, and non-fans, to see. You can add multiple iterations of Static FBML, and each one can have its own unique tab title. Plus, you can select which of your tabs you want visitors who are not yet fans to land on.

For example, you may want to display a welcome video greeting, have a sign-up form for a newsletter, or provide persistent rich-media content. Custom tabs are a great way to generate the view you want users to have when they visit your page for the first time.

An important point to note is that each tab on your fan page has a *unique* URL. This allows you to direct fans/nonfans to specific tabs on your fan page and perhaps even conduct an A/B test by using a link-shortening service such as bit.ly.

We'll talk more about applications the next chapter, but for now you can set the default view that people see when they visit your fan page from the fan page settings screen (Figure 7.1).

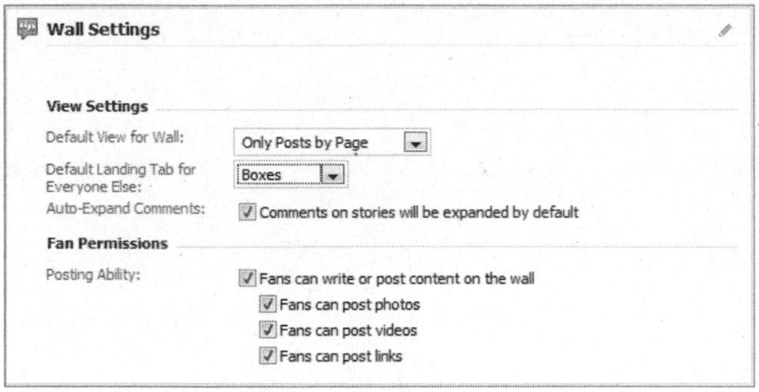

Figure 7.1 Fan page default view settings

For example custom landing tabs, see the following fan pages:

- www.facebook.com/vw: Volkswagen

- www.facebook.com/cocacola: Coca Cola

- www.facebook.com/Lacoste: Lacoste

- www.facebook.com/buddymedia: Buddy Media

- www.facebook.com/johnassarafpage: John Assaraf

- www.facebook.com/marismith: Mari Smith

- www.facebook.com/CarrotCreative: Carrot Creative (this page also has unique "fan-only" content).

Thursday: Understand Facebook Fan Page and Third-Party Applications

Facebook offers fan page administrators the option of adding a wide variety of helpful applications to fan pages. We discussed these applications briefly in Chapter 5, but we'll go over them in more detail here. The following are commonly used applications offered by Facebook for fan page administrators:

Discussion boards Here you can allow people to carry on a conversation on your Facebook fan page.

Events This is the destination for scheduling and promoting events on your fan page.

Photos You or your fans can share relevant pictures.

Reviews This is the location of user reviews of your product, brand, business, or organization.

Video Facebook's video platform is similar to YouTube, Vimeo, or other providers.

Notes This is a basic blogging platform that allows users and fan page administrators to write notes or blog posts and appear on fans' News Feeds.

Applications created by Facebook typically have a logo with a similar appearance to the one in Figure 7.2, with the Facebook logo at the bottom of the application's logo. This is the easiest way to tell whether an application was created by Facebook. It's an important distinction only insofar as these apps cover the most common scenarios and tend to get the most usage. So, they are generally mature applications that you can rely upon.

Figure 7.2 Discussion group logo

Some but not all of the functionality provided by these applications can be found in Facebook groups. You cannot embed a Facebook application of any kind in a Facebook group. You typically can include any of your applications on your fan page or profile with some minor configuration.

Even though Facebook offers a wide range of useful applications for many common marketing scenarios, it doesn't offer everything you may find useful for your specific situation. This is where third-party applications fit in—they can give you the quickest and most impactful new capabilities for sharing or gathering information from your fans or friends. Usually integration is a series of self-serve steps that don't require significant intervention, so you can try an app without assistance from your more technical colleagues. In many cases, third-party applications can be a great alternative to the time and expense of building your own Facebook application, which we'll cover in Chapter 8.

One of our favorite such applications (and one we've used several times for clients) is one of a number of polling applications. These apps help you run a simple survey on a Facebook fan page or profile and get feedback from visitors. Although a poll application isn't necessarily the best way to get statistically valid data, it is a quick way to get feedback to structured questions.

Facebook once offered its own Polls application but quietly removed it in late 2008. Several third-party application developers have created replacement poll applications to fill the void. The Poll application (`www.facebook.com/apps/application .php?id=20678178440`) works reasonably well for limited purposes and has a large user base. Others may be a better fit for your specific situation, such as Involver's Poll app (`http://involver.com/gallery.html`).

These are some other third-party apps you may want to install on your fan page:

Networked Blogs This app allows you to import your regular blog. It can be installed on your personal profile too, and comments port between your profile and fan page (See `http://apps.facebook.com/blognetworks`).

YouTube Badge Create a fully customizable widget with your YouTube videos or favorites (See `http://apps.facebook.com/youtubebadge`).

Facebook's Twitter app You have 420 characters to create an update on your fan page; by linking your fan page to your Twitter account, any time you update content on your fan page, it automatically posts as a tweet on Twitter, truncates the post at around 120 characters, and inserts a bit.ly link back to your fan page. (You can choose which content to post as tweets: status update, photos, links, notes, and events.) This can be an extremely effective strategy in terms of growing a large presence quickly on Twitter and then using this app to bring your Twitter followers onto your fan page. To track stats for any bit.ly link, just paste it into your browser's address bar and add a + sign at the end (See `http://facebook.com/twitter`).

Selective Tweet Status If you're active on Twitter.com as well, you may want to choose specific tweets to post as your fan page status update using this app, which works for personal profiles too. Note that if you use Facebook's Twitter app, it's best not to use the Selective Tweet Status app because you'll end up with double tweets when Facebook posts the same content to Twitter (See `http://apps.facebook.com/selectivetwitter`).

For a suite of fan page apps, see Involver.com (`http://involver.com`) and Wildfire Interactive (`http://wildfireapp.com`). For enterprise-level customization, see Buddy Media (`http://buddymedia.com`).

When seeking applications that will create a better experience for your fans or friends, be sure to temper your expectations. Third-party apps won't always work exactly as you want them to work—there may be a quirky user interface or a functional issue that frustrates you. You get what you pay for!

Friday: Measure the Effectiveness of Posted Content

Your fan page comes with a special analytics tool called Insights. When you view your own fan page—or any page you're an admin for—you'll see the "Insights" box just above your fans. You can see, at a glance, your "post quality" score in terms of numbers out of 10 and stars out of 5, plus the number of interactions this week. Click See All, and you'll find an array of metrics to view, including gender split, top countries, top cities, top languages, and more. You can drill deeper and see page views, numbers of discussion posts, number of mentions (@ tagging), and so on.

The data available under Insights may or may not be of particular use to you. However, it's certainly worth keeping an eye on the top-level stats to see how the quality of your posts and interactions are doing over time.

For a third-party analytics tool, see Fan Page Analytics (`http://fanpageanalytics.com`), which provides an interactive map of where your fans are around the world, other fan pages they are members of, and additional useful information.

Week 2: Learn About Facebook Connect, Widgets, Fan Boxes

We truly believe that history will judge the release and evolution of Facebook Connect as one of the most important developments for the Internet in the past 10 years. Why is it so important? It's a bridge between the Internet as we've known it and the social construct in which we all live. Let's start by reviewing the basics of Facebook Connect, some practical applications, and some of the implications. We'll also look at widgets and fan boxes, two other options for the integration of Facebook and third-party websites.

Monday: Understand Facebook Connect

Facebook Connect is a technology that allows developers to access data contained within Facebook and use that data in an external website, mobile application, or other type of computing device. OK, that may not sound terribly exciting to a marketer, but it truly extends the Facebook experience to the Web and back. It also makes a variety of common social features easy to integrate in an existing website without investments in new code or communications platforms. Consumers can enjoy a third-party website with the familiarity of the trusted Facebook platform as a supporting cast member.

Facebook Connect Highlights

When site managers commit to using Facebook Connect on their websites, they are making their lives much, much simpler. Here is a summary of the features of Facebook Connect that may be integrated with an existing or new website:

Single sign-on Users can be authenticated via their Facebook username and password. This eliminates the need for a site to use its own authentication system, which takes resources to build and maintain.

True identity Through Facebook, you can track a user down to a specific Facebook profile so you know you're likely dealing with a real human and not a bot or an anonymous character who can't be held responsible for their comments or actions on a website.

Friends and social distribution Facebook Connect allows you to pull in a user's list of friends to show other people who use the website. You can also use the friend list to encourage people to share content, items for purchase, or other information relevant to your organization through Facebook.

Social comments Comments, reviews, and discussions have worked for a number of very large companies such as Amazon, Yelp, and others. Facebook Connect allows web developers to integrate similar infrastructure into their own sites for the purposes of getting more discussion and repeated visits for a website.

Personalization Advanced integration of Facebook Connect allows website managers to create personalized experiences for site visitors based on Facebook profile data, demographic information, and geographic location.

For more information on Facebook Connect and some of its other features, visit `http://developers` `.facebook.com/connect.php`.

Tuesday: Understand the Facebook Connect Authentication Opportunity

In the early days of our programming careers, we specialized in a few key areas. As part of the process of building online communities and internal search engines, we constantly found ourselves having to build what we termed *transparent login* systems. These "duct-taped" solutions provided users with a seamless authentication scheme for surfing from one secure website to another one that was built, hosted, and maintained by different teams, organizations, or companies. Not only did these schemes address the multiple login issues that came with integrating multiple secure websites, but they also solved issues around server state, or *persistence*.

As a hypothetical example, say you worked at a health-care portal. It feels like a single site, but in the background there are actually three or four different sites built and maintained by completely different teams. The back-end systems that run these websites do not connect and would never be connected. However, you want to build online communities that require specific personal data from the authenticated user.

These transparent login systems typically consist of a few database tables in a SQL Server database that do nothing more than store user login information from all the different sites the user was traveling to and from in our little online partner ecosystems. You could write code that checked to see whether the user in question was allowed access to the data systems from a partner organization that you needed information from, in order to complete the process of building and displaying a web page. If granted access by the other system, you log them in via the programming code in a background process as opposed to making them log in manually. This is intended as a solution for a user experience requirement more than anything else. You couldn't effectively cast the illusion that a user was surfing on a single website or portal if they were being required to log in as they traversed different domains.

Simply put, *authentication* is the process of validating that an unknown someone from a trusted source is who they say they are. So, this process of having to manage users' authentication schemes became more prevalent as companies and organizations created more complex, interrelated networks of websites. Today this issue is not locked behind the firewall of enterprise intranets. We now have legitimate authentication, usability, and data portability needs on the open Internet. These needs can surface on business, social, informational, and educational websites alike.

Enter the "identity" movement. These are groups of people who started to look for a standardized way of building open systems to deal with the growing need to manage identity, access, and control of computer systems across multiple Internet properties and domains. Although many solutions have been created that take a healthy stab at solving these problems, none has been standardized. Moreover, the ones that could be considered "standard" and "open" tend to lack the support and/or features that would provide programmers and users alike with a compelling reason to adopt one system over the others en masse.

On May 9, 2008, Dave Morin, senior platform manager at Facebook, announced Facebook Connect on the Facebook Developers blog (`http://developers .facebook.com/news.php?blog=1&story=108`). Facebook Connect, although not open, is Facebook's answer for a standard authentication service that competes with several "standard" authentication systems such as OAuth, OpenID, OpenSocial, Windows Live ID, and others. More details were made public about the set of APIs on July 23, 2008, at Facebook's annual conference for developers before the system was made available to users in December 2008. The service enables Facebook users to log in to affiliated sites using their Facebook accounts to share information from such sites with their Facebook friends.

The service, also known as a *single sign-on service*, enables Facebook users to log in to non-Facebook sites using their Facebook account credentials. They can then share information from Facebook with their Facebook friends who use the same non-Facebook website, blog, or social network. Facebook Connect's identity management system should not be confused with models based upon "federated identity," such as OpenID.

While most people simply associate authentication services with a unified method of managing their sign-in activity across several websites, Facebook Connect does much more than simply letting users log in to a site by validating their identity via their Facebook accounts. When logging in with Facebook Connect, users bring their Facebook profile data with them. This means the website or blog they just logged into can allow them to find their friends who also use the same site. Furthermore, they can share information and experiences using the same features as they would on a Facebook application. With Facebook Connect, almost every feature that you can build with an application on Facebook can be offered through a third-party website or application using the service.

Wednesday: Decide How You'll Use Facebook Connect

So, knowing what you now know about Facebook Connect, how do you make the most of Facebook Connect on your website? First, don't force it. Facebook Connect has a wide variety of features that you can use for your site. Some will make sense for your site, and others won't. The good news is that Facebook Connect is a bit of a "grab bag"—you can pick and choose the tools you want and the level of integration you need with the site. You'll have to learn more about Facebook Connect to get a sense of exactly what you should use, or you should speak with someone who has used Facebook Connect for their website in the past.

Second, make sure the integration of Facebook Connect fits into the look and feel of your existing website in a way that adds to the overall experience and does not detract from it. Take the site login system, for example. If you don't have a good reason for users to log into your site—through content, personalization, or some other "carrot"—then users will likely not take the time to log into your site, and your abandonment rates will skyrocket. Login is a barrier that prevents people from using your site, regardless of how easy it may be.

Spend some time also thinking about how you can use Facebook integration through Connect as a feature that will make your site more engaging. Are you doing things in a way that will make users recommend your site to friends? Will your site encourage more interaction as a result of Facebook Connect integration? At a minimum, it should make the job of administering your site and new features considerably easier than building the technologies yourself or integrating third-party solutions.

This is probably also a great time to brainstorm with your web developers about the things you'd like to achieve with Connect. Your web developers are the people who are ultimately responsible for the stability and look and feel of your website. These decisions about social features, authentication, and the like, are major decisions that can have a positive impact on your site—but only if everyone is working together.

And finally as we've mentioned before, be sure you can collect usage statistics and other numbers that can tell you about the effectiveness of your site before and after the integration of Facebook Connect. If you do this, you'll at a minimum need to use some technical resources to do the integration work. Someone is likely to hold you to a high standard when it comes to the outcome of the decision. Did you get more users, more page views, more unique visitors, more comments, or more time spent on your website? You should scrutinize every major change you make on your website to better understand how those decisions impact important metrics.

Thursday: Measure the Benefits of Facebook Connect

So, what outcomes should you expect by integrating Facebook Connect into your site? At a minimum, exposing your website through the Facebook channel of more than 350 million people and counting will help your cause. Here are a few real possibilities that you may want to measure depending on your specific situation and goals:

Additional traffic By posting parts of your site or user commentary on Facebook, more people will be exposed to your website. And if Facebook continues to grow, this can become a significant part of your Internet marketing strategy.

Improved satisfaction If people who want to interact with your organization can do so in a variety of channels such as your website, social media, mobile devices, and so on, they'll be happier. It stands to reason they'll view you more favorably, and they'll be more willing to view future communications in a positive light.

More interactivity with customers Giving customers the opportunity to comment on parts of your site and share with Facebook friends will make your brand, product, or organization part of the social conversation. Facebook Connect makes this easy to integrate into an existing site, which can make the site a more attractive destination for users. Encourage conversation, and it will become a virtuous cycle that will give people more of a reason to think about you and talk about you.

More exposure of content/websites If Facebook evolves into a place where people learn about new things, you'll need exposure there to do effective Internet marketing. More exposure of your website is a good thing. Remember, there is no such thing as bad publicity.

Trust via global privacy settings Facebook Connect allows you to forget any concerns you or your customers may have regarding their privacy. Connect dictates the rules, and the consumer makes modification via security settings in their Facebook profile. Over time, expect Facebook to become more of a trusted entity for managing passwords and security settings over an increasingly social Web.

A great example of Facebook Connect in action is the site JibJab.com (http://jibjab.com), a company started in 1999 that offers humorous customizable digital greeting cards and videos. To quote Gregg Spiridellis, CEO at JibJab Media, "It took us *eight years* to reach 1.5 million registered users in the era of e-mail. It took us only *five months* to acquire the same number of users on Facebook."

Friday: Understanding Fan Boxes and the Wealth of Facebook Widgets

If Facebook Connect is too advanced for your needs, you can always opt for a lighter integration between Facebook and your website. This is where fan boxes and other types of Facebook widgets can be used. They're not particularly difficult if you can add a few lines of code to your existing website or blog.

Not to be confused with Facebook Boxes, a Facebook *fan box* is a mini-fan page that can be added to an existing website. Figure 7.3 is an example of a fan box for Mashable, a popular blog that we've referenced a few times in this book. You'll notice that it includes the latest content along with the total number of fans for the page and snapshots of a few of the randomly selected fans. All the content referenced in the fan box—both content and user profiles—is hyperlinked so the user can learn more on Facebook. The bottom includes a link that will send the user to the Facebook fan page, where they can choose to be a fan. If you use all the features of the fan box, you'll need a lot of real estate on your screen.

Figure 7.3 Fan box for Mashable

Facebook currently allows three major options for integrating fan boxes into existing websites. Users can attach a fan box to TypePad or Blogger (Google's blogging platform). Users can also attach a fan box to an existing website. Note that you can't do this for any fan page you happen to like. You must have administrator privileges for the fan page to add it to a third-party blog or website.

Similarly, Facebook allows people and companies to share content via badges. There are currently three types of badges—profile badges, photo badges, and page badges. These badges typically carry basic information about your presence with a hyperlink so visitors can click the badge and immediately view your Facebook presence. Badges are an interesting way to share that you have a presence on Facebook, but they are limited in that they carry very little information that a visitor can act upon. They are best used to accentuate a blog's design or content and not for an official company website in most cases.

Week 3: Integrate Your Efforts with Multichannel Marketing

Facebook and other social media marketing activities are great on their own, but they're truly at their best when integrated with a variety of other marketing efforts. Put differently, you shouldn't build a fan page or run advertising on Facebook with the expectation that social media will solve all your marketing problems. You should think about the opportunity of reaching hundreds of millions of targetable consumers via interactive, social media and consider how that can enhance existing marketing efforts.

Monday: Review Marketing Collateral

Sometimes, the biggest mistake companies make in their social media marketing campaigns is in failing to communicate to customers that they have a social media presence. You'd be shocked at the number of companies that fail to do the basics such as referencing a Facebook fan page or Twitter account on printed materials or in presentations. Building it isn't enough—you have to inform people of your efforts. So, the lowest-hanging fruit is simply to check your existing marketing collateral to see exactly where you aren't mentioning your social media presence. These pieces of collateral—print, online, and so on—should be changed to include your social media properties. Things like your Facebook fan page and Twitter account are becoming as essential to mention as your organization's website URL.

Tuesday: Establish Metrics to Inform Future Multichannel Marketing Decisions

Social media can certainly be an enhancement of outbound marketing efforts. If you're calculating outreach on a "cost per touch" basis, Facebook can be an incredibly efficient means of communicating with your customers. But you can't just say that to colleagues; you're going to need numbers to compare social media to offline marketing efforts. So, as we've discussed before, although in a different context, measurement is critically important.

For example, let's assume you are responsible for launching a new product, and you want to inform customers. You have a customer list of 2,000 e-mail addresses, 1,000 physical mailing addresses, and a Facebook fan page with 500 fans for your company. You also want to run a print advertisement in a trade magazine. You have a budget of $10,000 to spend on your launch communication along with a development resource who can make changes on your websites. What do you do? In an ideal situation, data would inform these decisions well before personality or intuition.

Your first priority should be to use the launch and the resources you have to learn as much as you can about the effectiveness of each channel. How do you do this? You measure how each effort works to get consumers to respond to your call to action. The following steps are similar to what we did to track the effectiveness of Facebook campaigns but will similarly help you gain intelligence across multiple channels:

1. Pick the marketing channels you'd like to use to reach customers.
2. Settle on a consistent call to action across your various channels so you're measuring like things in your campaign.
3. Set a unique landing page for each effort along with a means for visitors to convert to a greater level of commitment (purchase, lead, sign-up, and so on).

4. Make sure you can measure unique visitors and conversions of each of these landing pages for similar periods of time (campaign, month, week, day, and so on).

5. Set a time frame for the campaign along with a budget for each channel.

6. Establish a multichannel dashboard that you can use to track the outcomes on a time-series basis.

7. And finally, be sure to collect time-series data for each channel that can be rolled into campaign-wide statistics.

Unique Identifiers for Landing Pages

At a minimum, multichannel campaigns require unique landing pages for tracking results. Be sure that each different thing you try to measure has a distinct URL that is easy for a consumer to enter. There is no point in doing it if the URL is too difficult for a user to enter or if the user can figure out a workaround.

Wednesday: Use A/B and Multivariate Tests in Multichannel Marketing

As the campaign generates statistics, you'll begin to learn quickly which channels are more effective. Just be sure to measure on a per-unit basis—unique visitors per dollar spent, conversions per dollar spent, and so on. Look out for differences between the visitors and conversions metric as well. Some channels may be good at getting people to respond to you but not respond to the call to action!

What we're doing is essentially setting up an A/B test for multichannel marketing that can answer some questions for you. Is Facebook a cost-effective way to market your company/product/initiative? Can you retire or perhaps just deemphasize certain marketing tactics as part of your campaigns? You probably want a few examples of campaigns where you've had some success in one channel over another before making broad generalizations. But the technology is indeed there to measure the effectiveness of social media relative to other types of marketing you do. You just have to set it up in the beginning and separate the outcomes so you can have the intelligence you need in order to know what to do in the future. You'll learn more about this in week 4 later this chapter, when we dive into advanced analytics.

Thursday: Integrate Social Media and Web

In Chapter 2, we surveyed the social media landscape and talked about all the different services that are currently available to companies that want to reach out to customers. To summarize, Facebook and Twitter currently dominate the landscape, but a variety of other services can enhance your efforts, reach more customers, and provide search engine optimization benefits.

Hybrid and one-trick pony social networks like Flickr, YouTube, and Twitter are the best candidates for integration with Facebook. They don't really compete with Facebook, yet they have distinct benefits of their own that justify a separate social media presence on those networks. Pointing to content on those sites is natural and makes intuitive sense as opposed to posting content that resides on MySpace or another social network similar to Facebook.

But the other benefit of integrating third-party social media services is the search engine optimization (SEO) benefits of doing so. Search engines are increasingly indexing content that resides in social networks. And all the major social networks have major "search engine juice." That is, they're highly regarded as trusted sources of content on the Web. So, cross-posting content from one social network to another can be a very beneficial thing for your standing in search results—at least today. If this behavior gets out of hand, you can expect search engines to change their algorithms to deemphasize this as a viable little marketing trick. You can point to Flickr and YouTube pictures and videos by simply adding a link in the status update section of your profile or fan page. Twitter is a different story altogether. Facebook offers a Twitter application that provides some integration between the two social networks. Anything you post on a Facebook fan page can also simultaneously post to Twitter. So, you can conveniently maintain both your fan page and a corresponding Twitter account entirely through the Facebook fan page interface. Interestingly, it doesn't work the same the other way around—likely because Facebook wants you inside its social network and not another.

Real-Time Messaging: Facebook, Twitter, Google Buzz, or all of the above?

In late summer 2009, Facebook introduced a "Twitter-like" feature of including "@ replies" in the status update. This allows someone to direct a status update to a fellow Facebook user. Users simply type the "@" symbol in the publisher on either a personal profile or fan page and begin typing the name of a friend (or fan page, group, or event), then select the desired person/link from the dropdown menu, with up to six tags per update. The person (or fan page) being tagged gets the same content posted on their wall, thus providing additional real-time activity and visibility for both parties. This is an indication that Facebook is adding more "real-time messaging" features in Facebook that have been successful for Twitter.

Does that mean that Facebook will turn into Twitter? Probably not. Facebook is a rich canvas of status updates, personal information, pictures, events, and so on. Twitter, on the other hand, continues to build out its infrastructure for real-time short-form messaging of less than 140 characters. This currently gives Facebook the advantage of having a far greater percentage of valid consumer accounts. According to Mashable, a large number of Twitter accounts are either not used or likely spammers.

Add to all of this the February 2010 entry of Google Buzz (buzz.google.com). With Buzz, Google opened up the latent social network available in peoples' Gmail accounts. Think about it—everyone in your Inbox and Sent Items folder does indeed identify people in your social graph. Feature-wise, Google Buzz is a lot more like Twitter than Facebook. (Or, in fact, Google Buzz could be compared to FriendFeed.com which got acquired by Facebook in 2009: http://facebook.com/press/releases.php?p=116581). The Google Buzz product is built around status updates much like Twitter, and Google Profiles are, although included, a lower priority in the Google Buzz experience. The big difference between Google Buzz and Twitter is that users have unlimited characters for posting on Buzz, unlike Twitter. Google Buzz also allows you to integrate an existing Twitter account—so all your updates from Twitter can be populated on Google Buzz.

After tens of millions of users tried out Google Buzz within its first 48 hours, popular blogs such as Mashable.com and HuffingtonPost.com were quick to integrate a "Buzz This" button on their sites—see Figure 7.4 below:

Figure 7.4 "Buzz This" button

Nobody has the crystal ball that can tell you exactly what the right move is for real-time messaging for your business. Most companies with a social media presence have opted to play it safe and operate on both Facebook and Twitter, and surely we'll see some companies make a sincere effort to establish a presence on Google Buzz as well. With every new service comes another strategic consideration for you and your business and unfortunately more complexity. It's just another reason to stay informed to see exactly how your marketing time, effort, and money should be spent.

Friday: Explore Special Offers

So, you have your new fancy Facebook fan page, and you aren't sure what to do with it. We cover several great uses for the fan page in this book. However, you want to focus directly on one particular campaign tactic that has been deployed by others. We're talking about using Facebook to promote special offers to fans, using Facebook as the exclusive channel for access to these deals.

As with most, if not all, social media marketing campaigns, you need some signposts to measure success and challenges on your campaigns. Since this section of the book is presented in a case study type of format, you need to make sure you are comparing all these situations with similar yardsticks.

Since we are dealing with empirical information here, and not information derived directly from the subjects themselves, we will be covering five factors commonly used in these types of campaigns:

Reach How far does the information about the campaign travel on the Web? In other words, how many other websites talk about the Facebook special in question, and what size of audience do those sites have individually and jointly?

Relevance Does the special on the Facebook fan page support the intended focus of the brand, company, or organization for which it is being deployed?

Influence Among those who receive information about the special, who shares and passes along this information, and who do they share it with?

Authority How trusted is the source of the information? This strikes at the heart of whether the brand that is employing Facebook is trusted by its intended consumer.

Engagement This is a measurement of how involved the brand that owns the Facebook fan page is with the fans on the page. Included in this measurement is the actual size of the Facebook fan base with consideration about the size and reach of the managing brand being taken into consideration, of course.

So, we're going to keep this exercise simple and quick by using a scoring model of 1 to 5, with 1 being very poor and 5 being very good. Please know that this is not a scientific campaign. The scoring of the judging criteria is our opinion and our opinion only. We will run down the basics we find by reviewing the special offer on each Facebook fan page from the consumer's point of view.

Services: InstaWhite Smile

www.facebook.com/pages/South-River-NJ/InstaWhite-Smile/25861932423?ref=ts

InstaWhite Smile of South River, New Jersey, encourages its Facebook fans to contact Debbie in their offices for a "special price of $99." However, we should note that InstaWhite Smile doesn't specify whether this special is only for Facebook fans. This may seem to be of little consequence, but it's necessary to convey to your audience that they are getting a value on your fan page that is not available anywhere else.

By making your Facebook fans aware that your Facebook fan page is the only location to get a specific special or, better yet, *the* place to get the best specials, you not only encourage them to join up but also to check back more often and possibly share your page with friends, family, and peers.

Of course, InstaWhite Smile would need to have a reasonable number of fans for any promotion on Facebook to benefit its potential customers and, in turn, its business.

Unfortunately, in the case of InstaWhite Smile, it created its Facebook fan page and listed a generous special, but apparently the company overlooked the need to build a community. At the time of this writing, it has zero Facebook fans. Building your fan base on Facebook is covered in another chapter of this book. We can come to the conclusion, in this case, that the special offered by InstaWhite Smile is most likely not successful.

It would not be possible for this campaign to pick up any viral momentum simply because there are no followers on the fan page to share and promote the special offer. Doing a quick search on Google for *InstaWhite Smile Facebook offer* returns five results in total. This is a very poor showing in the most used search engine in the world, which reinforces the score of 1 awarded in this category. *Reach: 1.*

Clearly, the intended action one would expect would be to give potential customers a reason to use their services. Having a special offer correlates with this goal. However, the failings of the execution of this campaign forces a less than perfect score. One can't assume that simply being on message is enough to be supportive. In the case, the lack of proper execution hurts the score for InstaWhite Smile when it comes to relevance. *Relevance: 3.*

No one is getting the message here, so there can't possibly be even a measure of influence. *Influence: 1.*

Searching Facebook, blogs, and Google for mentions of the InstaWhite brand with negative words like *scam*, *fraud*, and *lawsuit* turned up no relevant searches. We'll give them a 5 here. *Authority: 5.*

Again, along with the theme from reach and influence, there is absolutely zero engagement with the Facebook platform in general from anyone at the InstaWhite Smile offices. *Engagement: 1.*

This gives InstaWhite Smile an overall score of 2.2 in our little Facebook special offer comparison.

Sports: The Pittsburgh Pirates

www.facebook.com/Pirates

Major League Baseball's Pittsburgh Pirates team advertises an "exclusive offer on tickets to our Facebook fans" for different games throughout the season. There are a couple of wins to note right off the bat with this campaign. First, the fans know immediately that this offer is specifically and exclusively for them. Second, the fans are motivated to visit the page often to share it with peers, family, and friends who are also Pirates fans.

With the Pittsburgh Pirates' Facebook fan page being a channel for these offers exclusively, interested fans become connected to the fan page in a way that makes it a necessary destination when looking for the complete picture about all things Pittsburgh Pirates. What fan would not be excited about discounts on tickets? The

Pittsburgh Pirates also really raise the bar by lowering the cost on some of these seats. In some cases, the Pirates have reduced ticket prices by 50 percent for their Facebook fan page followers. These kinds of specials are sure to get the attention of their ticket-buying fans.

The Pittsburgh Pirates brand comes into "the game" (sorry, couldn't help it) with a large fan base to share these deals with. By the time this book is published, the Pirates should have more than 60,000 Facebook fans, not to mention several sister, independent Facebook fan pages and Facebook groups. A quick search on Google for *pittsburgh pirates Facebook tickets special* returns more than 815,000 results in total. This is a very good showing in the search engine's results pages. *Reach: 5.*

The message for the marketing efforts for a professional sporting franchise should be "buy tickets to the games," and it is in this case. *Relevance: 5.*

Not only are the Pirates delivering the message to its audience of more than 60,000 on Facebook, but they have provided a channel for the story to be exported to more than half a million websites outside the Facebook.com domain. *Influence: 5.*

Searching Facebook, blogs, and Google for mentions of the *Pittsburgh Pirates* brand with negative keywords like *scam*, *fraud*, and *lawsuit* turned up several results in every case; however, there were no relevant searches that could be attributed directly to the franchise. Now there are many results that come up with these searches that may cause some confusion in the marketplace, but we'll still give the Pirates a 4 in the category for authority/trust. *Authority: 4.*

When it comes to engagement with fans on Facebook, this is where the Pirates organization really hits a home run. Not only do the Pirates spend to keep their fans updates on the latest happening with the team, but you can see that the fans respond in kind. *Engagement: 5.*

This gives the Pittsburgh Pirates an overall score of 4.8 in our little Facebook special offer comparison.

Housing: Prague City Apartments

www.facebook.com/pragueapartments

There was one particularly interesting point we wanted to make about the Facebook fan page offers from Prague City Apartments. On its main page, it cleverly calls out its specials with a creatively designed profile picture. It appears as two separate pictures when in actuality it s single file with its logo on top and an ad for "10% discount for Facebook fans" on the bottom.

This clever piece of media extends the "10% discount" offer not only to those who are already fans but to anyone who finds the company via a search. The reason for this is that Facebook displays your profile picture next to your search listing when you come up in its internal search results. We're not aware that the folks at Prague City Apartments intended for this to happen, but either way it is a win for them.

Although the Prague City Apartments have a relatively small following of just more than 200 Facebook fans, we're not convinced that it needs a really large following. Considering that you find more than 50,000 websites linking to the Prague City Apartment Facebook fan page or talking about it, we're comfortable with giving the top rating in this category when taking into account the size of the organization and the local nature of the business. *Reach: 5.*

The message for this campaign should encourage people to rent units, and it does. *Relevance: 5.*

Again, although the Facebook fan page has only about 200 followers, it has cultivated this channel into more than 50,000 return links and mentions on blogs and other websites. This is very impressive indeed. *Influence: 4.*

Searching Facebook, blogs, and Google for mentions of the *Prague City Apartments* brand with negative keywords like *scam* in particular turned up several results in Google; these sites were, in every case we found, warning tourists about traveling safely in Eastern Europe. These sites were not calling out the apartments specifically. There could be some trepidation by tourists about any housing provided in this part of the world based on personal prejudices or sites like the ones we found while conducting our tests. These issues must be given due consideration, so we give a 4 in the category for authority/trust. *Authority: 4.*

When it comes to engagement with the company's fans on Facebook, certainly it does an adequate job. For the most part, the fan page is used to deliver promo codes to interested parties for the Facebook fan page special. Prague City Apartments wins for the discount and loses for the page serving any other interesting purpose. The folks there answer queries from Facebook users in a timely fashion, based upon the time stamps of the conversation thread; however, we can only assume that the fan page would be all but dead if the prospective renters didn't use it to get access to their "10% discount" codes. *Engagement: 3.*

This gives the Prague City Apartments an overall score of 4.2.

So, there you have it—examples of offers from three different companies from three completely different industries. In the end, we find that success comes by actively engaging with your audience. After you spend some time cultivating your fan base and creating a special for them that is delivered on Facebook through your fan page, there a few last things to follow through on:

- Make sure you give them a reason to come back, with more of these kinds of special offers.

- Make sure the offers stand out on the page.

- Make the offers exclusive to your Facebook fans.

- Make sure your Facebook fans know that your offers can be found only on your fan page.
- Sprinkle on a lot of engagement, and you should have a winning recipe for your next Facebook special offer campaign.

Week 4: Conduct Advanced Analytics

Now it's time to take everything you've learned into account in a single view that informs you about the channels that work best to reach customers. The key to succeeding with advanced analytics is to record as many "molecular" statistics as you can. Get numbers on every little thing that happens every day, and you can always roll up the numbers into aggregate reports by time or channel to tell you what has happened. You can't necessarily control the products you are given to take to market, but you can discipline yourself to understand the impact of specific tactics in your marketing campaign. Let's look at an example campaign across a variety of different channels.

Assume for a moment that you're trying to drive sign-ups for a weekly e-mail newsletter for a fictional yet popular skateboard company. From other experiences and marketing campaigns, you know that every newsletter sign-up equals an average of an incremental $26.15 in annual revenue and $9.78 in annual profit. The newsletter is currently sent to 10,000 people, you added 400 new customers to it per month on average over the last year, and the monthly churn or unsubscribe rate of the list is 1.6 percent.

You are tasked to run a campaign that will get you to 20,000 subscribers within the next four months, which is a 10-time net increase in daily sign-ups from last year. This is quite an ambitious goal, and it will require you to bring as many resources as you can bear across a variety of outlets so you can find these new customers. So, your management team has provided you with a $10,000 marketing budget for this campaign. They also want you to do it, so you can't farm out this work to a contractor or marketing agency. The good news is that you have $1 per net new subscriber to spend to attract them across different tactics. It's good money but not enough for you to ignore costs, so you're going to have to do this efficiently. Management also wants to know the impact of establishing a Facebook fan page for your brand. You'd better get to work!

Monday: Brainstorm and Set Up

First things first, you need to settle on the tactics you're going to use to help achieve your goals. What tools can you use in the Internet marketing universe to generate these sign-ups as inexpensively as possible? Management has requested a Facebook fan page, so that's a must. Management has also set a goal of 10,000 new subscribers, so the other tactics you use must be effective. You'll need to run some Facebook advertising, but you will also need to look at traditional search advertising via Google AdWords,

Microsoft adCenter, and Yahoo's Overture in case Facebook isn't sufficient. You also have a hunch that a major publication helps you generate newsletter sign-ups, so you'll devote some budget to a $2,000 print advertisement that tests the cost effectiveness of print vs. the various online options.

Table 7.1 summarizes the different marketing tactics you will use for this campaign. Note a few things in this table. First, you aren't advertising exclusively on Facebook. Facebook is a great marketing channel, but it may not be the most effective for your purposes. It's better to put your eggs in a few baskets. You'll measure a few things across campaigns to triangulate the effectiveness of each. The total number of sign-ups and total cost gives you the absolute effectiveness of each tactic. The cost per subscriber is a derivative statistic that tells you the relative effectiveness of each of the ones where you devote marketing budget. The percentage churn by channel tells you the long-term effectiveness of each.

▶ **Table 7.1** Tactics for Fictional Campaign

Channel	Tactic	Measurement
Facebook	Fan page	Total number of sign-ups
	Click-through advertising	Total cost
	Impression advertising	Cost per subscriber
		Percent churn by channel
Google AdWords	Click-through advertising	
Yahoo Overture	Click-through advertising	
Microsoft adCenter	Click-through advertising	
Twitter	Maintain account and send occasional tweets about newsletter	
Skateboard 2010 Magazine	Print advertising	

Tuesday: Execute Your Strategy

The prep work and maintenance for each of these Facebook tasks is covered in previous chapters of this book. In this particular case, setting up a newsletter sign-up procedure directly on a Facebook fan page requires the marketer to change the default tab setting on the fan page to an iteration of the Static FBML app and create custom content with an opt-in box that entices a user to sign up. Although this is something that most Facebook application vendors can do inexpensively, it should be considered as part of the marketing spend for that channel and tactic. Click-through and impression-based advertising is recommended on Facebook in this case to determine which results in better outcomes on a cost per subscriber basis. Subscribers found in these two ways may have different characteristics that will generate a different outcome, and that may inform future marketing/advertising decisions on Facebook.

Advertising on Google AdWords, Yahoo! Overture, and Microsoft adCenter is largely self-serve much like Facebook advertising, although the key is to run ads on inexpensive keywords that also generate enough traffic to be meaningful. This tends to be more challenging on Google—the large amount of traffic on Google has resulted in a more mature auction model and thus higher prices than alternatives from Yahoo! and Microsoft. But it can be done with patience and experimentation. For Twitter advertising, Adly Inc. (`http://ad.ly`) recently launched an advertising solution for in-stream advertising services and comprehensive analytics (`http://analytics.ad.ly`). To build your targeted Twitter following, you might use a tool such as TwitManage (`www.twitmanage.com`) and use that channel to "tweet" an occasional message to remind followers of a marketing offer or campaign such as the one in this example.

For each channel and tactic, you'll want to have a separate landing page that you can measure to tell how each is doing. This can be done by setting up a separate referring identifier for each channel that you can use to track the total number of sign-ups as well as assign individuals to the channel from which they visited you. Just make sure you keep the landing pages the same—slight differences in the requirements for sign-up can have an impact and can make the numbers harder to analyze. Keep as much as you can consistent so you can make accurate judgments of how each channel contributes to the goal.

Wednesday: Set Up a Dashboard and Collect Data

Comparative data will tell you which channel is the best at generating sign-ups. Which does best when you are optimizing for the best "bang for the buck"? Which is most expensive? Which provides you with the longest-lasting benefit? Similarly, if you analyze the behavior of customers from each channel and tactic, you can better understand churn and the long-term impact of the marketing effort. Time series data will help you tweak individual campaign tactics to optimize your ad spend.

The best way to do this is to create a spreadsheet with separate tabs for each tactic and track the numbers aggressively and on a regular basis, preferably daily. In each, you'll enter data on the daily performance of each tactic—total cost, number of clicks, number of new fans/followers for the Facebook fan page and Twitter, number of new newsletter subscribers, and so on. Remember, you're doing this to optimize the performance of each channel so it can contribute as best it can. Optimization only takes place by paying attention to what happens on a daily basis and making tweaks and adjustments to your tactics—be it new ad copy, different targeting options, retiring underperforming ads, and so on. You can only do this by looking at the numbers on a daily basis and working to fix issues as they arise. No matter how good your ads may perform, they can always do better. You'll know you can't optimize your campaign further when the numbers peak and begin to reverse.

Aggregate numbers need to be collected on a separate tab designed to show a rollup of all the numbers for which you can effectively compare tactics. The summary of metrics in Table 7.1 is a good start because those are the best metrics for judging how incremental investments impact your ability to attract new people. Figure 7.5 is an example of such a summary view that will help you assess how different channels contribute and how they differ from one another. All these numbers should be a summation of numbers that you are recording daily or weekly on different tabs of your spreadsheet. This way, every outcome is recorded, and you're analyzing the full set of available data to make better marketing decisions as your campaign progresses. The value in this view is the ability to look at campaign tactics across similar metrics to determine their relative effectiveness.

	Ad Spend	Clicks	Impressions	eCPC	eCPM	CTR	$/Subscriber	# New Subscribers	% Sub/Click
Facebook Clickthrough	$ 287.89	1,185	1,489,012	$0.24	$ 0.19	0.08%	$ 0.32	908	76.6%
Facebook Impression	$ 422.72	2,245	2,117,655	$0.19	$ 0.20	0.11%	$ 0.29	1,453	64.7%
Google Adwords	$ 987.09	1,243	267,845	$0.79	$ 3.69	0.46%	$ 1.91	517	41.6%
Microsoft AdCenter	$ 189.35	487	224,090	$0.39	$ 0.84	0.22%	$ 0.81	235	48.3%
Yahoo Overture	$ 357.58	564	281,953	$0.63	$ 1.27	0.20%	$ 2.03	176	31.2%
Print Advertisement	$1,500.00	241	50,000	$6.22	$ 30.00	0.48%	$ 19.23	78	32.4%
TOTALS	$3,744.63	5,965	4,430,555	$0.63	$ 0.85	0.13%	$ 1.11	3,367	56.4%

Figure 7.5 Multichannel dashboard summary

Thursday: Analyze Data and Revise Campaign Spend/Tactics

So, how does the data in Figure 7.5 inform future decisions? To quote Elizabeth Barrett Browning, "Let me count the ways!" This summary has a wealth of information ready for your interpretation.

First, you can see that you've spent $3,744.63 so far, or a little more than 37 percent of your budget. You have attracted 3,367 subscribers through these channels to date at a cost of $1.11 per subscriber. So, you're doing well, but you aren't quite at the goal of $1.00 per new subscriber. You have an effective cost per click of $0.63, which is good, but the number could use improvement. The effective cost per thousand impressions (CPM) number is fantastic at $0.85, and 56.4 percent of people who click your ads become new subscribers, so the offering appears to be fairly enticing to customers. Overall, it's a pretty good start, but there is always room for improvement.

Compared to the other channels and tactics, Facebook advertising is doing the best by far across all major metrics—cost per subscriber, effective cost per click, and impressions cost. Good performance in the final column, % Sub/Click, tells you that these visitors are most responsive to the offer once they view the landing page. Of the three search engine opportunities, Microsoft adCenter has performed the best, although it has contributed very little to the overall number of new subscribers with a mere 235. That's the catch on effective Internet marketing—sometimes the absolute numbers suggest that the tactic isn't necessarily worth your time. Google provided new subscribers at a much higher cost of almost $2 each, but the advantage there is that more than 500 were found in that channel.

You may also notice that the print advertising campaign hasn't done terribly well so far. Numbers on that are by far the lowest of every tactic, yet you've spent the most money on it. This begs the question—how did the online campaigns do by themselves? Figure 7.6 is a second assessment of the summary data, but with another row to show the performance of the online campaigns.

	Ad Spend	Clicks	Impressions	eCPC	eCPM	CTR	$/Subscriber	# New Subscribers	% Sub/Click
Facebook Clickthrough	$ 287.89	1,185	1,489,012	$ 0.24	$ 0.19	0.08%	$ 0.32	908	76.6%
Facebook Impression	$ 422.72	2,245	2,117,655	$ 0.19	$ 0.20	0.11%	$ 0.29	1,453	64.7%
Google Adwords	$ 987.09	1,243	267,845	$ 0.79	$ 3.69	0.46%	$ 1.91	517	41.6%
Microsoft AdCenter	$ 189.35	487	224,090	$ 0.39	$ 0.84	0.22%	$ 0.81	235	48.3%
Yahoo Overture	$ 357.58	564	281,953	$ 0.63	$ 1.27	0.20%	$ 2.03	176	31.2%
Print Advertisement	$1,500.00	241	50,000	$ 6.22	$ 30.00	0.48%	$ 19.23	78	32.4%
TOTALS	$3,744.63	5,965	4,430,555	$ 0.63	$ 0.85	0.13%	$ 1.11	3,367	56.4%
TOTAL MINUS PRINT	$2,244.63	5,724	4,380,555	$ 0.39	$ 0.51	0.13%	$ 0.68	3,289	57.5%

Figure 7.6 Dashboard summary: online

What this tells us is that if we continue running our online campaigns and perhaps add budget to them, we'll hit our goals. We simply need to redirect some of the money we've devoted to print advertising and put it in a place where it will be more effective.

Now, we're not picking on print advertising just to poke fun at the magazine industry. In every campaign you run, you'll have at least one channel and tactic that performs poorly compared to the others. Sometimes that is a traditional channel like print advertising, and other times it will be an online channel or tactic. You'll have to decide whether the underperforming tactic is truly important to your overall strategy or whether you can get by without it. In all of these cases, it's better to not make big financial commitments early. You're better off holding the decision as long as you can assess the performance of your ads across different channels. Just make sure the ads get a statistically valid number of viewers before making any snap judgments.

Friday: Report Outcomes

There is nothing quite as powerful as walking into a management review and saying with confidence, "If you give me $6,457 and 75 days, I'll hit your goal." But that's exactly what you're able to do when you commit to building a dashboard the right way. The dashboard is all about building the knobs and dials so you can calibrate a campaign to its maximum efficiency. You know how much money goes in, you know where it is spent most efficiently, you spend it, and you know what will come out. It works the same for newsletter subscribers as it does for e-commerce or any other outcome you need as long as you have the tools for measurement and the commitment to do it.

You may be working with a few limitations—a legacy marketing campaign, less budget than you truly need, a halfhearted commitment to Internet advertising, suspicion of social media. But all of that is OK. Numbers are largely unimpeachable. You can change perceptions with data and even show return on investment or other metrics that management will expect to see from you. Here are some final tips for reporting that will help you succeed when sharing information about your campaigns:

Chart time series data to show progress Odds are you'll bumble along in the beginning, but you will get better. Show people how you've progressed.

Admit mistakes and things you've learned along the way Sometimes management just wants to see that the company has gotten smarter by running such a campaign.

Try to demonstrate return on investment Customers, mailing list subscribers, Facebook fans, and Twitter followers all have some economic value to your business.

Share success stories Don't be afraid of other companies' success stories. Tell people about the things other companies do to succeed with social media.

Suggest other ways to use the medium If you're running a marketing campaign, look out for ways to conduct better customer service or track customer relationships with social media. Be on the lookout for new opportunities that will help your company prosper.

Customized Experiences via Facebook Applications

When Facebook opened itself to third-party developers in May 2007, it ushered forth a new era in social application development. According to Facebook representatives, the company attracted more than 500,000 developers in the first year of its developer platform. That said, the early gold rush of Facebook application development has faded as Facebook has matured. Nonetheless, there are still opportunities that warrant the development of specialized applications with a marketing purpose.

Chapter Contents

Facebook Applications: A Brief History

Think back a few years to the spring of 2007. Facebook was just emerging as a viable mainstream social network. It had been released to people outside of educational networks just six months prior in September 2006, and it boasted a user base of just 20 million people. Facebook's biggest competitor was MySpace, which had emerged as the world's most popular social network. A new social media application, Twitter, was all the rage of the South by Southwest Interactive trade show. Isn't it interesting how things change so rapidly in the world of the Internet?

Yet it was in this environment that Facebook announced its developer platform on May 24, 2007. In stark contrast to its chief rival MySpace, which was not friendly to third-party application developers, Facebook announced an application programming interface (API) that developers could use to tap into the social context of Facebook. Developers could now tap into the social graph of users and create applications of all types that would allow people to interact in new and interesting ways. In addition to the functionality provided by these apps, developers could integrate advertising and conduct financial transactions. But the key was the propagation of messages on users' News Feeds (sound familiar?). Any application that a user installed would kick off a message that would appear on their friends' News Feeds.

This viral feature of the first Facebook applications created a whirlwind of activity. Developers seeking to become part of "the next big thing" flocked to Facebook by the thousands. A wide range of applications were created—casual games, social utilities, personalization apps, nonprofit apps, and so on. Buzz grew so strong, a site called Adonomics.com emerged to measure the growth and even valuation of individual Facebook applications and the companies behind them! (Today you can see similar data at www.appdata.com.) It's probably no coincidence that Facebook achieved significant growth in its user base just after launching its developer platform.

As apps were released on Facebook, some opportunistic developers took more liberties than others to take advantage of the Facebook developer platform. In the early days, application "invites" were a key way to encourage viral adoption. A developer would simply require a user to invite an unlimited number of friends to use the application before unlocking desired functionality. If users didn't want to invite friends, they wouldn't be allowed to get the full benefits of the application. Further, developers could kick off News Feed items for the most casual use of their applications. So, clicking a button in an app would both perform a necessary or desired function and put a message on the user's News Feed. This was great for the developer but increasingly annoying for friends of Facebook users who ran these third-party applications, especially since Facebook provided little recourse to people who didn't want to see these messages. So, two things that were once interesting benefits of third-party applications became an annoyance to users.

Facebook responded in three ways. First, it no longer allowed applications to let users invite all of their friends for applications. Strict limits were placed that restricted the number of permitted invitations based on the popularity of the application and the rate at which users accepted invitations. Second, Facebook gradually added new controls that would allow individual users to "hide" News Feed messages from certain Facebook friends and applications. Later, Facebook would also place severe restrictions on the exact wording of calls to action that did make it to the News Feed; any apps that did not comply with the Facebook policy would not be "approved" and thus couldn't be discovered in search or propagate virally through the News Feed.

This had a few implications. The lack of limitations on invitations and News Feed messaging had allowed the earliest applications developers to grow their user bases tremendously. Viral messages sent out from a small number of users actually had the impact of reaching millions of second- and third-level friends. It was also uncommon for users to "uninstall" applications once they were used. So, the outcome was a few early application developers with large and rather sticky audiences. When the restrictions went in, it became much more difficult for new developers to build a similar user base—they actually needed a real viral idea! So, as a result, Facebook applications lost a bit of their luster. The "apps bubble" came and went in just months—a few winners stood, but a lot of other developers were left wondering how to create their own viral success on Facebook.

Featured Case: How Causes, Zombies, Werewolves, and Vampires Changed the Course of Facebook Applications

Blake Commagere is a social applications pioneer, working as a developer at Plaxo, a social network for businesspeople, and on his own building Facebook applications such as Causes, Zombies, Werewolves, Vampires, and others. We caught up with Blake to get his thoughts on Facebook applications—then and now.

Q: *Talk a little about the early days of developing applications on the Facebook platform.*

A: Causes was a beta partner on the platform, so at first we were just exchanging IMs with the platform team, sharing emails, testing new ideas like "mock Ajax," and giving them feedback. It was incredibly exciting—we all knew this was a new idea and game-changing event, and it was insanely busy and fun. Additionally, the growth potential of a product had been wildly underestimated, even by those of us with experience working on viral products like Plaxo. I remember having comments in my code for Causes that read things like "Oh, when this gets to 100,000 users, this has to be optimized." My optimistic estimates put us at hitting those numbers within a month, which would mean for an aggressive but reasonable pace at which to optimize portions of the product. I believe we hit 100,000 users on Facebook Causes within two days, and that meant some very aggressive scaling and optimization plans.

Continues

Featured Case: How Causes, Zombies, Werewolves, and Vampires Changed the Course of Facebook Applications (Continued)

Q: *You had a few huge viral hits. What do you think were the keys to your success?*

A: The keys to success were twofold: the ability to recognize potential for a particular application on the platform and the ability to rapidly adapt that concept as the platform changed. The platform history is littered with the corpses of products by people who could not or would not adapt their product as the platform evolved. The platform has changed dramatically and will continue to change dramatically, and you *must be* willing to adapt to it.

Q: *What happened to your applications?*

A: I was part of the Causes team; they still run and maintain the app, and it is doing extremely well. My other hits—the Zombies, Vampires, etc., games—are now owned and run by ohai, a company I cofounded.

Q: *How does the Facebook application development environment differ today from the early days?*

A: Initially, the platform changed much, much quicker. A platform like this was completely new, and the team at Facebook iterated at such a rapid pace that we developers had far less time to alter our applications to bring them into compliance with the API changes, and so on.

We now have much more detailed documentation, the capabilities of the platform have significantly expanded, and Facebook is communicating its product road map to developers. Initially it was this crazy experiment where we all—both Facebook and the developers—were learning together how a platform like theirs could and should work.

Q: *Where do you see the best marketing opportunities in social media today?*

A: It really depends on the brand being marketed. I think celebrities have really found a great way to market themselves on Twitter.

Celebrities like Dane Cook and Tila Tequila were really pioneers for that type of marketing on MySpace, but the design of Twitter better represents the asymmetrical relationships we have with celebrities.

For bands, MySpace is your strongest marketing opportunity. For location-focused service, the iPhone is a phenomenal platform because it has built-in location services available to developers. Facebook has grown to become such a huge service that for any brand it represents an extremely strong marketing opportunity.

Facebook Apps Today

Although Facebook placed a number of restrictions on applications, it also created a variety of other ways for marketers to get into the News Feed of consumers. We discussed a number of those tactics earlier in the book—fan pages, profiles, automatic News Feed updates, Highlights, Suggestions, and so on. Marketers have a wide range of options, and many of those options are not anywhere near as complicated as establishing a new Facebook application to support a marketing campaign. Furthermore, whereas applications aren't absolutely necessary to create a Facebook presence, a good application strategy is critical for a presence on mobile platforms such as the iPhone, Google Android, the Palm OS, and Windows Mobile. So, mind share when it comes to specific branded applications tends to be in favor of mobile devices over Facebook.

The one place where applications have been very successful on Facebook is in the casual games category. As of October 2009, a quick scan of the top applications on AppData.com reveals that 8 of the top 15 most installed applications are casual games. As the Facebook platform continues to mature and integrate more rich media content, expect these games to get gradually more advanced over time. This also means that the bar to create an interesting game will continue to rise over time.

All of that said, there are still a few cases where it may make sense for you to create a specialized Facebook application to enhance a marketing campaign:

Launch of a new product or service You can introduce a product through an application that shows off the value of your product in a creative manner.

Immersive branding Apps can provide a multimedia, interactive, or gaming experience that gives a user a positive and reinforcing experience with your brand or product.

Logical brand extension via the News Feed and/or profile Certain businesses have products or services that more naturally lend themselves to specialized applications that reinforce the overall value proposition.

In each of these circumstances, you're looking to use the application as a clever call to action that makes the user do something that reinforces your business or brand message. The applications themselves can serve an entirely different purpose, but at the end of the day, users of the application will be exposed to one of your marketing messages in a clever way—assuming you don't force the brand or the product onto the customer too aggressively. This is where creativity really comes into play as much as any other place in Facebook marketing. It is rare to find an application that succeeds virally without some humor or interesting angle on a product or service. You can't just overtly sell your product to consumers via a Facebook app and expect it to be a viral hit. The execution of a clever idea is a necessary success factor to create a successful marketing initiative through Facebook applications.

Featured Case: When Rabid Fans Build Viral Apps for You

One of the most impressive Facebook application marketing successes today didn't come from a corporation. It came from a rabid fan. The James Avery Charms application allowed users to send images of charms created by jeweler James Avery to one another as virtual gifts. As of October 2009, the James Avery Charms application had more than 87,000 active users and almost 4,700 fans. It was created by Michele Caldwell, a website developer and IT support specialist for adWhite, an advertising agency in The Woodlands, Texas. We took a few minutes to talk with Michele about the application and why she created it.

Q: *Tell us about the app you created, the James Avery Charms application.*

A: I created an app on Facebook that allows people to send images of James Avery charms to their friends. The app can be added to a person's Facebook page and shows all the charms people have sent them.

Q: *What made you create the James Avery Charms application?*

A: I was at home recovering from major surgery in January/February 2009, and I had just gotten my own Facebook account. Friends started sending me "gifts," so I got curious about how I could create my own app to send others "gifts." One of the gifts I had collected was made using Gift Creator on Facebook. I found out it was easy to create your own gift app.

Q: *How did you build the application?*

A: I just went to Gift Creator, and a wizard took me step-by-step through the process. I started out by adding a few images of charms from James Avery's website, and then I ended up adding a lot more, around 150 of them.

Q: *Did anyone from James Avery reach out to you after you created the application?*

A: Yes! I was really excited. Last month I got contacted by the general manager of direct channel. He said he wanted to talk to me about how we can work together and thanked me for being such a big fan, and we e-mailed back and forth a few times, but I have yet to talk to him in person.

Q: *Have you spoken with any other James Avery fans as a result of creating the application?*

A: I get Facebook messages from fans all the time, mostly asking me how to add the app to their sidebar or some other technical question. I've not spoken with any in person.

Q: *What are your future plans for the application or other applications? Has it been a fun experience?*

A: It has been a fun experience just to see how quickly it grew. More than 2.5 million charms have been sent as of this date! That totally amazes me. Unfortunately I don't have time to work on it, or even respond to most e-mails I get about it, because my day job keeps me so busy. I knew I would never get paid for doing it. I don't want fame or notoriety. I just did it as a fan of James Avery for the purpose of passing the time while I was home recovering from surgery.

The Consumer Experience of Facebook Apps

Before we get into common types of Facebook applications and the mechanics involved in building or integrating an app into your campaign, let's first examine the customer experience of applications—discovery and installation.

Discovery

Contrary to popular belief, it's actually somewhat difficult for Facebook users to find an app without a notification from a friend. Why is that the case? Well, for one, Facebook is fundamentally driven by the social context of the News Feed. Most communications in Facebook happen in the News Feed, which is good for all of us because that's what users see first upon every login. But it does mean that for an app to propagate and have a chance to be a viral success, it will need to send enticing yet useful messages through a user's profile, which alerts friends via the News Feed. In that sense, it is similar to a Facebook fan page or any other marketing tactic you'll use with success. Apps can also be found through search—either through Facebook's search or through a traditional search engine. But it is pretty rare for users to seek a Facebook app in this manner. Users may also find apps in four other ways:

- When friends become a fan of an application on Facebook. A message announcing this will appear in the News Feed.

- When a friend uses an app to post directly on their friends' Walls, as shown in Figure 8.1. (Depending on privacy settings, friends of friends or even everyone on Facebook can see the app Wall postings.)

Figure 8.1 Pillow Fight

- Via Facebook advertising, where you'll run an ad specifically to get people to look at your application.

- Through Facebook's app recommendations, which is found at www.facebook. com/apps/directory.php or by clicking the Applications button in the bottom left of the Facebook home page and then clicking Browse More Applications. Figure 8.2 shows the way Facebook presents application recommendations to a user.

But all told, the most common and most cost-effective means for an app to propagate on Facebook is via "app-driven" messages that are routed through a user's profile and then to their friends' News Feeds.

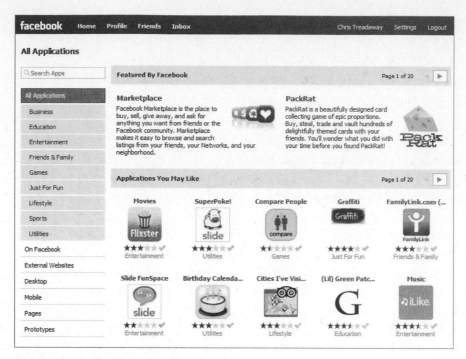

Figure 8.2 Facebook application recommendations

Keys to Getting Your App Discovered

So if discoverability isn't guaranteed, how should you build a consumer-facing Facebook app to make it as viral as it can be?

Get it right the first time If you have a novel concept, you have to be sure that the experience people have with the app is right and encourages viral behavior. If you fail to do it the right way, you'll miss an opportunity. Remember, people make knee-jerk reactions to things they see and experience on Facebook. Make sure the knee-jerk reaction is enjoyable and in your favor the first time because there really are no second chances.

Build an app that requires regular visits The more visits, the more opportunities you have to get on News Feeds, and the more opportunities people have to become a user of your app. Regular visits also breed loyalty among users.

Encourage sharing/announcing app events via the News Feed Engaging apps are typically at their best when friends install apps. That's why they're called *social apps*! You can kill two birds with one stone by adding notification features to your app that will get reminders on people's News Feeds. Just don't go overboard, because it's a fine line between annoying people and being informative.

Launch thoughtfully To make an app successful, it's critical that you seed the application with friendly users who understand that you're just getting started. People you don't know may ignore the app if it doesn't have many users, so start strong with people who will test the app and give you feedback. Meanwhile, they'll count toward your active users metric, which will tell others that your app is worth investigating.

Monitor outcomes As with other Facebook marketing efforts, measuring success on an ongoing basis will help you learn quickly what is working and what is not working. If you find that you aren't adding users quickly or that people aren't using your app regularly, you may be able to make a tweak or two to optimize performance.

Finally, remember that poor execution works harder against you than good execution works for you. Do things the right way and the way that dovetails into your goals and objectives for the app, and you put yourself in a position to succeed.

Installation

Now let's review the installation process. Once users have discovered an application and the user clicks the View Application link, they're sent to the application's home page. Figure 8.3 is the home page for Red Bull's branded rock, paper, and scissors social game. This layout may look very familiar to you—it doubles as the fan page for the app so people can become fans, write on the Wall, rate the application with a review, and see other friends who are using the app. All of this information can indeed play a role in whether or not the user chooses to install the application.

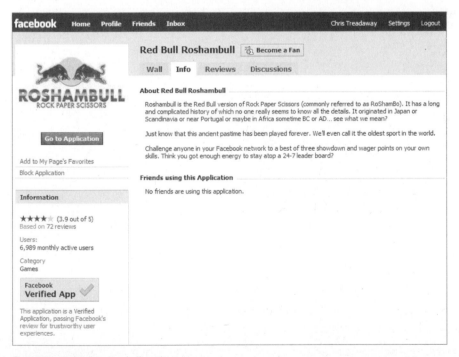

Figure 8.3 Red Bull Roshambull app home page

To view or install the app, the user must click the Go To Application link in the upper left of the screen. At this point in this particular application, the user then sees the home page of the app (Figure 8.4). Red Bull Roshambull also henceforth appears in the list of applications accessible from the Applications button in the bottom left of the screen (Figure 8.5). This is also the place where users can uninstall apps that they no longer use.

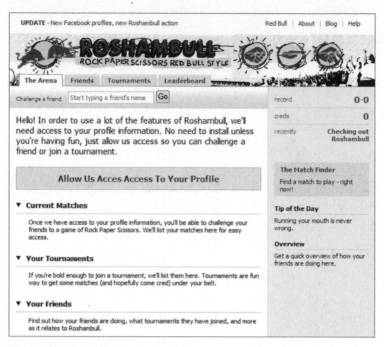

Figure 8.4 Roshambull Facebook game

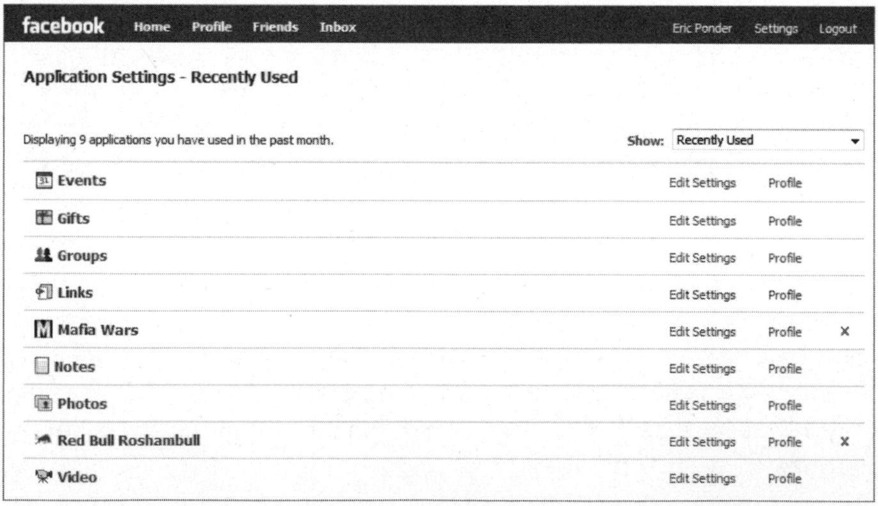

Figure 8.5 List of applications

In the case of Red Bull Roshambull, this social game has very little utility without inviting another Facebook friend to play the game. This is unusual—Facebook has cracked down quite a bit on apps that require invitations to be functional. So don't get terribly excited, because you may not be able to get away with a similar scheme for your app. For a user to invite friends to play Roshambull, the app must first get permission from the user to access profile data and friend lists. Clicking the Allow Us To Access Your Profile link brings the user to Figure 8.6.

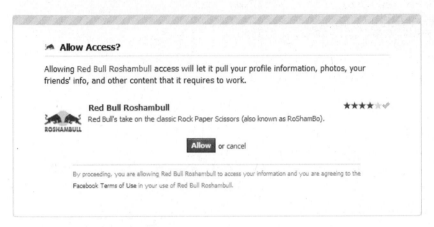

Figure 8.6 App requesting profile data

This seemingly draconian message in many cases appears to be a lot more severe than it really is. The app is requesting access to profile data that it may use in a variety of ways to make the app fully functional. The message is a bit of a catch-all—it doesn't spell out exactly how profile data will be used. It doesn't say how/if messages will be sent through a user's profile, which may then annoy friends. It doesn't suggest one way or another if messages will be sent through notifications and how regularly those messages may appear. So, it is fairly limited and somewhat scary for users to read.

Sadly, as an app developer, you don't have an opportunity here to share any further detail with concerned users. The screen is a standard setting for the Facebook development platform, and it can't be significantly altered. In this sense, uncertainty about how profile data will be used and how other apps in the past have misused Facebook are the biggest barrier to installation. In 2010, there is also a fair amount of "app fatigue" from users. Either they don't want the hassle of using a new app or they don't want to deal with the risk of offending friends with frivolous News Feed messages that benefit the app creator more than the actual user. So, keep all of that in mind as you balance the needs of having your app spread virally and also keeping people happy. There is a happy medium, and failure to hit that happy medium may affect the success of your app.

Types of Facebook Applications

So, what types of Facebook applications are most popular today? That certainly depends on who you ask. Some demographic groups respond to different types of applications, while others don't. The following are the different types of applications that currently have the highest number of users. This list is intended to give you some high-level ideas of the types of concepts that may resonate with your customers in case you are considering an application of your own.

Social games By far, the most Facebook applications today are social games. These are applications that intend to entertain the user first and foremost, not necessarily sell them anything. That said, the in-game experience is often enhanced through virtual goods, which are often sold to users for real money. This is the primary monetization scheme for social games on Facebook, although some also sell advertising. The top social game producers are currently Zynga, Playfish (acquired by Electronic Arts), and Playdom. Few "branded" social games have achieved significant popularity, although Red Bull had some modest success with the Roshambull application (`http://apps.facebook.com/redbullroshambull`), which is the branded rock, paper, and scissors game app we highlighted earlier in this chapter.

However, a few large companies have introduced branded elements into social games for marketing purposes. This is similar to paid placements in movies or television shows—a company interested in reaching a certain audience will pay to have a branded item placed into the game to enhance game play in some way. Expect to see more of this over time instead of actual fully developed and new social games that need to catch fire to meet marketing objectives.

Quiz apps Popularized in late 2008 and early 2009, a variety of quiz applications were designed by a wide range of companies to capture answers to simple questions from users and share those personal details with other friends on Facebook through the News Feed. It sounds too simple to warrant something as seemingly complex as an application, but there is no shortage of quiz apps on Facebook. Why would someone write a quiz app? Engaging quiz applications have occasionally generated a large audience, which the producer of the app could use either to monetize through advertising or to offer products and services to users of the app. One company, LivingSocial, created a huge user base with simple apps such as the Pick Your Five series that allowed users to pick their five favorite things (movies, celebrities, TV shows, sports teams, and so on) and share that information with other Facebook friends. Again, it sounds way too simple and perhaps sophomoric. But Living Social was able to tap into a user's desire to express themselves on their profiles and share information with friends in a systematic, predictable, and somewhat socially acceptable manner. There have been several attempts from companies to create branded quiz applications, but few have succeeded in creating a large and lasting user base.

If you want to avoid creating your own Facebook quiz, just build your own using a "quiz-building" application. Several of them are available for free on Facebook. Check out QuizPlanet!, Quiz Monster, QuizYourFriends.com, or a variety of others to see what meets your needs. But beware—if you don't write the app yourself, you're beholden to the specific limitations and rules by which those apps were created. You can save time, but you won't have ultimate control over how the app is used and the wording that propagates on users' News Feeds.

Personal/virtual gifts In the early years of Facebook gifts, Facebook controlled the gifts that were available for free and for purchase. Applications emerged to help developers and brand managers create their own gifts so people could give each other hugs, pats on the back, and other virtual gifts like the James Avery charms described earlier in this chapter. The same situation was the case for identifying family members—parents, siblings, cousins, and so on. Out of that need was borne the We're Related application (now FamilyLink), which had more than 20 million monthly active users in early November 2009. In both cases, Facebook has recognized the need these apps fill and has added new platform features for developers that make for a better consumer experience. Users can now just use Facebook's features, and they won't need to install or use an app if they want to identify cousins or siblings or share a virtual hug. In a sense, apps written by third-party developers have given Facebook ideas about product/platform enhancements, and it has responded with similar functionality.

Widgets Widgets are Facebook apps designed not to run as a consumer "app" experience but rather as part of a fan page to customize the look and feel for a consumer. There is no installation process for a consumer. These apps instead run inside a fan page automatically and are presented to the user via a tab of their own or the Boxes tab. Why would someone go to the effort of creating an app just to customize a fan page? The functions offered through Facebook fan pages are fairly limited and cover broad scenarios that are consistent with the rest of Facebook—posting photos, links, comments, and so on, and interacting with other people. If you need to do anything else in particular, such as creating a sign-up form, for instance, you'll need to use a Facebook app such as Facebook's own Static FBML. You don't necessarily have to build your own custom application for this. You can also look for apps that do what you need via a search engine or look at examples of other fan pages that do the things you need to do. You may just find that you don't have to build anything yourself—you can just reuse and/or modify something that has already been released for general use.

Conceptually it's also good to think about what you want to achieve with your application. Most folks are motivated by one of the following goals:

Building a viral hit You may want to create an engaging application that people will enjoy using repeatedly and will recommend to friends either directly or by allowing messages to propagate via the News Feed.

Introducing new functionality An app can offer an experience through Facebook that provides relatively unique new social features or provides similar benefits but with a unique distribution angle that makes more Facebook users more aware of it than competitor applications.

Extending the brand in a new way An app can also utilize brand assets in a slightly different way that is engaging or interesting to the target market.

Providing entertainment for the sake of brand/product loyalty Some apps help people enjoy themselves or pass time by interacting with your brand or with other consumers through games, interactive experiences, and so on.

Optimize Your Fan Page with Apps

In Chapter 5 we discussed all the basics of setting up your Facebook fan page. To make your fan page more compelling and engaging for your fans, you can add any number of third-party apps. All fan pages come with the default Facebook apps: Links, Photos, Videos, Notes, and Events. Often, new fan pages may not have other apps by Facebook like the Discussion tab or Reviews app added, and you'll need to manually add them.

To add apps to your fan page, look just below your image, and click Edit Page. Scroll to the foot of the page, click Browse More under Applications, and search for an app you want to add. You can also browse the Apps Directory at `www.facebook.com/apps/directory.php` and then click the Page button to go the section with apps that can be added to fan pages (which is the vast majority of apps!). Click the app you want to add, and you'll almost always go to that app's fan page; look for the Add To Page link.

Once you've added an app to your page, it's not always obvious what to do next. Go back to your main fan page, click the Edit Page link under your image, and you'll see all apps added to your page in alphabetical order. Click Edit App. Each app is different as to how you can configure the settings. Usually there is a help section or a simple tutorial. Be sure to also click and check the application settings for each app; this is where you have the option of adding a tab and publishing to your fan page Wall, and the News Feeds of your fans.

These are some of our favorite apps for fan pages that you'll get most mileage out of:

Static FBML We mentioned this app in the previous chapter; to reiterate, it is probably one of the most vital components of your fan page because you can add your own fully customizable content. FBML is Facebook's own version of HTML. This app allows you to simply paste in code and give the app your own name, which becomes the tab title. One of the most popular uses of the Static FBML app is to create a *landing tab* (or *canvas page*) specifically for users who have not yet joined your fan page to land on. On that landing tab, you can also include rich media such as a video and perhaps an opt-in box for a free giveaway. Another benefit to the Static FBML app is you can install multiple iterations of the app. In other words, you might have one landing tab as a welcome message and another with details of your services. By way of example, see Gary Vaynerchuk's fan page (`http://facebook.com/gary`), the Oprah Winfrey Show (`www.facebook.com/oprahwinfreyshow`), Four Seasons Hotel and Resorts (`www.facebook.com/FourSeasons`), and RED (`www.facebook.com/joinred`).

Extended Info This app, shown in Figure 8.7, also allows you to insert custom HTML. The only drawback is you can't change the name of the app title. What we like about this app is it can be added to the Wall (the main page your fans see), and the app also automatically inserts a vertical scroll bar when you add more content. You can find the Extended Info app at `http://apps.facebook.com/extendedinfo/`.

Figure 8.7 Extended Info app

Networked Blog If you publish a blog, this app is exceptional for pulling in your blog feeds and allowing your fans to comment on those imported posts. The app can also be added to your personal profile, and any comments shown on your personal profile will also show on your fan page, and vice versa. Networked Blogs also provides the opportunity for even more "viral visibility" because Facebook users can join and follow your blog whether they are a fan on your fan page or not. You can find this app at `http://apps.facebook.com/blognetworks`.

YouTube Badge Many of the Facebook YouTube apps tend to be a bit buggy. However, we've found the YouTube Badge app (see Figure 8.8) to be most reliable and flexible. You can select from various types of video (Tag, User, Playlist, Favorites) and choose how many videos to display.

Figure 8.8 YouTube Badge app

Plus, when clicked, each of the videos opens in a new window and goes right to the YouTube page. You can find this app at `http://apps.facebook.com/youtubebadge`.

Facebook to Twitter As mentioned in Chapter 7, this is Facebook's own app that allows you to post to Twitter. There's huge power in using this app to bring your Twitter followers back to your fan page. You have 420 characters in the Facebook publisher to create content, and when you have this app applied to your fan page, your posts get truncated at about 120 characters and posted out as a tweet with a shortened (bit.ly) link to your fan page. You can find Facebook to Twitter at `http://facebook .com/twitter`.

Selective Tweets To reverse the process in the previous app (posting *from* Twitter *to* your Facebook fan page), this app works wonders because if your tweet volume is high, you don't need to clutter up your fan page with excess content. Rather, you can select which tweets get posted as your fan page status update. If you're also using the Facebook to Twitter app, you can temporarily adjust the settings so as not to double post. You can find the app at `http://apps.facebook.com/selectivetwitter`.

Posterous Posterous is an excellent, free, quick blogging platform that allows you to easily create various types of content posted via their website or by e-mail. This platform also gets great Google indexing, which is good news for your search engine optimization. If you're using Posterous anyway, you may as well add the Facebook app to your fan page and get additional viral visibility from your content. You can find the app at `http://apps.facebook.com/posterous/facebook`.

Notes Notes is a default Facebook app, but it bears mentioning that there are myriad uses for the app. Certainly you can create a rich-text note directly in the app, add images, and post. The Notes app also allows you to tag any of your friends. (As a respectful policy, we do recommend only tagging your friends provided they are actually mentioned in the note.) But the power behind the Notes app is it allows you to import *any* RSS feed. You could import your regular blog feed here instead of using the Networked Blogs app if you wanted. Or, you could get creative and import the "likes" of your Twitter favorites RSS feed, as shown in Figure 8.9. This allows you to quickly and easily push content from Twitter (using a blend of your favorite content producers' tweets along with your own) and interact on the fly wherever you are, including on your mobile device.

Figure 8.9 Imported Twitter favorite with fan engagement

For additional Facebook fan page apps, you might like to check out Involver's suite of free and paid apps: `http://involver.com`.

What You'll Need to Build a Facebook Application

As we mentioned earlier, Facebook applications are built in Facebook Markup Language (FBML). It's the successor of Facebook Query Language (FQL) and works in conjunction with the Facebook API. It is similar to Hypertext Markup Language (HTML), the default programming language on the Internet. Rather than being used to write standard web pages, FBML is only used for building Facebook applications and performing other tasks on Facebook. To use FBML, you minimally need to have an application that allows you to use HTML/FBML for your profile. We'll talk more about that when we talk about hosting later in the chapter.

Some of the things you can do with FBML include sending e-mails to other Facebook users, embedding videos or images in pages, creating dashboards, building games, building forms, displaying headers, and other tasks. FBML is not a completely new language. It allows the use of regular HTML tags, making it extremely flexible for the programmer building the application or feature.

Speaking of programmers, we're going to assume you're not one. This book is targeted squarely at marketers, so we're assuming you have exactly zero experience writing code. With that being the case, we'll talk about how you get someone to build an application for you on Facebook. Rather than talking about building applications, markup language, specific server configuration settings, and PHP/MySQL thingama-jigs, we'll focus on what you should expect when building a Facebook application, following best practices, hiring a programmer, and managing the project.

 If you want to learn how to program FBML, we recommend any number of other books on the subject, such as Nick Gerakines' *Facebook Application Development* (Wrox, 2008), Richard Wagner's *Building Facebook Applications for Dummies* (Wiley, 2008), or Jesse Stay's *FBML Essentials* (O'Reilly, 2008).

Also, take a look through Facebook's handy "Get Started" app tutorial at `http://developers.facebook.com/get_started.php?tab=tutorial`. There, you'll see the step-by-step process for building an app, including a handy tutorial, the anatomy of an app, and an overview of the guiding principles.

Best Practices

Whether you get an internal team or a third-party vendor to build your Facebook application, you'll still need a solid understanding of best practices when it comes to designing, building, and deploying Facebook applications. After all, you can't possibly expect to effectively manage this project if you don't have a reasonable foundation when it comes to understanding the core tenets of what it takes to build a good Facebook application. We're going to briefly cover three major areas when it comes to this topic: speed, user experience, and terms.

Speed

It's important to make sure your application is built to run efficiently on the Facebook platform. As with any application that you build on the Internet, the speed at which a page loads into a user's browser is one of the single most critical elements of execution when it comes to the user's perception or enjoyment of your application. Because you're dealing with an application programming interface when building Facebook applications, paying special attention to the techniques used to cause your application to render quickly on a user's profile is especially important. You need to pay close attention to this aspect of your application, because the fact that you're going through an API means the web browser has to wait twice as long to retrieve information and display it to your user than it would with an application that doesn't use an application programming interface.

Granted, in many cases we are dealing with seconds or even milliseconds when talking about transactions between applications. However, users have little to no patience on the Web, and the time adds up quickly when someone is waiting for their browser to render the web page they are waiting on. It's important that you take the most efficient path possible to grabbing data and processing information you need and bring it back to your web pages so your users are presented with the most responsive experience possible.

So, here are five of the most important tactics for producing lickety-split applications as recommended by Facebook:

- Use FQL instead of the API whenever possible. The reasoning here is that the API is nothing more than a wrapper on top of FQL. FQL gives you more direct access to the data you need.

- Make sure the application preloads the FQL queries. This is a smart technique when programming with any language. You never want your page to load partially, wait for data, then finish loading.

- Ajax, or asynchronous JavaScript and XML, is another technology that can be used to improve the perception that a page is loading quickly. On Facebook, Ajax is implemented as Facebook JavaScript (FBJS). It allows the programmer to load data and implement processes in the background of a web page while other parts of the page are loading.

- Stash what you can in the cache. Caching is the process of storing data or a file locally on a user's computer for easy access later. By doing this, your application does not have to continually reach out across the Internet to retrieve information that doesn't change during a user's session. Although there could be several things you can store temporarily in the cache, we recommend at a minimum that you store the CSS and external JavaScript files you use in your applications.

- Build smart navigation, and use pages effectively. Don't throw everything plus the kitchen sink on any page of your application. Learn how to use pagination so your user can move from relevant sections of your application with a minimal amount of page load on each window.

User Experience

User experience (UX) is defined as the quality of experience one has when interacting with the design of something. This is not limited to Facebook applications or even web pages. For example, a person has a bad user experience when sipping out of a leaky travel mug. You want to make sure your users have a good experience with your application.

When taking into account user experience as it relates to the design of your Facebook application, you must think about the needs of your user, any constraints your company has from a business or brand point of view, and any limitations or needs technically related to the application and your goals.

Generally you should always consider ease of use, information design (intuitiveness), the structure of the elements on your page, aesthetics, and overall functionality. When designing a Facebook application, there are several specific elements to ponder:

- Make sure your application doesn't require users to install third-party applications to use your application.
- Don't force users into logic loops if they opt out of performing a task that you deem valuable.
- Don't force users to spam their friends in order to enjoy the features of your application.
- Engage with your users.
- Allow users to engage with each other.
- Keep your application fresh by fixing UI issues that inevitably arise, and update the app on a regular basis to encourage repeated use.

Terms

Lastly, you need to make sure Facebook is happy with what you're doing with its platform. After all, we must remember that we are all guests in their house, so to speak, when we use the Facebook platform. As such, it's just good manners to understand the house rules and abide by them. After you've come up with a concept for your application, it is well advised that you read through the developer principles and policies (http://developers.facebook.com/policy), including the statement of rights and responsibilities listed at the top.

On a very high level, you need to know that Facebook takes user privacy, spamming, lying, cheating, copyright, pornography, hate speech, and intellectual property very seriously. Stray from any of these areas in a manner that is counter to Facebook's guidelines for acceptable use, and you should expect swift, unapologetic action from Facebook to correct the situation for their users and remove your application from Facebook altogether.

Hire a Programmer

Now that you have some understanding about what you need to be considering when designing and deploying your shiny-new Facebook application, let's talk about getting someone to build it for you. Hiring a really good programmer who specializes in any language is difficult process. We don't want to overwhelm you, but at the same time, this process needs to be taken seriously. There's a very high price to be paid for hiring a low-quality programmer. Do your homework, check references, and be sure candidates can back up any claims they make in regard to success and experience.

Assess Your Candidates

Qualified developers should have the expertise and the experience to be able to discuss any aspect of the Facebook application development process covered in this chapter. Furthermore, they should be able to expand on any of these topics with relative ease. Now, we're not looking for perfection here. If a programmer doesn't define UX exactly as we do here but clearly shows that they understand that UX is the practice of designing something to the benefit of the user, you're probably in good shape.

The candidate needs to have a fairly deep understanding of these principles, which in turn will show their level of experience, and ideally success. Ask the programmer how she would enhance the performance of a Facebook application.

Next, you're looking for technical competence. Have the programmer show you at least three applications they have built in the past. The applications should be live on the Facebook platform. Use these applications, and let your gut tell you whether the performance is where it needs to be. Does the navigation make sense? Is there a logical progression in the data structures or the application's narrative?

On a more fundamental level, have some basic tests that you give to all applicants in order to consider them seriously for the position. These should include the following:

- Embed a live video feed in a Facebook profile.
- Allow comments on a live video feed.
- Pull some basic profile information (name, city, and ZIP code) from the Facebook friends of a logged-in user account.
- Connect to a third-party data source, pull data from it, and display data in a Facebook application.

If you have any peers or acquaintances with Facebook development experience, ask the candidate to give you some samples of the Facebook-related code they have written and have your friend review it. Although there are many "right" ways to skin a cat when it comes to programming, making it difficult to identify the "best" code, it is certainly easy for an experienced programmer to identify poor programming practices.

One more thing—ask the candidate questions that will give some insight into their work ethic and habits. Questions should be direct and clear such as "If you committed to a deadline and started to realize that hitting the goal would be a challenge, how would you react?" You are looking for a two-part answer here. First, the programmer needs to communicate to you and the rest of the team that the deadline is in jeopardy with some explanation about why the issues have arisen. Second, the programmer needs to indicate that, unless the situation is an impossible one, they will still work diligently to hit the original deadline. Change is inevitable, so communication is key.

Manage a Development Project

Best practices for project management have been written about in a dozen formats or more. But at the end of the day, it's not which project management method or project development method you choose that determines success. The management of the overall project life cycle, the work ethic of the team members involved, leadership, and discipline have a much greater impact on the success of a project than the project management philosophy that is employed.

If you don't have any project management background or experience, then you don't want to take this part lightly. As critical as the programmer's job is when it comes to building your Facebook application, the manager on the project arguably has a much larger impact on the overall success of your endeavor. If you're going to take on the role of project manager for your Facebook application projects, it's critical that you manage the crucial steps in the project life cycle.

Scope and Goals

Before you run off expecting to build an application that will solve all your company's problems, first come up with some tangible, realistic goals that you want the application to reach. These objectives will determine features that will direct the development of your app. Specifically, what technical features of your Facebook app support the business objectives you have? What is the minimum bar necessary to achieve those goals and to give users a good experience with your application? What can users do with the Facebook app and how? How will communication flow through the app, e-mail, Facebook notifications, and the Facebook News Feed?

It isn't an academic exercise to do all of this up front. It's a necessary task that you'll need to conduct to avoid building the wrong thing and then rebuilding it later. Every hour of a developer's time is costly, especially if you make a mistake and have to make changes. Start out with a good idea of what you want, and document those requirements. You may need to make a change or two as you go, but at least you'll cut out a lot of unnecessary time having your developer help scope your application and write your requirements.

Research as many apps as you can in the genre you're planning to build as well as apps with features you want to emulate. Make a list of such apps—with the URLs to the app pages—and a corresponding list of features you like so you can present this information to your developer.

As you consider what you're going to build, also remember to use the right tool for the right job. Facebook applications are great experiences inside the social network/social graph. So, you can succeed if your goals are about acquiring users or monetizing through virtual goods or third-party advertising inside your app. But Facebook apps won't solve all your problems, especially if you are looking to drive product sales, extend the reach of e-mail marketing campaigns, or drive traffic to your website. You often will need a combination of Facebook and other social media tools or your own website to make your marketing campaign work as designed.

For example, let's say you have a mandate from your management team to create a Facebook application that will generate an additional 120 online sales of your product. That's a great idea, but if you're asked to do this exclusively through a Facebook application, you may have some trouble. One reason is that Facebook does not currently allow you to add a shopping cart to a person's profile. So, a goal of having your Facebook application drive the immediate sales of your product may be asking too much of the Facebook application, no matter how good it is. It makes more sense to use the Facebook application to drive traffic to a landing page on your website.

So, in this case, you actually need both your Facebook application and your landing page to work properly. The Facebook application can be measured for the effectiveness of pulling people into the website, while the landing page itself must be optimized separately with different copy and layout to ensure that customers convert at the highest rate possible. This difference is important to understand when defining goals and ensuring that the application *and* supporting cast members are scoped properly. Sometimes you need more than just a one-man band.

Additional Deliverables

In addition to the functions of your application, you will need to ask your developer for a number of other things to ensure that a new developer can take over the project in a worst-case scenario or in case you choose a different developer for the next version. Be sure to include the following as you define the scope of your project:

- A copy of any source code created to build the application
- The addition of one of your employees as a developer of the application so you can conduct administrator tasks
- Project files and documentation related to the project
- Hosting information for your application
- Database structures related to your project

Your developer should also perform any configurations necessary through the hosting provider to ensure that the app is up and running properly before finishing the project. Facebook requires all new apps to be approved before communications propagate across Facebook and before the app can be found in a search. Oftentimes, Facebook disallows apps from being approved because of the violations of the developer terms of service mentioned earlier in this chapter. Don't sign off on completion of your application until the approval process has been completed. Otherwise, you may build an application that never launches to its intended audience.

Project Planning

Project planning involves not just hiring people for tasks you can't complete but also securing necessary resources, assigning responsibilities, and defining and securing budget if it is necessary. Depending upon the size of your project, it is important that you define what specific tasks are required in order to produce the finished product. You should estimate the time and effort required for each task, identify dependencies between different activities, and map out a realistic schedule for the overall project. Make sure that you involve your team when estimating how long the different activities will take and the inconveniences associated with them. Define critical dates and associated milestones. Make sure all this information is written to the project plan, including any relevant budget information, and get sign-off for the overall project from your key stakeholders.

Communication and Project Tracking

After you've done all this work to determine the scope, define your deliverables, and create a project plan that all necessary parties agree to, you must have open and effective communication if your project is going to be successful. Transparency and leadership are critical. It doesn't do anyone any good if you have a well-defined project plan, the scope, and tasks assigned if no one on the team knows what those tasks are or when the milestones hit.

As the project plan is being executed, you must track the actual results of your team's efforts and the specific tasks completed by the different members of your team as they are mapped out on the project plan. Not only are you looking for individuals who are hitting their goals according to the project timeline, you are also herding cats. In more complex projects, there are many times when some tasks intersect with other tasks being completed by different team members. If someone on the team gets off track and falls behind, it can hold up the efforts of the entire team and create a negative impact across the entire team in a cascading manner. Not only does this cause the project to fall behind schedule, but this can also create monetary and morale issues. Your job is to motivate team members to stay on track. In the case that problems crop up, it's your job to mitigate the negative impact on the entire team by reassigning resources or making changes to the project plan.

Change and Risk Management

This brings up two other important responsibilities related to project management: change and risk management. Even when scope and project planning are conducted under the best of circumstances, stakeholders often change their mind about what they want out of an application. This could be because they see changes in the marketplace, because the underlying business changes, or because they had a barbecue at their cousin's house this weekend and Uncle Frank came up with some great ideas that the team hadn't considered.

Sometimes situations demand changes in your approach that may impact scope, timelines, or deliverables that you once thought you needed. Changes like this and other events can adversely affect the successful outcome of your project. When possible, it's critical the project manager identifies risks and notifies the appropriate stakeholders of the situation as soon as possible. Sometimes you're willing to take a risk to make a change, and other times you won't be willing. The project manager, more than any individual on the team, can have a great deal of impact over the ultimate success of the project. Communication is key to making it work.

Debug Your App

If you are relatively new to the software development business, you are probably not familiar with bugs—identifying them, classifying them, and prioritizing them. It's an art to find them, so if you have a talented tester nearby, you'll certainly want some help. Once you've found your bugs, two main concepts help to drive changes to applications: severity and priority.

Severity is assessed by determining what happens for a user, without making any qualifications about the veracity or importance of the bug. In other words, what does the user experience? A numerical scale is used to classify each bug, and numbers are assigned independently of and before priority is assigned. For example, we use the following broadly defined scale for our applications:

- *Severity 1*: Browser or app crash, data loss: a fatal bug that causes the app or browser to terminate or data in the application to be lost

- *Severity 2*: Usability problem: app too difficult to use and/or too little information given to the user

- *Severity 3*: Feature Loss: important feature from last version inadvertently left out in current version

- *Severity 4*: Inconvenience/layout problem: process in the app not streamlined, poor layout, too much information given to the user

- *Severity 5*: Personal preference: no apparent problem for the user, but someone on your team (or you) prefer(s) that the app behave differently

Once all bugs have been identified in a sweep of the app, you can sit down with your team to assign a *priority* to each of the bugs. Priority is a determination of how quickly you'd like to fix the bug, and it is usually assigned in a group setting where people with different opinions can share their thoughts on the importance of each bug. We use the following priority scale for our applications and websites:

- *Priority 0*: Urgent, must fix immediately

- *Priority 1*: Very important fix but not immediately urgent

Continues

- *Priority 2*: Important fix that should be completed in the current version before official release

- *Priority 3*: Not a necessary fix for this version. Fix it if we can get to it; otherwise, add to next version and reprioritize alongside other bugs

- *Priority 4*: Feature enhancement or change that should be part of the next version

- *Priority 5*: Feature enhancement or change to consider for a future version

One final point regarding debugging your app. If you are seeking the perfect application or website, you may be disappointed by just how long it takes to release. Most commercial websites have minor issues that the developers or business managers don't like on the site. The reality of the Web today is that there really is no such thing as the perfect app or website. Conventional wisdom in the software business is that if you've released an application or website without minor bugs, you've released it too late. So relax, but make sure you knock out major issues so you're happy with the outcome.

Monetize Your App

It's one thing to create a fun, popular, and viral app. It's another to create an app that actually makes you money. Of the 300,000+ Facebook apps, only a small percentage of them are currently being monetized. You may be happy with the viral visibility and user data your app provides. But we suspect you'd also like to know about ways to generate revenue from your app!

It should be noted your efforts may be better spent utilizing Facebook's primary features such as the fan page, social ads, Facebook Connect, and existing apps to further expand your reach and monetize your own products and services. However, if you do go the route of developing your own app, Facebook suggests five popular business models for monetizing your app, detailed at this web page: http://wiki.developers .facebook.com/index.php/Common_Business_Models_for_Facebook_Applications.

In brief, the five models are as follows:

- *Advertising*: By optimizing the data that Facebook provides their app developers, you can serve highly targeted ads on the canvas page of your app.

- *Freemium (by subscription)*: You provide the basic access to your app for free but offer an upgrade level that users need to pay for.

- *Virtual credits/virtual goods*: Users purchase or earn virtual credits.

- *Affiliate fees*: Earn a commission from items users buy via an affiliate link on your app. For example, the Virtual Bookshelf earns money when users purchase books linked to on Amazon.com.

- *Merchandising*: Offer items such as mouse mats, mugs, caps, T-shirts, and so on, with your brand/app/logo.

You can find articles about application monetization on the Facebook developers wiki here:

```
http://wiki.developers.facebook.com/index.php/Articles_About_Application_
Monetization.
```

In addition, third-party providers to help you monetize are listed here:

```
http://wiki.developers.facebook.com/index.php/Third_Party_Providers_
to_Help_You_Monetize
```

> For some time, Facebook has been beta testing various payment systems inside the platform. Only a small number of apps have integrated the virtual currency system (Facebook credits) successfully, but this could be the way of the future for many apps.

The Future: Applications on Mobile Devices

We've covered the present of Facebook apps; certainly we're beyond the early days where there weren't many rules. Some of the opportunities for fast viral growth are gone. The bar is higher today than it was. But it doesn't mean that Facebook apps will necessarily fade into obscurity. In fact, they may enjoy a renaissance.

Remember that Facebook has more than 350 million users, and the social network continues to grow at a rapid pace. The installed base of the Facebook platform is rivaled only by the Web, by Windows, and by SMS today. No other platform comes close to the reach of Facebook. At the same time, smartphones are continuing to grow in popularity. Increasingly, consumers want a mobile web experience regardless of where they are.

The popularity of Apple's iTunes and the App Store tells us that there is already a huge market in third-party mobile applications. Google has created a similar applications marketplace for Android phones, and Microsoft is doing the same with Windows Mobile. When three industry giants all go after the same market, you have to think there is truly an opportunity! Many of these apps run outside the social context that Facebook so uniquely and comprehensively provides.

Similarly, a variety of third-party apps have attempted to build a social network around mobile applications such as location-based services. These applications allow the user to invite friends to join through the phone's contact list. It is a social network of sorts, but it isn't anywhere near as comprehensive. Many active Facebook users have far more Facebook friends than cell phone numbers.

Consider these Facebook mobile stats:

- More than 65 million active users are currently accessing Facebook through their mobile devices.

- People who use Facebook on their mobile devices are almost 50 percent more active on Facebook than nonmobile users.
- More than 180 mobile operators in 60 countries are working to deploy and promote Facebook mobile products.

There are a few possibilities for the evolution of mobile apps that utilize social graph data from Facebook:

Facebook Connect–enabled sites that behave like mobile apps There is nothing keeping developers today from building sites that are purposely optimized to run as apps on mobile devices. Facebook Connect (which was covered in Chapter 7) would pull in required social graph data and allow for communication with friends and across News Feeds.

App compatibility through Facebook Mobile Facebook Mobile runs on a wide range of mobile devices (iPhone, Blackberry, Palm, Android, Sidekick, Windows Mobile, and others). This app displays a wide range of data that is exposed on Facebook—the News Feed, status updates, profiles, and other friend activity. But Facebook Mobile does not allow third-party apps to run through Facebook Mobile and run on the mobile device as they run on Facebook. Should Facebook see an opportunity in extending the dev platform fully to mobile devices, we would expect future compatibility between third-party Facebook Apps and Facebook Mobile.

A Mobile Facebook app container Alternatively, Facebook could release a simple "app container" for each type of mobile device that taps into the user's social graph on Facebook. This container would be fully customizable to a particular brand or look and feel. It would act as a "platform" of its own but would allow for Facebook and mobile development with one simple, comprehensive effort. This would reduce the confusion and effort necessary to target different mobile devices, and it would also allow developers to focus on creating better apps that users will enjoy.

Facebook applications are a great way to extend your brand experience beyond the provided features of the Facebook platform. It just takes a little creativity and patience to navigate the rules and standards that have evolved after the first few years of third-party social application development. It is truly multidisciplinary—you'll need to scope an app properly, enforce a great customer experience, and manage a development effort to get it in the right place. If you don't, your time, money, and energy will be wasted, and you'll have to find a new Facebook tactic to engage with your audience.

The Analytics
of Facebook

9

Social media is the latest big thing in marketing, but it's even better when impact can be shown not just with strong opinions but with numbers to demonstrate successes in customer engagement, satisfaction, increased page views, and even return on investment (ROI). In this chapter, we'll review the basics of analytics so you know what to track and what is important.

Chapter Contents

Keep Score with Metrics and Monitoring

Imagine this scenario for a moment. You are sitting outside a conference room waiting to give a presentation to senior executives of your company about the progress you've made with social media. They wanted you to present one slide with all the details of how you've done, and they want you to speak about how your company has fared relative to your competition. What belongs on that one slide? Better yet, how can you communicate the value of what you do in five minutes? What will convince them that you've succeeded and that they should trust your plan? This is why metrics or key performance indicators are so important. Although a cynic might say that numbers can be distorted to tell whatever story you'd like, statistics is also the preferred language of executives. So, what statistics matter most in social media? To understand all the metrics that truly matter, you need to step back and learn the basics of Internet marketing.

First, you should understand that everything your customers, partners, and so on, do on your website(s) is recorded in a massive log file. This log file is a bit cryptic, but fortunately you don't have to interpret it. Web analytics tools take care of this for you by generating readable reports by date and metric. Figure 9.1 is an example of such a report from Google Analytics. If you don't currently manage or get reports on your company's website traffic, you should try to get your hands on one to understand what appears in reports, how often they are generated, and how your company views them. For years, Internet-based businesses have watched these numbers very closely. But now, businesses of all kinds have concluded that the Internet says a lot about the health of a product, brand, or business unit. The best way to get familiar with the nomenclature, reporting, and intelligence generated from these reports is to dive in headfirst.

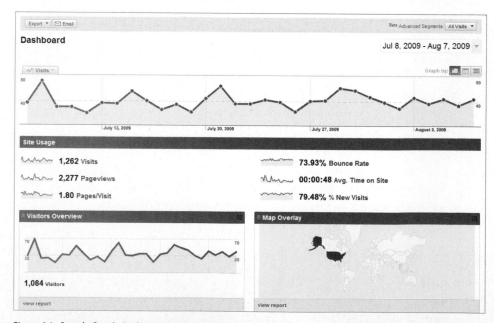

Figure 9.1 Sample Google Analytics report

Table 9.1 summarizes the basics of unique users, page views, and abandonment or bounce rates. When someone visits your website or social media presence on a given day, that person is regarded as a new unique user. With that unique user, you (by definition) also get your first page view—this can be a visit to a landing page, your home page, or any other page on your site that is indexed by a search engine. Some of these users will find something else of interest on your site and click another link to go to another page. This gives you another page view but not another unique user. Other users will get what they need from the page they found on your site, or they'll be disappointed in what they see. So, they'll move on to another destination on the Web or shut down their browser altogether. This behavior is known as a *bounce* or an *abandonment*.

▶ **Table 9.1** Basic Internet Marketing Metrics

Statistic	Definition	Meaning
Unique users	# of distinct people who visit your site on a given day	Awareness of your site
Page views	# of distinct pages viewed on a given day	Stickiness of your site, value of site's content
Bounce rate	% of people who view one page on your site and then leave	Whether people are truly interested in your site/content
Time spent on site	Amount of time in minutes the average user spends on your site	Whether your site is truly a destination or a pass-through

These basic Internet marketing metrics are important, but they don't even begin to tell the entire story about the health of your Internet presence. Analysis is necessary to look at a few of these numbers in combination with other metrics or on a time-trending basis. Individually, we call these second-level metrics *derivative statistics* because they are created by looking at some of these numbers on a relative basis or by combining some of the statistics to see how the site performs over time. Some examples of derivative statistics are page views per unique user, money/subscriber, click-through rate, cost/click, clicks/hour, fans/day, and so on.

How do derivative statistics help you learn more about the use of your website? It's really a matter of looking at your performance critically and as objectively as possible. If you are hoping for a particular outcome, you're less likely to consider that your site isn't performing as well as it could. We tell people all the time that most Internet marketing and social media campaigns are not optimized, no matter how much you think they are. So if you start with the assumption that you have to improve something in your presence, you'll be more likely to find things to fix.

Whatever you do, don't be a cheerleader for your Internet and social media effort. Your job is to find problems and fix them proactively. Think critically about what you're doing. Look for hints of declining performance or ways you can make great performance even better. If you're creative and thinking critically about your job, you'll identify issues before your colleagues. That's a much better situation than the alternative.

For example, you may have a directive to make your website more engaging for users. You get a report saying that you've had a 40 percent increase in unique users, from 1,000 to 1,400 per day over the last month. Page views are up from 2,225 to 2,661. It's time to celebrate, right? Wrong. Although your unique users metric is up, your page views per unique user metric is actually down 17 percent. You've attracted more people to your site, but they're also not sticking around! So, you've succeeded with one metric but failed in the one that actually matters to you. Digging another level beyond the obvious is the key to figuring out what is really happening.

So, how do you begin to collect all the data that you will need to generate derivative statistics and gain intelligence from all the numbers? The easiest way to get started is to create a dashboard in a spreadsheet such as Microsoft Excel. This dashboard will be the one place where you keep a daily record of everything that has happened from the start of your project. Suffice it to say that your dashboard will be your best friend and the one file you simply can't afford to lose—so be sure to back it up regularly or keep it in an online backup service like Windows Live Mesh.

Every individual piece of data that you can collect about your website and social media effort belongs in the dashboard. What are those metrics that are so handy? We've covered them throughout this book, so odds are you are already aware of what you'll need. If you're running a fan page, you'll want to know what your fan count is at the same time every day. The same metric applies to groups or friends of a profile. If you're running advertising campaigns to drive traffic, you'll want to know how much money you spent, how many clicks it generated, and how many impressions you got for your money. Remember, it's all about having the discipline to collect numbers every day so when the time comes, you'll be able to analyze outcomes and drive intelligence from a cryptic set of numbers.

If it's a multichannel marketing effort—such as using Facebook ads to drive website hits or using Google ads to increase your Facebook fan count—you'll want to collect those numbers individually by using the interface provided for reporting. Different analytics services (Google, Facebook, and so on) keep daily data for different periods of time, so if you don't get data on a timely basis, you can lose it altogether. Therefore, make a commitment to capturing all the data you can every day. You can always disregard unnecessary data later after you determine what you really need. Different services also automate parts of the process for you as well. Google Analytics, for example, can be set up to generate reports for you and automatically send you updates via e-mail or on demand. Going into this, you'll just want a good strategy for acquiring voluminous data on a consistent basis and with a consistent time period in mind. You may not see the benefits of this up front, but you'll be happy you did it when the time comes to analyze your progress.

Executive Management of Internet Marketing and Social Media Progress

If you're an executive managing an Internet marketing or social media effort, you are in a tough position. On one hand, you are ultimately responsible for the success and failure of this marketing program. On the other hand, you don't have time to become an expert. That's why you've hired staff, a contractor, a consultant, or an agency to help you. You are almost entirely reliant upon these people to make it work.

Nonetheless, you really need to understand the basics of Internet marketing metrics and derivative statistics. Those responsible have all the incentives in the world for telling you that things are going well and all the tools at their disposal to tell whatever story they'd like. Make sure you ask probing questions to learn exactly what is happening. Here are a few other tips:

- Learn the process. How exactly is success and failure judged by your people?

- Ask for time-trending data. What is your performance over time? Week by week? Month by month?

- Demand comparative data. How do you do vs. your competitors? Understand that you won't get comparative metrics across the board, but you should have a basic idea of how your competitors drive traffic.

- Seek iterative improvements. How are your people assessing themselves critically and making improvements on the fly? And do they do so in a way that keeps the data consistent and comparable on an apples-to-apples basis?

- Look for numbers that show progress. Your people should be able to tell you which data indicates progress. Make sure you understand what they're saying, and probe!

If you're working with someone in your company who is assigned to this work for the first time, you may need to be patient with them as they're learning. Experts, consultants, and contractors should know most of this already—if they're the caliber of professional that you deserve for your business. Ask difficult questions, and apply the correct level of understanding based on the stated qualifications of the person responsible.

And finally, keep in the back of your mind a few important quotes about statistics:

"Facts are stubborn things, but statistics are more pliable." —Author unknown

"Statistics are like bikinis. What they reveal is suggestive, but what they conceal is vital." —Aaron Levenstein

Let's walk through building a dashboard together. Figure 9.2 is the beginning of a dashboard we built for a client with an established brand name that was interested in increasing the community on its Facebook fan page.

	A	B	C	D	E	F	G
1		FB Uniq Users	FB Pg View	FB Fans	Twitter Followers	FB Fans/Day	Twitter/Day
30	28-Apr	9	30	517	453	1	4
31	29-Apr	11	26	522	461	5	8
32	30-Apr	23	54	523	460	1	-1
33	1-May	12	32	533	470	10	10
34	2-May	4	6	534	477	1	7
35	3-May	10	22	538	479	4	2
36	4-May	8	23	544	482	6	3
37	5-May	4	8	547	488	3	6
38	6-May	3	7	549	491	2	3
39	7-May	5	8	557	492	8	1
40	8-May	4	14	559	492	2	0
41	9-May	2	3	561	494	2	2
42	10-May	2	4	565	498	4	4
43	11-May	6	20	568	503	3	5
44	12-May	3	4	573	511	5	8
45	13-May	10	27	577	513	4	2
46	14-May	4	16	584	511	7	-2
47	15-May	10	27	587	519	3	8
48	16-May	3	5	593	522	6	3
49	17-May	2	4	601	525	8	3
50	18-May	8	25	623	528	22	3
51	19-May	7	21	632	530	9	2
52	20-May	16	36	642	545	10	15
53	21-May	6	11	658	550	16	5
54	22-May	8	17	665	555	7	5

Figure 9.3 Basic dashboard for Facebook and Twitter

In this simple case, we wanted to capture the daily total number of Facebook fans (column E) the client had, along with some metrics on how the Facebook fan page was being used through unique users and page views (columns B and C). At the time we started the project, the team had a secondary objective, to see how increased social media engagement on Facebook would impact the company's Twitter presence, so we added column F to track the total number of Twitter followers per day. That's it—the basics of a dashboard. Pretty simple, eh?

If that were it, the job would be very easy. But these numbers by themselves offer a lot more insight when you keep up with the data collection process and update the dashboard regularly. Take, for example, the incremental fans/day metric. Figure 9.3 shows the basic dashboard but with new columns for net new incremental fans per day. It's really pretty simple—all you do to calculate this derivative statistic is subtract the total number of fans you had yesterday from today.

1		FB Uniq Users	FB Pg View	FB Fans	Twitter Followers	FB Fans/Day	Twitter/Day
30	28-Apr	9	30	517	453	1	4
31	29-Apr	11	26	522	461	5	8
32	30-Apr	23	54	523	460	1	-1
33	1-May	12	32	533	470	=E33-E32	10
34	2-May	4	6	534	477	1	7
35	3-May	10	22	538	479	4	2
36	4-May	8	23	544	482	6	3
37	5-May	4	8	547	488	3	6
38	6-May	3	7	549	491	2	3
39	7-May	5	8	557	492	8	1
40	8-May	4	14	559	492	2	0
41	9-May	2	3	561	494	2	2
42	10-May	2	4	565	498	4	4
43	11-May	6	20	568	503	3	5
44	12-May	3	4	573	511	5	8

Figure 9.3 Dashboard with fans/day metric

Figure 9.4 is a chart of this basic metric over the first month of the project. What does this simple chart tell you? It says that you inherited a presence that was generating somewhere in the ballpark of four fans per day. It says that you did "something" right starting around May 17. It also says that the impact of that "something" appeared to wear off a bit about a week later, but the overall effort appeared to, at minimum, double the number of incremental fans you could generate for the fan page per day. Not bad at all.

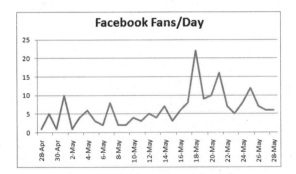

Figure 9.4 One-month chart of Facebook fans/day

One other observation you may have made regarding this chart is spikes in the data. This is both a positive and a negative. It is good to see spikes because you can see the direct impact of things you do on individual days. We like taking notes in the comments field for a cell in a dashboard spreadsheet just to remind ourselves what happened on that particular day. It certainly helps after you've run a campaign for a long time and you can't remember what you did on what day! One negative of this chart, however, is that you can get distracted by the high and low spikes. Sometimes, you didn't have to do anything at all to see a major spike upward or downward. Someone who closely manages or scrutinizes the process may want an explanation when in fact this is just normal noise. If you are looking at the data every day, keep in mind that you are just going to have good days and bad days. You'll also have days of the week or holidays that naturally just don't do as well. You may notice in Figure 9.4 that there are dips in the data on May 2, 9, 15, and 22. What is the one thing these dates all have in common? They are Fridays and Saturdays—two days when you'd expect people to spend less time online and on Facebook.

Now how can you gain intelligence from the data? You can drive yourself crazy looking at daily spikes in data, which may drive you to "overoptimize" your site. Trends are perhaps better detected when you employ the use of moving averages. We talked about moving averages in Chapter 6, "Month 3: Creating Demand with Facebook Ads." The idea behind moving averages is that they can help you see and visualize longer-term trends. If long enough, moving averages also help you largely eliminate circumstances such as weekends, holidays, and so on, that can skew results and give a clearer picture of the health of a site or campaign. The key is to get a moving average for a long enough period of time. For example, a four-day moving average wouldn't work because some of the moving average data would incorporate weekends while others wouldn't. Because you want your data to be as clear and consistent as possible, we recommend 7-, 14-, and 28-day moving averages for almost all Internet marketing work.

 To calculate a moving average, simply pick the amount of time you want, and take the average outcome for that metric over that period. For example, a seven-day moving average would be calculated by averaging today and the last six days of results. That number would be "today's seven-day moving average metric," which you will then need to recalculate tomorrow and every day thereafter.

Figure 9.5 shows the same one-month chart of new Facebook fans as Figure 9.4, but it includes another line with the smoothed-out seven-day moving average (DMA). Now the chart gets a lot more interesting. You can clearly see that the fan page was minimally effective with little/no maintenance in the first half of May. The campaign work done in mid-May was very effective, but the 7 DMA line is trending downward. If your goal is to get a consistent eight new Facebook fans per day, the jury is still out regarding your success. If the goal is 10 to 12 new Facebook fans per day, you'll need to employ at least one new trick to consistently reach your goals. Longer moving averages, such as 28- or 56-day moving averages, help you determine the success or failure of campaigns that are designed to run for a long period of time. As with all your data,

be sure to collect as much information as you can on the various externalities that take place—things that happen either inside or outside the Internet marketing campaign that can impact results. You'll want to know exactly how certain activities impact performance.

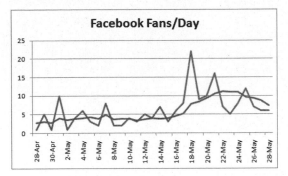

Figure 9.5 One-month chart of Facebook fans with seven-day moving average

Over and above moving averages, we also like to compartmentalize important data into weekly, monthly, and quarterly views to analyze the success or failure of a project. Take, for example, Figure 9.6, which is a summary of advertising outcomes for another client that wanted to grow its number of Facebook fans. For this particular campaign, we recommended Facebook advertising as a means to get the word out about a revamped Facebook fan page. You'll notice in the first few weeks we learned a lot about what customers liked and didn't like about our advertising. In weeks 3 and 4, we raised the advertising budget with the lessons learned from weeks 1 and 2. We found opportunities to get more efficient with ads, so we pulled back some ads and added others in week 5. Over time, we found more fans with less advertising spend, and we acquired those fans more efficiently over time at a small marginal cost. When you can find fans at $0.27 each and you can communicate with them ad infinitum for years to come, you've done a great job! We don't know whether it is coincidence, our great partnership, or dumb luck, but our primary point of contact at the client was promoted during the middle of week 5!

	Ad Spend	Clicks	Cost/Fan	Fans	Fans/Clicks
Week 1	$ 52.50	213	$ 0.59	117	55%
Week 2	$ 47.50	201	$ 0.39	151	75%
Week 3	$ 97.72	475	$ 0.43	255	54%
Week 4	$ 80.00	458	$ 0.39	231	50%
Week 5	$ 35.00	202	$ 0.27	160	79%
Week 6	$ 35.00	236	$ 0.22	188	80%
Week 7	$ 35.00	194	$ 0.27	160	82%

Figure 9.6 Summary advertising data by week

Facebook Return on Investment and the Mayo Medical School

Return on investment is perhaps the harshest yet most aligned measurements for a social media campaign. Why? In large part, we're still in the early days of social media. A lot of the benefits are soft because nobody really knows where Facebook, Twitter, and other social media services are headed. Is this the new way of doing business or just a fad? Nobody knows for sure. As a result, you'll have different perspectives on social media that will drive different opinions. Some managers/executives in an organization look for fairly immediate ways to generate a short-term ROI. Others see the real and potential long-term benefits enjoyed today by establishing an effective presence and connecting with consumers. One thing is certain—nobody has a crystal ball that can tell you definitively what a Facebook fan is worth. Nobody knows how Facebook will change or modify its platform to allow for different and more engaging marketing opportunities.

That said, some organizations have grappled with the issue of ROI for Facebook. The Mayo Medical School is one example. Barbara Porter is the assistant dean for Academic and Student Affairs at the Mayo Medical School. When discussing the benefits and ROI she's seen with using Facebook, she describes how it has enabled the school to save time and money on its new student orientation process. Since the Mayo Medical School has adopted Facebook as part of its orientation process for new students, the school has seen a savings of more than $20,000 per year. This is because the team-building exercises that are traditionally required to integrate new students into the culture of the school are no longer necessary.

"Facebook has really changed how we do orientation at Mayo Medical School," she said. "We no longer have to operate with the assumption that nobody knows anyone."

Porter spells out two primary goals the school is reaching toward: first, socialization and team building among the students, and second, saving money for the program so the school can reallocate it for better use elsewhere. Porter claims that because of Facebook, "the teamwork has already been established. They've camped! They've planned camping trips before they ever get to the medical school."

Porter explains, "The positive impact number one [is that] they come as a coalesced team, and two, it saves us money."

Before the school created its Facebook page, the school spent a considerable amount of time learning each student's name along with some of their particulars so the student could be welcomed into an environment where they felt like someone was paying attention and cared. "We didn't want them to feel isolated," Porter said.

Things have certainly changed since those days. Now Porter finds that the students know everybody in their class when they arrive at school. For example, each entering class has a Facebook fan page named for their graduation year that they are invited to upon appointment to the program. Everybody who gets appointed is a member of the page because they want to make sure they know their future classmates, events, and school-related information.

Since the page now allows students to mingle virtually and even meet in person long before the first day they arrive on campus, they are well acquainted with each other at a much earlier point in time relative to previous school years.

"You know, our student body is nationwide," says Porter, "so the kid from California already knows the kid from Tampa. The kid from New England already knows the kid from Phoenix."

The end result (her ROI) is that it saves Barbara Porter and the rest of the staff in the Office of Academic and Student Affairs the effort they used to expend to get new students acclimated to the new school culture at the beginning of the school year. With this newfound freedom and time, she and the rest of her team can devote their efforts toward things like speaking with the incoming students about the health-care system in America or spending additional time on the curriculum.

The Academic and Student Affairs Department does look at the analytics in relation to their fan page, user profiles, activity, behavior, and traffic. However, all these metrics roll up into their overreaching goals of saving money and increasing the effectiveness of their socialization efforts. By monitoring their users through analytics and responding appropriately to the results, Facebook has become an effective platform for the school to address socialization needs earlier in the process and away from their campus. Now they can spend time on new activities "as opposed to the time and money we used to spend on socialization," confirms Porter. This is invaluable to the school "because it is important that they recognize and know each other and are able to build that teamwork that is such a value to the school and the Mayo Clinic."

This is not to say that embracing Facebook as a primary tool in the orientation process was a walk in park for the Department of Academic and Student Affairs. Like many people who are introducing social networks into their team processes, Barbara has her naysayers. The responses from those unbelievers are pretty typical of the criticisms one hears at other organizations. Typically they are the result not of experience but of ignorance. Our advice is to expect this from some members of your team and don't let it stop you. Most objections are easily overcome.

Besides, the best cure for those objections is success. Look for small successes early on in your campaign to demonstrate the value of your efforts. Additionally, having a good grasp on the analytics piece will show the team that you are not shooting in the dark. Once you remove these obstacles early in your efforts, the rest of your efforts will be easier to sell to the rest of the team. This is critical to your success, and we'll talk more about this in the next chapter on organizational considerations.

As a result of Barbara's success, she can go straight to the core of the content she needs to be sharing with the new students when they arrive on campus. "You know, actual curriculum content," Porter says.

"We really marvel at the savings and the ability to focus on the things that, I won't say really matter, but give us a jump start on curriculum. It gives us a jump start on other orientation things that are specific to Mayo Clinic that they would not have been able to get."

Clearly the Mayo Medical School understands the value of Facebook. But it's not enough to just know that it can benefit you or your organization. You have to seek out areas where you can operate more efficiently using the social graph of the very people you're trying to reach or service. Be creative. Find ways where you can provide a richer and better experience with Facebook in a more efficient manner than your organization had been previously.

224

Featured Case: Kevin Hillstrom, Ambassador for Social ROI

Kevin Hillstrom spent more than 20 years in the retail industry, including stints as vice president of database marketing at Nordstrom, director of circulation at Eddie Bauer, and manager of analytical services at Lands' End. Today, he is one of the most outspoken advocates of social media analytics and ROI, and his blog Mine That Data (www.minethatdata.com/blog) is one of the most-read database marketing publications of any kind in the world. We caught up with Kevin recently to learn his perspective on social media ROI today.

Q: *You've been an outspoken champion of ROI for social media and other Internet marketing channels on your blog, Mine That Data. What do you think that people both understand and fail to understand about Internet marketing in 2010?*

A: The biggest misunderstanding, in my opinion, is that online marketing and customer behavior are best analyzed on the basis of "campaigns." The reality is that customer behavior is generally consistent over the long-term and is fluid in the short-term. Take a sample e-commerce brand. Of all customers who purchased in 2009, about 35 percent will purchase again in 2010. Among those who purchase in 2010, the average customer will purchase two times, buying an average of three items per order. These metrics seldom fluctuate much. In other words, over the long-term, a business is reasonably consistent and predictable. Yet, online marketers tend to analyze campaign performance, and this is a place where performance is very fluid. We attribute orders to the activities that we think caused the order to happen, giving us a false sense of "what works" and "what doesn't work." In reality, we attribute orders that would normally happen anyway to our marketing activities, thereby over-inflating the importance of our marketing activities, causing us to execute "more marketing activities"!

Q: *Much of your career has been focused on online retailing. Where do you see Web 2.0 and social media technologies being best utilized today to help sell products?*

A: I believe social media technologies are best used in customer service. Honestly, I don't see much utility in getting sale and promotional messages in 140-character bursts. I see a ton of utility in a customer service employee using Twitter to help a customer who had a problem with the shipment of her order. I work with companies that actively listen to customer issues and then proactively respond to those issues in an effort to please the customer. This use of social media, while not glamorous, often works well. In my analytics projects, customers who have interactions with live human beings almost always have significantly greater long-term value than do all other customers, even after controlling for prior purchase habits.

Q: *Critics may say that ROI for social media is a longer-term pursuit. Your thoughts?*

A: I disagree. To me, "longer-term pursuit" means that something doesn't appear to be working today, so let's just keep doing fun social media stuff until we can prove it is working. It is not hard to demonstrate that social media activities deliver ROI; we simply have been told too often that we can expect huge levels of ROI when the reality suggests that ROI is more modest. There is absolutely nothing wrong with saying that social media was used to solve 124 customer service issues in November. There is absolutely nothing wrong with saying that we have a corporate blog, and subscribers to the corporate blog ordered 96 times in November, spending $9,600 against a cost of $1,000 to maintain and staff the blog. These aren't breathtaking numbers. But the numbers clearly support doing more, and the numbers generate a profit. Remember, companies are in business to generate profit! So, don't be frustrated by small numbers; use them to demonstrate profitable outcomes. Your CFO would rather you demonstrate $2,000 of social media profit than execute a gaudy radio marketing blitz that cost $1,000,000 and lost $50,000 profit. Be content with what you have!

Q: *Some companies have begun to use coupons and other enticements to attract customers via social media. Do you think that is an effective tactic?*

A: Absolutely not. I always say that coupons, discounts, and promotions are taxes that are placed upon brands for not being remarkable. When you tie a coupon to social media, you are acknowledging that social media isn't working to your expectations, so you want to cheapen your brand to make it appear that social media actually works. Again, be content with small gains. Lower your expectations. Under-promise and over-deliver. You don't need to hit a home run with social media, though unfortunately, everybody is looking for social media home runs that seldom exist.

Continues

Q: *Where do you see online retailing in five years? More or less integration with Facebook and other types of social media?*

A: I see much more integration with Facebook and other types of social media. I believe that social media will become a hybrid of enhanced customer service coupled with the utility that people get from using tools like Microsoft Word, Excel, or PowerPoint. When is the last time that somebody asked you to prove the ROI of using Microsoft Excel? Who asks you to prove the ROI of your monthly broadband Internet fee? Honestly, I think that social media becomes another "utility," if you will, like the telephone you use in your office, electricity, Internet access, or software tools like Word, Excel, or PowerPoint. It just becomes part of the lives of those who choose to partake in it. And that is a good thing!

Measure Engagement with Insights

Facebook provides in-depth analytics on your fan page that allow you to consistently edit your approach for greater results. These analytics appear on every fan page only when an administrator views the page, as shown in Figure 9.7.

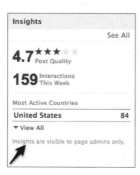

Figure 9.7 Fan page Insights

When you click See All, you'll see a variety of stats, graphs, and interactive data. At a glance, you'll see the total interactions this week that are comprised of your fans' Wall posts, "likes," and comments. Your post quality shows you how engaging your posts are to your fans, and your star rating compares your post quality to other pages of similar size.

You can then view graphs of the fans that interact with your page via interactions per post, post quality, posts, discussion posts, reviews, and mentions. By moving the horizontal slider, you can zoom in and out and see a wider or narrower perspective, such as weekly, daily, or hourly. Plus, you'll see the number of fans by gender, age, country, and language. Along with just the fans who actually interact with your fan page, you can also view the dashboard for all fans of your page (see Figure 9.8).

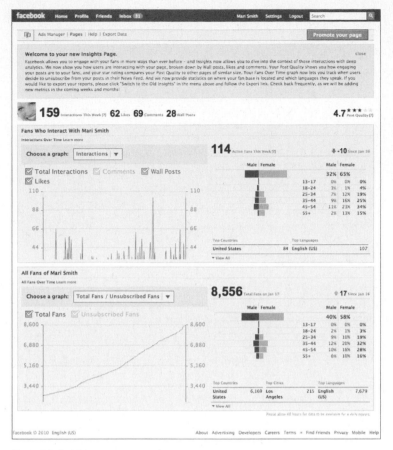

Figure 9.8 Insights page

When reviewing your total fan base, you can navigate through seven different graphs that show trends in user acquisition and subscription:

Total Fans/Unsubscribers This is the total number of fans over time, overlaid with the total number of fans who have chosen to hide your posts in their News Feed (unsubscribers).

New/Removed Fans This is the number of people who have become a new fan of your page or stopped being a fan of your page. (Important note: Facebook currently only allows users to join a maximum of 500 fan pages; it's possible some fans leave your page because they are close to the limit. However, more likely they have not found your content to be relevant in their News Feed, and instead of hiding the posts, they simply remove themselves as a fan.)

Top Countries This is the growth of your fan base over time broken down by country.

Demographics This is the growth of your fan base over time broken down by age and gender demographics.

Page Views This is the total number of times a page was viewed per day.

Media Consumption This is the total photo views, audio plays, and video plays for the content you have uploaded to your page.

Unsubscribes/Re-subscribes This is the total number of times fans unsubscribed from your page and the total number of times fans resubscribed to your page.

To export your fan page analytics, select Switch To The Old Insights in the menu, and follow the Export link.

Sysomos, a social media monitoring and analytics firm, put out a fascinating study of 600,000 fan pages as reported on TechCrunch.com (www.techcrunch.com/2009/11/28/facebook-fan-pages-77-percent). The study found that 77 percent of those fan pages analyzed have fewer than 1,000 fans. Only 4 percent of fan pages have more than 10,000 fans. What we find fascinating about this particular study is this golden nugget on TechCrunch's post: "…unlike on Twitter, where popularity is correlated with how many times you tweet, Facebook fan pages tend to be updated only once every 16 days."

When analyzing your fan page Insights, we can assume your primary objectives are to increase the total number of fans and to increase the engagement rate (frequency of interactions) of those fans. With a creative Facebook ad campaign and/or integrated Twitter promotion or other social media platforms, along with promotion on your blog, websites, e-zine, e-mails, and so on, you should see an increase in fans. But that's just part of the equation. You need to provide consistent, relevant, quality content; otherwise, most Facebook users who do join your page may never come back after that initial action.

As Facebook points out, "Page admins who post meaningful content will retain fans, while admins who post spammy or low-quality material will lose fans and subscribers."

And, to quote TechCrunch, "…that's really the big difference between Facebook fans and Twitter followers. On Twitter, you follow someone because you want to hear what they have to say. On Facebook, you fan them just to show your support of affinity. Too often, it's a throwaway gesture." Though this may be true for certain fan pages and for certain individuals, we tend to disagree.

The secret to creating a highly active fan page that ultimately drives other key performance indicators such as opt-ins (e-mail subscribers), blog subscribers, product sales, and paying clients, is to demonstrate you genuinely *care* about your fans. Definitely update far more often than the average of every 16 days! Respond promptly to fans' questions, comments, suggestions, reviews, and so on. Plus, involve your fans—ask questions, and conduct surveys and polls. You can even ask them what types of content they most want from you or, if you were to run a contest, what prize they would most want to win.

Insights is also used by marketers and applications developers to measure the success of Facebook applications. The same suite of demographic data is available, along with other metrics specific to the application. To get this information, you must first be listed as a developer of a Facebook application. Then, go to `www.facebook.com/developer`, and click the application that you want to learn about. On the right side of the screen, you should see a Statistics link. There, you can find Usage Statistics—the number of active monthly users for your application, the total number of users you've earned for the lifetime of the application, the number of Wall posts people make about the application, and the number of reviews you've received. The User Response tab includes information on how certain metrics pertain to the application relative to the statistical norm across Facebook. For example, some apps are better than others at getting people to respond to real-time notifications. Other apps inspire people to respond to those same messages and report them as spam. These are important marketing insights that can give you an idea of how well your application is meeting customer needs. The problem is that this data is currently made available only to "official developers" of an app, and it's buried alongside a variety of numbers that would only be interesting to a techie. Ah, the joys of being a 21st century marketer.

When Facebook Isn't Quite Enough: Landing Pages

Let's now turn our attention to landing pages. Landing pages are webpages explicitly set up to encourage visitors to become leads for your business. Usually there is an attractive enticement on the landing page—sign up for free information, a newsletter, free quote for something, and so on. These aren't new; they've been around for a long time. But as the Internet has matured, people have focused more time and energy on landing pages because they are the best way to map a campaign to a clear business objective.

Like landing pages on the Internet, successful landing pages on social media are similarly based on conversions to a business objective. On Facebook fan pages, it's the conversion of the visitor into a fan. On a Facebook profile, it's the conversion of the visitor to a friend. On Twitter, it's the conversion of the visitor to a follower. If you've failed to convert the person, it doesn't necessarily mean that you've lost that person forever. You may have caught the person on a busy day. That person may be back another day to visit your site and make the commitment you want them to make. This is why thinking too short-term can be dangerous with social media—positive reinforcement of your brand works online just as well as it works with print media. Sooner or later, repeated positive interactions with your brand or product will have a great impact on your business and future marketing plan.

A few examples we've alluded to earlier in this book are for companies that effectively blend social media with other web properties. In those cases, customers are informed about a marketing program via social media, but the landing page actually resides elsewhere on the Web. Why is this the case? For one, Facebook and Twitter offer limited platforms for a new web presence. Some things are just easier to build on the Web than on a proprietary social network. The Web is also much more accessible than Facebook or Twitter. Companies want to reach as many consumers as possible, even the Luddites who aren't on social networks yet. Finally, if a landing page lives on the Web, a company can point numerous demand generation/advertising approaches to the campaign. This helps the company learn more about who responds best to the marketing offer and how different types of Internet media can be used to reach customers more effectively and inexpensively in the future.

> ## Featured Case: Bill Leake of Apogee Search
>
> Bill Leake, CEO of Apogee Search in Austin, Texas, knows quite a bit about Internet marketing and landing pages. He's been solving search engine optimization problems and running paid search campaigns for clients for many years. We caught up with him to ask some questions about landing pages and the future of Internet marketing.
>
> **Q:** *What business objectives are best met by using landing pages? What are the biggest advantages to effectively using landing pages in an Internet marketing campaign?*
>
> **A:** A normal website is somewhat like a multipurpose vehicle, in that it has many functions, whereas landing pages can function like a sports car or a work truck, in that they have one primary function. Multipurpose vehicles rarely win contests for both speed and strength, and the pages on your website rarely will win conversion contests by themselves. Constructing landing pages allows you to tailor conversion-oriented messages to particular personality types, about particular products, highlighting particular offers or deals. Effectively using landing pages in Internet marketing campaigns can give you a five- to tenfold increase in conversion rates over simply using your existing webpages.
>
> **Q:** *What are the most common mistakes you see when people create their own landing pages?*
>
> **A:** Four things:
>
> - Not clearly thinking through their message and audience (who am I trying to reach, and what am I trying to get them to do?)
> - Not having adequate (let alone compelling) calls to action
> - Failing to build several landing pages
> - Failure to devise and execute a test plan
>
> **Q:** *You've had a lot of successes with Internet marketing clients. Can you tell us about one of your best success stories, without naming names, of course?*
>
> **A:** Picking out one from the hundreds is a tough task, but I often find myself mentioning our client that helps out pregnant moms with no insurance. We'd built them up a multimillion dollar business, and their landing pages were converting visitors to leads at an eye-popping 21 percent. After one of our landing page optimization campaigns, that click-to-lead conversion rate on their forms went down to 13 percent. And our client was thrilled. What

happened? We doubled their phone calls by focusing the forms to encourage phone calls rather than web leads, and sales went up 54 percent. Remember, for many of us, we're trying to get people on the phone, and if we can skip the whole web lead step, that's often a good thing to do.

Q: *How do you see social media evolving to meet lead generation and customer acquisition needs? Is it a replacement for the Web and search engine marketing, an enhancement, a fad, or something in between?*

A: I see it as an enhancement of search engine marketing. Competent search engine marketers know that the ideal form of marketing involves a combination of trust and need. SEO and PPC marketers have always been great at the need (since they are geared toward folks who are searching for what they have to sell), but have struggled with trust and credibility issues of the brands they represent. For instance, I may be looking for a satellite TV installation and find myself on a landing page that markets what I'm looking for but be uncomfortable as I don't know the brand. Social media marketing is blending rapidly with search (witness the ever-increasing number of reviews that Google pulls up in its search results), and social media marketing adds the trust and credibility element that search marketers are looking for. When you combine "I need this" with "my social network says this vendor is OK," you have an incredibly powerful combination.

Q: *What do you suggest that people who are new to Internet marketing and landing pages do educate themselves?*

A: Reading this book is clearly a good start. I also recommend subscribing to the Apogee Search Marketing blog and newsletter—the blog is at www.apogee-search.com/blog.

There are some tremendous industry resources out there like MarketingProfs that have new, fresh content. Google has some great content under its Google Website Optimizer section. I also recommend reading one of the numerous "Internet marketing glossaries" out there for a definition of terms.

Bill Leake, a former McKinsey & Co. consultant, has been driving provable revenues through web marketing since the mid-1990s when, as part of the management team at Power Computing, he built the first company to sell $1 million over the Internet. As CEO of Apogee Search, he has guided the company from inception to its current position as one of the 20 largest independent Internet marketing agencies in North America, with hundreds of happy, referable clients.

Bill also serves as president of the Austin Interactive Marketing Association and as chairman of the Search Engine Marketing Professionals Organization (SEMPO) North America committee. Bill received his MBA from the University of Texas at Austin and his BA from Yale University.

Conduct Tests for Greater Results

Success with landing pages depends a great deal on tweaking your conversion rates using a variety of tactics designed to let data drive your decision making. The great thing about the Web is that sites, buttons, layout, and advertising can be updated or changed quickly, and you can track outcomes based on those changes. The science and process behind optimizing your site based on these changes is known as *A/B* or *multivariate* testing, which we covered in detail in Chapter 6.

To review, A/B testing may sound like a complicated concept. But in reality, the concept is simple. It's used to test the effectiveness of two pieces of creative to see which one results in a better, faster, or more inexpensive response from customers. This isn't particularly difficult when you can change the design of a logo or an e-commerce website and see what the outcomes are with data from your web analytics reports. Contrast this with the physical world. If you owned a storefront, you'd have very little data to rely upon unless you monitored the activity of every customer *and* you found a way to read their minds!

Take, for example, A/B testing for advertising. Your objective is to see which of two ads are more effective than the other. Effectiveness in this case will be measured by total cost, clicks, cost per click, and ultimately lead generation cost (measured as total cost divided by form submissions).

You want to test two ads to see which performs better than the other. These two ads are henceforth known as A and B, and you treat them as subjects to which you have no particular emotional attachment. The different advertising copy points to a single landing page on the Internet—a page that is kept consistent throughout the entire A/B test. It's critically important to isolate a single variable for an A/B test to work properly. Then it's simple: you run the advertising for long enough to know conclusively which ad is superior. The collective response of your "subjects"—that is, customers—will tell the tale, and the results will come in the form of relatively unimpeachable statistics.

Ideally, you'd like to see tens of thousands of impressions over at least a week before drawing any conclusions. If you're running smaller campaigns with far fewer subjects, you may have to come to conclusions with far less data. Although that isn't preferable, it's probably OK in most situations. Just understand that the more you run an A/B test, the more reliable your data will be. And if you're doing some A/B testing, you are better off than doing no A/B testing at all.

 If you have a few different options, feel free to run them all at the same time. Although it's called A/B testing, you can run an A/B/C/D/E all at the same time. Just keep a single outcome variable so you can see whether A, B, C, D, or E wins.

Your Facebook fan page has its own landing page too: existing fans always land on your Wall by default. But you can select which tab nonfans land on; we recommend choosing a tab with your own custom content created with the Static FBML app mentioned in Chapter 8, "Customized Experiences via Facebook Applications." Now, this is something important you'll want to note: every tab on your Facebook fan page has its own unique URL. This essentially means you could conduct an A/B test by shortening the long URLs for the two tabs you want to test with a trackable service like bit.ly. That provides you with the number of clicks per tab (though it won't count traffic coming from any other sources where you're not using the bit.ly links). Then, if you had an opt-in box on each of the tabs, you could conduct a reasonable split test to see which opt-in is more effective. You wouldn't be able to tell which tab (landing page) was most effective in converting fans, though; that test may be best conducted one tab at a time.

Multivariate testing is similar to A/B testing in that you are testing to see which landing page is more effective. The difference is that you are simultaneously testing for a number of variables. This can be any number of things: the placement of your Buy Now link, the text you've included on your site, the design or layout of the site, and so on. You'll need to randomly serve different landing pages at the same time—so a user at a particular point in the day can be served different iterations equally. You just need to maintain randomness, so things such as time of day, geography, or day of week don't impact the data. Remember, you are looking to keep as many things equal or consistent as possible.

I really like using multivariate testing when I first assess what is happening on an existing web property. It is a scattershot approach that helps you quickly test new ideas or theories that people have about improving important customer metrics on your website once they get there. You can try different combinations of text, imagery, icons, and the like to determine the mix that gets the right customer response. Data will often let you know what things don't work. This will narrow down your multivariate testing to the best ideas, which you can then isolate in individual A/B tests where you keep everything else consistent with the exception of the creative that you are trying to analyze. The advantage you get from this approach is that you move beyond opinion and into facts backed by data.

What all of this implies is that you can spend a lot of time tweaking your web properties to optimize for the outcomes that are important to your business. Some people probably think that is terrible, but others may think this is a great opportunity. It's why we've spoken earlier in this chapter about the importance of truly knowing your strategic objectives for your website. What metrics are important to your business? Why do you have a website or social media presence? Every business has a different answer to these questions. You can be the person to align your web presence and social media effort to things that truly matter at the executive level.

Organizational Considerations

Organizations of all types are waking up to the possibilities of social media. But the overall importance of social media and the tactics you use will largely be based on what your organization is and how it views marketing, customer engagement, risk, and being on the "cutting edge." It will also impact access to resources, who you can hire, how quickly you can act, and what you ultimately need to get things done. In this chapter, we'll look at roles universal to any organization and how different types of organizations can best utilize social media.

10

Roles and Responsibilities

In any organization—large corporations, government agencies, sports teams, startups, and so on—the difference between good and great is in the people who make up that organization. It's critical that people be properly evaluated and that they have the room to make decisions on behalf of the organization based on its goals and management philosophy. So, it stands to reason that one of the most important first steps to making your social media and Internet marketing campaigns succeed is in picking the right people.

Let's first talk about the roles that need to be filled to run a successful campaign. These are functions that someone must fill at various points of the development of a campaign to ensure that different perspectives are heard throughout the process.

The "general manager" The person responsible for overseeing the overall campaign. This person should be able to do any of the business tasks necessary to conduct a social media marketing campaign, although the person doesn't necessarily need to be an expert in all of them. General managers should know enough to manage the process and be willing to learn things they do not know. In larger organizations, this person should also be available to "backfill" someone who is out because of illness, maternity/paternity leave, disability, or another reason.

The "brand manager" The person responsible for the stewardship of the brand. This person is the spokesperson for the brand. The brand manager ensures that the tone of the campaign or social media presence is in line with what the brand represents. This is also the person who makes sure that the campaign doesn't go too far to potentially threaten brand sanctity or customer perception.

The "business requirements gatherer" The person responsible for understanding the broad needs of the campaign across different stakeholder groups in the organization. This person is in tune with things that are happening in the organization and is probably the one colleague who does the best job networking within the organization. This is the person who collects all the feedback and translates it into a product that everyone can enjoy, but sometimes the result of this work is a compromise that nobody really likes. But possibly the most important role of business requirements gatherers is that they can integrate the social media campaign into other marketing efforts for maximum benefit. As we've discussed earlier in this book, you are much more likely to succeed when you use social media to enhance your marketing across different channels.

The "creative" The person responsible for turning rough business concepts into something interesting, edgy, and engaging. This involves a process of brainstorming, concepting, and presenting ideas to management for a new campaign. It's a role that demands both the creation of new ideas and the wherewithal to bring them to life through the use of imagery, icons, graphics, and sometimes copy. The person is oftentimes a loud and vocal critic of the brand manager, who is decidedly more conservative about the use of organization assets, trademarks, brands, and so on.

The "reporter" The person responsible for gathering statistics on the performance of the campaign across all types of media (social media, websites, others) and for sharing coherent reports on results. This is a role that is highly analytical and almost requires a stats junkie in a best-case scenario. Reporters should have enough skills with spreadsheets and with data analysis to create compelling reports and perhaps come up with some of their own that clearly tell the tale. It is often handy to make this person agnostic to the success or failure of the campaign. Just the facts, ma'am.

The "technical lead" The person responsible for managing staff, consultants, or vendors responsible for custom web development required to support your marketing campaign. Much like the general manager who is responsible for turning out a coherent marketing campaign, this person is responsible for communicating with developers and other technical personnel to ensure that customizations are done as effectively and inexpensively as possible. This isn't necessarily the person you'd invite to your next cocktail party, but the technical lead can help you do amazing things with Facebook apps, Facebook Connect, and your website.

The "executive sponsor" The executive at the organization who is ultimately responsible for the success or failure of the effort. This is a little tricky—in some organizations, failure is defined as an embarrassing problem that results from the execution of the campaign. In other organizations, failure is defined as whether very specific numbers are reached—number of leads, costs per touch, and so on. As you can imagine, in the former case there isn't as much pressure to perform, but there is more pressure to "draw between the lines." In the latter case, there is more pressure from a marketing metrics perspective and more scrutiny over whether social media is a viable marketing tactic. You'll have pressure in your role if you are overseeing your campaign—exactly where will depend on how your organization views social media.

These roles don't necessarily need to be filled by different people—most organizations won't have the luxury of a large qualified staff to handle different roles. But the responsibilities are fairly consistent across just about all campaigns regardless of organization type or scope. And sometimes these roles are filled by third-party vendors or consultants who have specific expertise that is not available in your own organization.

Vendors vs. Employees

Everyone is likely busy at your company. So, you probably have a choice to make: do you assign tasks to employees, or do you hire vendors to fill gaps in your organization? The first and most fundamental question is always, "Do you have enough money and knowledge to hire a vendor that you can trust to do the job?" If you're lacking the budget, you'll have no choice but to get colleagues to share the workload. There is certainly a risk inherent in that approach—if your project is the lowest priority of a group of tasked colleagues, it probably won't succeed. There are also advantages to having vendors you trust, because you've worked with their employees in some other capacity over the years or because you have gotten a good recommendation from a friend.

But the choice of vendor or employee is really a strategy just like any other. If you believe social media to be the future of marketing as we do, you can easily justify bringing the capability in-house. It's a long-term investment, and it's better to keep that knowledge around the watercooler. However, you can accelerate the learning curve a bit by hiring the right vendor or consultant to share what they know with you and your team. Few people in most organizations have run successful social media marketing campaigns in the past, and even fewer have the breadth of career experiences that make them ideal candidates for a new campaign. But your colleagues probably have skills here and there that easily transfer with a little assistance.

Aside from reasons mentioned, there are a few other considerations for your decision to seek help from a third-party or choose to run your own Facebook marketing or social media campaign. We'll explore these next.

Use In-House Staff

Using in-house staff may be a viable option for your campaign if any of the following are true:

- You have faith in your people to figure it out.

- Social media execution is not critical to your success in the short-term. You can endure some failure and experimentation without significant impact to your business or your brand.

- You want a long-term capability, and you suspect that your employees will not leave. If you think that institutional memory will indeed stay with your company, it's a good idea to invest in your people.

- You think your team can handle it without help.

Get Help from a Vendor or Consultant

On the other hand, you should consider getting outside help for the campaign if any of the following are true:

- You are skeptical about your team's ability to get the job done effectively without assistance.

- Social media is important in the short-term but not terribly important long-term, so you need a quick shot of immediate expertise

- Your employees simply don't have time. Social media maintenance can be very time-consuming if done well. A vendor or consultant can be a good "gun for hire" to help alleviate stress on your people.

- You need insurance—someone who can provide help if it is needed. Of course, you can always use this insurance to deflect blame if you need, although it's rarely a great idea and not generally good business, although I recognize that it happens.

- You've tried but failed to meet business objectives using social media, and you need someone to fix your problems.

If you do decide to hire a third-party to assist with your effort, consider that social media is now established enough that most qualified professionals will have demonstrable success stories under their belts. Find out the companies they've helped. Talk to a few of their clients. Ask difficult questions about expertise, work style, and responsiveness. Keep in mind that a cottage industry of social media professionals has sprung forth over the past few years. Some consultants are truly qualified and can do a great job for you. Others are shameless self-promoters who do a better job of marketing themselves than they could ever do for you. It's far too easy to make a mistake and hire the wrong person if you haven't done your due diligence.

Three Tough Questions for Vendors

The world of social media consultants, experts, and the like can be very difficult to navigate. How do you know you're really dealing with someone who has the skills and talents to help you? Ask three probing questions to get the answers you need, and dig deeper if necessary:

1. "What are your qualifications as a social media expert?" Find out exactly why the vendor thinks they're qualified to represent your business. You're looking for a few things here— time in the business, skills, and third-party validation that you're dealing with a true expert.

2. "What problems have you solved for your clients?" Learn the breadth and depth of the vendor's expertise. Ideally, you'd be dealing with a vendor that has shown the capacity to create innovative solutions for a wide range of problems.

3. "Who have you helped, and can I talk to a few of your former clients?" Success stories usually create rabid fans. Ask to talk to a few of them. When you do, probe to get a sense of exactly how the project went and whether the client and vendor are still on good terms.

A quick search on a popular search engine will also tell you quite a bit of information. Look for blog posts, articles in various web publications, and social media activity. If someone isn't terribly active on the Web and social media, that's probably not the right person to help you. Find out by doing your homework before you agree to sign a contract.

How Facebook Works in Different Organizations

If you've read the entirety of this book, you understand that Facebook marketing and social media can be fairly simple. But typically larger organizations are just now beginning to grapple with social media and the issues of transparency and communications. Legal concerns or approvals can send even the fastest-moving project into the weeds and can significantly impact the customer experience of a campaign. In some cases, it's better to be certain and deliberate than opportunistic and cutting-edge.

Now let's turn our attention to the specific challenges that affect decision making in different types of organizations so you can be aware of the dynamics around you or with your colleagues in other types of organizations.

Government

All around the world, government employees and management are beginning to understand the power and the opportunity of using social media where traditional communications have dominated for many years. The reasons are similar to a lot of the themes we've covered in this book—immediacy of communications, low cost, reach, the ability to edit or change something if a mistake is made, and so on. Social media usage is already as pervasive as e-mail in some demographic groups. All of it makes social media very appealing, especially for communities where citizens are more "tech-savvy."

The meme of Government 2.0 has emerged to cover these issues broadly as the concept grows in popularity. We're in a perfect storm for social media in government for a few reasons:

Maturing social and Web 2.0 technologies Facebook, Twitter, and other social media technologies are ostensibly competing platforms, and they are beginning to mature, so there is less technical risk associated with using these products.

Increased pressure on government to modernize Senior government officials are beginning to read about cases where the private sector has saved money or increased revenues using social media, and they look to employ similar practices for their agencies.

Potential for cost savings New technologies, if properly harnessed, can dramatically reduce the cost of traditional marketing and communications.

Election of Barack Obama It can be argued that the 44th President of the United States was the first elected with the support of social media as campaign officials mobilized millions of people to vote.

But interestingly, government policy has not exactly caught up to the realities of social media, crowdsourcing, and user-generated content. For instance, many government agencies forbid employees from blogging because of the risk that an employee will say something that may be perceived to be official government policy. Then the statement or position taken by the blogger/employee becomes a potential legal liability for the government. The more you see situations like this, the easier it is to understand that policy makers aren't necessarily trying to get in the way of progress as much as they are trying to balance risk with opportunity while minimizing unintended consequences. But again, overall it is a big weakness of social media that none of us can truly divide our professional and personal lives without a lot of work and care.

So, what types of government projects can Facebook and social media assist? Earlier in this book, we suggested that social media can in some ways be considered as another marketing channel—akin to e-mail, a phone line, or a paper brochure—except that social media is inherently interactive and provides a means for people to communicate with each other inexpensively and in real time. In that sense, the government can use Facebook and social media to quickly and effectively communicate via the social graph—both to citizens and to spread the word from citizens to one another. Take, for example, the work that NASA has done with its Facebook presence; you can find its fan page at www.facebook.com/nasa.gov. NASA achieved quite a following with thousands of fans who receive regular updates on what is happening there (Figure 10.1), photos (Figure 10.2), articles, and other information on space and aeronautics science. NASA also shares a variety of links to other sources of information on the Internet and in social media. It uses the Boxes tab (Figure 10.3) to encourage conversation and to link to parts of the NASA.gov website that may have been buried or hard to discover otherwise. But perhaps most interestingly, NASA also shares the Twitter accounts where you can keep up with real astronauts.

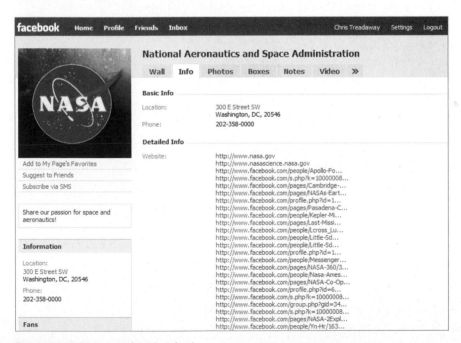

Figure 10.1 NASA resources from the Info tab

Figure 10.2
NASA pictures

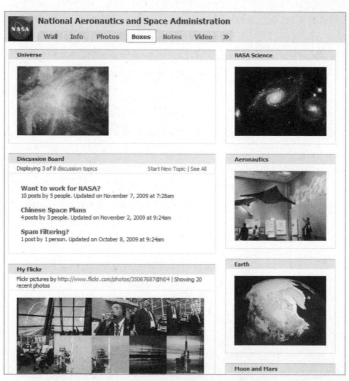

Figure 10.3
NASA Boxes tab

Government 2.0 and Social Media Projects

How can Facebook and Web 2.0 technologies help with common government tasks? Here are a few ways that government agencies can use Facebook, Twitter, and other social media technologies today:

Routine communications Informing citizens of new programs, city amenities, events, changes in traffic, utilities or facilities upgrades/repairs, and so on

Urgent communications Notifying citizens of dangers, the presence of fugitives, details on Amber Alert cases, severe weather, and so on

Decision-making transparency Using social media to keep people updated on important dates and meetings for community decisions, city council meetings, requests for feedback from the community, and so on

Crowdsourcing ideas Keeping tabs on citizen opinions and responses to controversial situations

Compliance and licensing Reminding citizens to pay property taxes, renew licenses, renew voter registration records, and so on, which all happens via old-fashioned postal mail today but could be cheaper and more effective via social media

Similarly, government organizations can use social media as a platform for people to communicate with one another. Take, for example, the U.S. Air Force page at www.facebook.com/USAirForce. The page defaults to the Wall, where a variety of people from all over the world comment on their love for the Air Force or their loved ones who are serving. But interestingly enough, there are two U.S. Air Force fan pages currently—the other is at www.facebook.com/pages/US-Air-Force/134276840326?. One is apparently backed by folks in the Pentagon, while the other originated from Colorado Springs, the home of the Air Force Academy. One has more interactivity, the other more content. Same organization, two official Facebook fan pages. Hey, nobody said that coordinating efforts is easy and that social media actually brings people to a consensus.

Oftentimes, an early-adopter government employee who uses a social media product will introduce an idea for how the government agency can use Facebook or a competing product. But it may not necessarily have the attention of senior officials because the effort is early, has very few users initially, or just simply isn't on the radar of important issues. A "pilot" project will be run because interested employees have a passion about the opportunity and they want to take the initiative to try something new. This employee will get approval from the manager, who is often a progressive, forward-thinking person.

We've seen it happen numerous times in government agencies that a project like this will then get popular—it will gain traction through citizen usage or appreciation by a supportive niche of citizens. But unlike businesses that may see something like this as an opportunity and perhaps become overzealous about overusing it as a marketing channel, popularity tends to have the opposite effect in government agencies. A large following or fan count demonstrates success, but ironically senior government officials will want to then step back to ensure that it fits into other government initiatives and that many of the risks are identified and mitigated. The attorneys enter, and ultimately the project looks a lot different than it did originally. In the end, it sometimes then misses the mark with the very people the project was intended to serve.

So, what do you do if you are a government employee looking to inject Facebook or other social media into your outreach to citizens? First, make sure it can work in your community. Although social media is becoming increasingly popular worldwide, your community may not respond well to government communications through social media. Second, talk to citizens, and solicit their feedback as you would for any other new program. Even small focus groups with friends and family can tell you a lot about how people will perceive your ideas for social media. Next, stay focused, and set attainable goals for your effort. Part of the solution is making sure that you are doing things the right way, and as we've mentioned previously, this may require some experimentation along the way. Finally, understand the internal environment in your agency. Anticipating future problems early in the process will help you make good decisions that will benefit you later.

Featured Case: GovLoop, the Social Network for Government 2.0

If you're in a government agency or other organization, you certainly aren't alone as you navigate Government 2.0. In fact, there is a social network available for you to meet other government employees who similarly are seeking interesting ways to take advantage of social media and Web 2.0. GovLoop (www.govloop.com) is perhaps the biggest social network available for Government 2.0 professionals. We took a few moments to talk with GovLoop founder and president Steve Ressler about his site and trends in Government 2.0:

Q: *Tell us a little about GovLoop in your words.*

A: GovLoop is the "Facebook for government" currently connecting more than 21,000 federal, state, and local government innovators.

Q: *What gave you the idea for GovLoop?*

A: I was a public servant for five years working in various departments including the SSA, Department of Education, and DHS. I always saw agencies re-creating the wheel and wished there was a way to connect with other departments on a peer level. With the rise of social networking technology, I saw the way to create the platform I always wanted—and thus GovLoop was born.

Q: *How would you characterize Government 2.0 in 2010?*

A: Government 2.0 is in adolescence. It has seen some success, has generated a lot of buzz, and has great promise. The trick is transitioning into adulthood—how do we go from 30 great Government 2.0 examples in 2009 to 300 in 2010 and 3,000 in 2011?

Q: *As you've observed the Government 2.0 community, where have you seen successes? Have you noticed any common themes for successful stories/projects?*

A: Lots of great successes I see every day on GovLoop. *Armed with Science* is a great podcast out of the DOD. Sensorpedia at Oak Ridge Labs is fantastic. The City of San Francisco does great things with open data and its open 311 initiatives. The common themes I see are strong business need, passionate and amazing leaders, and a willingness to take risk and iterate.

Q: *Where do you see Facebook fitting into the future of Government 2.0? What opportunities do you see?*

A: Facebook fits in well for the future of Government 2.0 as an extremely important channel to communicate with citizens. The purpose of government communications is to reach the citizens—in the past that may have been flyers in libraries or in-person meetings that then evolved into TV ads, radio spots, and government websites. Facebook is part of the next wave of venues where citizens live their lives, and it is important for government agencies to spread their information and act in these communities.

On GovLoop, members use social media such as blogs, videos, and forums to discuss best practices and share ideas on improving government. GovLoop won the 2009 AFCEA Bethesda Social Media Award and was a finalist for the 2009 ACT/IAC Intergovernmental Solutions Award. Ressler is also the cofounder of Young Government Leaders (YGL), a professional organization of more than 2,000 government employees across the United States.

New Military Social Network: milBook

The U.S. military recently launched a social networking site called milBook, a sort of Facebook clone for organizational information. The site has more than 18,000 members, is more oriented toward collaboration than socialization, and has extensive security levels.

The idea behind milBook (which along with wiki and blog tools is grouped into something called *milSuite*) is for the Department of Defense to get a dose of Web 2.0 flavor, said officials for the Army's MilTech Solutions group. "milSuite's aim is to provide those serving our military the same experience they take for granted in the public domain, behind the security of a firewall," explained Justin Filler, deputy of MilTech Solutions.

Nonprofit

Facebook has undoubtedly contributed greatly to a huge surge in nonprofit awareness, fund-raising, and causes. Currently, more than 30,000 nonprofits have Facebook fan pages.

The strategies for successful fan engagement are essentially the same as for-profit businesses: provide consistent valuable information, invite fans to contribute their thoughts freely, respond promptly, add multimedia content, and so on. Plus, you can regularly make fans aware of fund-raising activities, providing clear instructions for how fans can help and get involved more, both online and offline locally.

And, as with corporations and government, nonprofits also need to ensure there are solid policies in place for what can/cannot be shared, who's managing the Facebook content and fan activity, whether there is a voice/face of the nonprofit or simply the organization.

Facebook has a special page as a resource for nonprofits and other organizations for social good at www.facebook.com/nonprofits.

To quote Facebook on this special resource page, "We built it to help you harness the power of Facebook and bring positive change to the world. Facebook empowers nonprofits by enabling them to mobilize communities, organize events, increase fundraising, reduce costs with free online tools, and raise awareness through viral networks."

Causes App

Through the popular application Causes (Figure 10.4), more than $16 million has been raised since 2007, benefiting more than 300,000 different causes. Causes has become the leader among a growing number of social networks used by nonprofits. The app is free for nonprofits to use, but it does cost the organization staff time to develop and maintain.

The Causes app is available at www.facebook.com/causes. Also see www.causes.com.

Through the Causes app, both Facebook users and nonprofit fan pages easily join or create their own cause, invite their friends and network to contribute, chart their impact, create leaderboards, and more.

One great addition to the Causes app is the Causes Exchange (http://exchange.causes.com), where users share ideas about how best to use the app. A great example of providing new ideas for fundraising approaches came with the launch of the Birthday Wish, where users were encouraged to ask their friends to support a specific Cause rather than get them a birthday present. This seems such a simple and obvious idea, yet Birthday Wishes alone has apparently generated well over $1 million.

Figure 10.4

Causes app page

Here's an excerpt from the Causes Exchange blog regarding the Birthday Wishes feature:

> *Brad Sugars says he believes that cancer can be defeated, one birthday at a time.*
>
> *On his 38th birthday this year, Mr. Sugars, a skin cancer survivor and chief executive of the professional coaching firm ActionCoach, decided to raise money for the Cancer Schmancer Movement, a nonprofit organization devoted to the detection and early treatment of the disease.*
>
> *With a few quick clicks on Facebook, Mr. Sugars installed a program called Causes on his profile page and asked each of his 3,000 friends on the social network to contribute at least $38. Within a few weeks, more than 50 had given—some generously. By matching each donation, Mr. Sugars raised nearly $8,000 for the charity.*
>
> *"They make it so easy to do this," he said. "This is a way to challenge people to go do something good."*

HTTP://EXCHANGE.CAUSES.COM/2009/11/CLICKING-FOR-A-CAUSE

Example Nonprofits on Facebook

Beth Kanter, a respected nonprofit technology and social media authority, wrote an informative case study on her blog about the Red Cross's social media journey. Red Cross came under public attack for the way it handled disaster relief efforts after Hurricane Katrina. The organization then hired a social media manager (Wendy Harman), who helped to roll out a comprehensive, fully integrated social media policy and develop a powerful operational handbook. You can find the full case study, along with an excellent 109-page slideshow here:

```
http://beth.typepad.com/beths_blog/2009/07/red-cross-social-media-
strategypolicy-handbook-an-excellent-model.html
```

The following are several examples of nonprofits of all sizes successfully using Facebook to heighten awareness, strengthen their support, and raise funds:

- *Red Cross*: www.facebook.com/redcross
- *UNICEF*: www.facebook.com/unicef
- *Susan G. Komen for the Cure*: www.facebook.com/susangkomenforthecure
- *LIVESTRONG*: www.facebook.com/livestrong
- *Greenpeace*: www.facebook.com/greenpeace.international
- *Weston A. Price Foundation*: www.facebook.com/pages/Weston-A-Price-Foundation/58956225915
- *Pancreatic Cancer Action Network*: www.facebook.com/JointheFight
- *Modest Needs Foundation*: www.facebook.com/pages/Modest-Needs-Foundation/46172034338
- *Electronic Frontier Foundation (EFF)*: www.facebook.com/eff

Featured Case: Kane Swift and One Kid

With the help of his parents, as a fifth-grade science project, Kane Swift set up a fan page to directly support Susan G. Komen for the Cure called "One Kid, One Cure, and the Power of Social Networking." He got more than 1,200 fans and raised $400 in just one week so far. We need more kids like Kane!

www.facebook.com/pages/One-Kid-One-Cure-and-the-Power-of-Social-Networking/244652584233

Education

Given that Facebook started at Harvard University (in 2004 by three Harvard students) and for the first two years of its existence only those people with a .edu e-mail address could access and create a profile on Facebook, it stands to reason that education plays a large part of the Facebook ecosystem. When Facebook opened its doors to companies and ultimately the general public starting in 2006, many students who were active on the site in those first couple of years were very resistant (at first!) to the masses coming onto the site and changing the overall user experience of this "walled garden." However, as time wore on, tens of thousands of fun third-party applications sprung up, Facebook kept adding useful new features, and the original members found they could expand their network as they wanted and control their experience with the granular privacy settings.

Now, in 2010, with the sheer volume of users, the amount of time they spend on Facebook and the vast range of personal information they share, more and more organizations, including schools, colleges, and universities, will find themselves using Facebook to coordinate activities and distribute information.

Facebook's primary features of events, groups, and fan pages all work just as well for the education field as they do the commercial and nonprofit sectors. With consistent, relevant updates and proper engagement, schools, colleges and universities can easily expand their reach to recruit more students for full classes, boost morale, bolster student/teacher relationships, and even help improve grades.

As with nonprofits, Facebook also has a specific resource page to support educators in making the best of Facebook. See www.facebook.com/education.

Featured Case: Emergency Notification via Facebook

Communicating with students via text messaging has been an integral part of school systems for a while. Now, with the prevalence of social networks, being able to reach thousands of students via Facebook and Twitter is more important than ever.

Oregon's Pacific University (www.facebook.com/pacificu) integrated student notification via Facebook and Twitter using Ominlert's e2Campus (http://e2campus.com). Along with alerts via e-mail, RSS feeds, and text messaging to mobile devices, a service like e2Campus includes the ability for institutions to reach thousands of students and teachers with one click via Facebook and Twitter. As we talked earlier in this section about the sheer amount of time users/students spend on Facebook, with the ability to send alerts via Facebook, schools can increase their outreach for important communication. As reported in a CampusTechnology.com article:

According to Lee M. Colaw, vice president of information services at Pacific University, letting e2Campus contact students in emergencies through Facebook made sense. In fact, students had already requested it. When he conducted follow-up assessments on how the e2Campus system was working, Colaw said, students had suggested that the best way to reach them was via Facebook. Students said that they themselves were already re-typing and sending out university messages via Facebook. "We thought it would be more professional," Colaw said, "if the message came straight from the university instead."

http://campustechnology.com/Articles/2009/01/23/University-Links-Twitter-Facebook-with-Notification-System.aspx

Achieving Marketing and Recruitment Goals

Some schools may not be as hip to all the new Web 2.0 and social media marketing strategies. Or, they'll at least have a presence on Facebook in the form of a group or fan page, but the school may not know how to optimize their social network activity to achieve measurable results. There is a fine art to utilizing Facebook to connect with current students, empower teachers, promote the school to gain more enrollments, and track and measure your success. This is a specialty field that we're now seeing specialty services cater to. For example, BlueFuego, Inc., conducts a "social web audit" for colleges and universities to see how they're currently utilizing the social Web, and then it provides a social web strategy, training, and implementation support, with a heavy focus on the Facebook platform. Clients such as Abilene Christian University (`http://facebook.com/welcometoacu`) and Bentley University (`http://facebook.com/bentleyadmission`) are now engaging with hundreds of incoming students, attracting new leads, and providing customer service around the clock! Learn more at `http://bluefuego.com` and `www.facebook.com/BlueFuego`.

Example Schools, Colleges, and Universities on Facebook

Here are a few examples to learn from:

- *Stanford University*: `www.facebook.com/stanford`
- *University of Michigan*: `www.facebook.com/universityofmichigan`
- *Harvard University*: `www.facebook.com/Harvard`
- *Thunderbird, School of Global Management*: `www.facebook.com/ThunderbirdSchool`
- *Sewickley Academy*: `www.facebook.com/SewickleyAcademy`
- *Fresno Pacific University–Graduate School*: `www.facebook.com/graduatedegree`
- *Fresno Pacific University–Student Activities*: `www.facebook.com/pages/Fresno-Pacific-University-Student-Activities/110898556037`
- *SuperCamp, an academic summer camp for sixth grade through college students*: `www.facebook.com/SuperCamp`

Startups

Social media is a potentially huge opportunity for startup businesses, especially those that need to sell or market to consumers. Startups are often the most cost-sensitive organizations of any you'll find. But where startups are poor in cash resources, they are generally willing to try anything and work hard at new things that may help the business succeed. Social media is a good fit because much of it is built to be self-serve. Everything we've discussed in this book is designed to help you cut your learning curve and be effective as quickly as you can.

Generally speaking, marketing for a startup isn't about perception or the basic blocking and tackling associated with communicating messages to customers around the world. It is a much more surgical approach—how do you reach customers who are willing and able to adopt or buy your products and services? It's about transactions and finding qualified leads. It's about introducing new concepts to the marketplace that are bigger, better, faster, or more efficient than alternative ways of doing things. And all of that needs to be done cost effectively.

For unrecognized brands created by new, often unproven startup businesses, it can be very difficult to make a big splash. Consumers generally don't know who you are or what your products do unless they have experience doing business with you. Your brand(s) are not yet established, and they carry little to no meaning once you get outside of the relatively small and friendly group of family, friends, business colleagues, and early customers who keep up with you and want you to succeed.

So, all in all, you are a relative unknown fighting against all the other noise on Facebook, not to mention competitors who may be engaging with customers on Facebook and social media. In that sense, it is relatively easy to get a small and loyal following for your efforts early, but it is decidedly more difficult to scale once you've exhausted people who are at least a little familiar about you. How do you go beyond that first 100 or so people? You'll need much more than 100 people to show the world that your product is at least minimally important.

With a hat tip to Geoffrey Moore, we suggest that the answer certainly begins with your early adopters—people who will appreciate your work well before others realize on their own just how wonderful you and your product(s) or service(s) are. How can you identify and branch out from your early adopters?

Focus to keep early adopters happy Fill a niche, do it very well, engage regularly, and listen intently to your customers. Grow after you do one thing well, and don't get too ambitious early, because it may dilute the message that you are trying to promote.

Ask for support to get them involved A lot of people like to be associated with a success story from its humble beginnings. Appeal to them by asking for their help to promote you or your company to their friends and colleagues. Oftentimes you'll get assistance. Don't be afraid to ask for support—just don't overdo it because you may offend someone if you're too persistent.

Advertise to find and target new people As discussed in Chapter 6, Facebook advertising is perhaps one of the most effective and inexpensive ways available to target specific people based on profile data that they have entered voluntarily. Fortunately for you, this means that you can run ads targeted at people who live in a particular city, targeted at people who work in a company that you are trying to sell, or targeted at people of a certain age who fit the profile of early adopters for your product.

Be consistently useful for the customer first All too often, companies get so focused on their own needs that they forget to focus on the customer. The temptation is too great to send more marketing messages out through social media, and soon enough the ratio of marketing messages to useful content gets out of whack. Then customers abandon the social media effort. Just be sure to help the customer first and sell last. Make it a soft sale, and you'll do a lot better.

Finally, some companies don't use social media specifically as a marketing channel as much as they use social media to enhance an existing or new product. Social media isn't just the social graph—it is the social context through which you can deliver or receive real-time communications, identify validated users, and bridge between the web and social relationships. In certain cases, use of a product or service that is integrated with social media can help sell the very product you're trying to market. There are also opportunities to create new products and services using the social graph and data that can help modernize old businesses. If you go down this path, just remember that Facebook is similarly looking for new and interesting ways to make money. Facebook will always have competing interests between fostering a healthy, vibrant developer ecosystem and creating economic value for itself, not unlike Microsoft in the early days of the PC platform. You'll have to pay attention to industry news and events to know exactly how and where you can innovate.

Local Business

Local business owners similarly have a real opportunity to market to consumers in new and unique ways through social media. The reasons are simple—communications are easy and inexpensive, local customers can express themselves as a fan or a supporter of a local business or popular local product, and new customers can be found through Facebook's ad targeting features. Savvy local business owners are already using Facebook, Twitter, and other types of social media to promote themselves. In some cases, local businesses are bypassing traditional marketing and advertising altogether in lieu of social media marketing.

One of the primary reasons that social media is so popular with local business is the personal nature of Facebook and the social graph. Many local businesses have built a loyal clientele by getting to know their customers on both a professional level and a personal level. Local business owners aren't just shopkeepers—they are also neighbors, community activists, and friends. As Facebook has become mainstream, more and more people have created profiles and become Facebook friends with clients and business associates. The clear delineation we've had between our professional and personal lives continues to weaken because it just takes too much time and effort to keep everything separated in the world of Facebook.

Perhaps Facebook's communications platform is just as valuable to local business owners as the social graph. One common scenario for local business marketers is the need to prepare an e-mail newsletter weekly or monthly to keep customers informed. Without Facebook, an e-mail newsletter would need to be created using Constant

Contact or another vendor that specializes in e-mail marketing. These solutions typically cost a local business no less than $25/month and involve a steep learning curve. With Facebook, a local business owner can bypass e-mail marketing altogether and route communications through the Facebook fan page or a Facebook group. It's all designed to be self-serve, and it's free.

What other types of things can be done on Facebook? How should a local business take advantage of Facebook today? Many of the themes are the same as we've covered previously in this book, although effective applications may be different based on the type of business and the amount of time a local business owner has for marketing:

Customer interaction Facebook allows local businesses to share interesting stories and anecdotes and respond to random status updates in an effort to be more personable or human.

Customer service Local businesses can use social media to respond to product questions, concerns, or feedback.

Deals, coupons, and offers Facebook offers the opportunity to promote standing or special offers and coupon codes through the Facebook fan page or another part of the social network.

Real-time notifications Businesses can notifying customers of important business news, updates, new items, sales, and other relevant things as they happen.

Personal recommendations Facebook provides a forum for encouraging customers to talk about good experiences or make personal recommendations about your company or your products. This can range from overt compliments delivered via status updates to more subtle approval via your fan page.

Any of these can be executed with fan pages, groups, or even personal profiles on Facebook—and the overall experience can be accentuated by intelligently using other social media tools. Local businesses will want to consider a variety of the previous options that best resonate with customers. It will take time and energy to maintain your social media presence—so don't launch it and leave it alone for weeks at a time. Customers will notice your attention to detail and your commitment to keeping things up-to-date. Over time, you may just get customers responding to other customers' needs—a small community of helpful people bound by a common interest in your local business.

Facebook advertising is a particularly interesting way for local businesses to introduce a new/revamped Facebook fan page or other type of presence to local customers. It's the most inexpensive way for local businesses to target local customers and inform them—and in doing so you target people who you know have a Facebook account as well! Facebook ads can similarly point to websites, Twitter accounts, or other online destinations, so they're a good tool to gain customer awareness for just about anything you want to do online.

Where are things headed in the future? Facebook is certainly going to become more location-aware, especially as the social media experience becomes a mobile social media experience. Most smartphones are currently equipped with GPS technology, and so as long as they are web-enabled Facebook and other applications can know where your customers are. Expect the worlds of social media and location-based networks to continue to advance, giving local businesses new and increasingly effective ways of reaching connected consumers.

Some Final Tips on Facebook for B2B Marketing

Another consideration to keep in mind is the type of product you are selling. Take, for example, two cases—one an enterprise software product startup and the other a hamburger at a new fast-food restaurant. One requires a business-to-business (B2B) campaign—marketing business products/services to an audience driven by business goals (make money, save money, and so on). The other is a campaign targeting consumers who are mostly motivated by some combination of needs in Maslow's hierarchy of needs (`http://en.wikipedia.org/wiki/Maslow's_hierarchy_of_needs`). One transaction is tens of thousands of dollars. The other is five bucks. The sales cycle in one is very long—months if not years. The sales cycle in the other is the time it takes to drive by a restaurant.

Clearly, there are obvious differences in these two campaigns. Business-to-business marketing is more trust-oriented. A company and its stewards simply won't make a decision to adopt your product or work with your company without a pretty good idea that you can deliver on your value proposition. Consumers, on the other hand, will take a chance on a new product, or a new hamburger in this case, if they like what they hear. There is far less at stake over a $5 decision than a $50,000 decision. You won't get fired over picking the wrong hamburger over lunch, but you may get fired for choosing the wrong enterprise software product for your company.

So, how do you address this with your campaign? For B2B marketing, you're looking to use social media to establish a position in the market—a voice that speaks to specific pain in the marketplace. You should have a perspective on industry events, news, and developments. Commentary needs to be professional, on message, and consistent. Conversation should be encouraged, and metrics should track the amount and the depth of this conversation. You don't (and really can't) execute this type of marketing strategy without social media technologies—blogging, blogger engagement, Facebook fan pages, Twitter, and so on. Social media is the means by which you communicate your unique perspective to the world, and it is where you make your mark as a startup.

On the consumer front, you're tapping into a different need entirely—what former *Wired* journalist Brad King refers to as "The Cult of Me" (`www.thecultofme.com`). It is the notion that Web 2.0 technologies and social media have made everyone a "publisher." People use this capability to express themselves, so much so that egocentrism has to some extent gone mainstream. "Power users" on social media use status updates, shared links, photos, videos, associations with brands/companies, and so on, as a new form of self-expression that is both interactive and influential. People see what their friends like/dislike, and they form their own opinions based on what friends say and do. It isn't unlike trends in fashion—but it's far more encompassing, and it is part of our new digital lives.

In fact, a new term springing up now is *people to people* (P2). Some say we are moving away from business to business vs. business to consumer, and now everyone is in the business of people to people. You may hear some social media pundits saying, "People don't make friends with a logo, a product, or a bricks-and-mortar building... people make friends with people." This is the fundamental shift caused by social media prevalence. The more open, transparent, engaging, and genuinely caring a company—of any size—can be, the more success it'll glean from its social media/Facebook marketing efforts.

So, in closing, keep the following rules in mind as you build your campaign:

- Entertain your followers.
- Interact with customers.
- Maintain your social media presence.
- Inform people.
- Reach out to new customers or markets.

And perhaps most important: Fight the urge to oversell.

People won't engage with you unless they really like the product and you're providing the user with some value—entertainment, utility, or personal identification with your brand/company. Good luck!

Resources

Throughout this book, we've pointed out hundreds of great examples, case studies, and other information in an attempt to help you think creatively about how social media can solve your specific marketing problems. And although this book helps with your Facebook marketing initiatives, social media is bigger and broader than just Facebook. In addition to our website at http://facebookmarketinganhouraday.com, *we thought we'd give you a cheat sheet of third-party resources that can help you keep up with the ever-changing worlds of Facebook and social media.*

Appendix Contents
Companion Website
Other Reading Material
Social Media Tools You Can Use

Companion Website

The *Facebook Marketing: An Hour a Day* companion website—www.facebookmarketing anhouraday.com—has a blog and links to a Facebook presence that complements this book and its content.

Other Reading Material

If you're interested in reading more about social media and trends in Internet marketing, check out some of these books and popular blogs:

Books

The Facebook Era: Tapping Online Social Networks to Build Better Products, Reach New Audiences, and Sell More Stuff by Clara Shih (Prentice Hall PTR, 2009)

Trust Agents: Using the Web to Build Influence, Improve Reputation, and Earn Trust by Chris Brogan (Wiley, 2009)

The Whuffie Factor: Using the Power of Social Networks to Build Your Business by Tara Hunt (Crown Business, 2009)

Groundswell: Winning in a World Transformed by Social Technologies by Charlene Li and Josh Bernoff (Harvard Business School Press, 2008)

What Would Google Do? by Jeff Jarvis (HarperBusiness, 2009)

Free: The Future of a Radical Price by Chris Anderson (Hyperion, 2009)

Crush It: Why NOW Is the Time to Cash In on Your Passion by Gary Vaynerchuk (HarperStudio, 2009)

Social Media Marketing: An Hour a Day by Dave Evans (Sybex, 2008)

Socialnomics: How Social Media Transforms the Way We Live and Do Business by Erik Qualman (Wiley, 2009)

Blogs

Mashable: www.mashable.com

ReadWriteWeb: www.readwriteweb.com

Seth Godin blog: http://sethgodin.typepad.com

danah boyd blog, apophenia: www.zephoria.org/thoughts

The Next Web: www.thenextweb.com

Chris Brogan blog: www.chrisbrogan.com

Social Media Examiner: http://socialmediaexaminer.com

All Facebook: www.allfacebook.com

Inside Facebook: www.insidefacebook.com

Social Times: www.socialtimes.com

TheKBuzz: www.thekbuzz.com

Social Media Tools You Can Use

The list of possible social media tools you can use grows daily. It can be overwhelming to try to keep up with the rapid changes and growth; however, we will attempt to list a few of our favorite tools here that have been around for a while or that we have had positive experience and results with.

Blogging Two of the most popular blogging platforms today are TypePad and WordPress. It's a personal choice, and there are arguments for both platforms. Both offer free and paid levels. Going with the paid levels will offer you more ability to customize and optimize for SEO. WordPress.com is the free version, hosted by WordPress and doesn't allow for as much customization; WordPress.org is the version you host yourself and allows you the ability to use a vast array of templates, widgets, and plug-ins.

Linking Twitter to Your Facebook fan page There are currently two ways to do this. Either you can configure the Twitter application (http://apps.facebook.com/twitter) on Facebook to post to your Facebook fan page or you can run the Selective Tweets application (http://apps.facebook.com/selectivetwitter) that will do the same thing as long as you add the #fb tag to your Twitter posts. If you tend to post a lot of tweets, the Selective Tweets app is ideal. Alternatively, you can choose which tweets to post to your Facebook fan page via TweetDeck (http://tweetdeck.com) or HootSuite (http://hootsuite.com).

OneForty Thousands of Twitter management applications have emerged to help people and companies understand and unlock the value of their Twitter accounts. OneForty (http://oneforty.com) is a repository of these applications, which are categorized and rated by individual users.

uStream.tv Want to enable live streaming of an event and include comments and other social features in the user's experience? Fortunately, there is a platform for that. uStream (http://ustream.tv) is that platform, and it's even already integrated with Facebook and Twitter!

URL-shortening services Once used just for shortening long URLs shared via Twitter, a variety of URL-shortening services are now providing a full suite of analytics so you know exactly how these links are shared across social media, how often they are clicked, and so on. Awe.sm, bit.ly, and others offer such analytics, and in some cases they also allow brands to establish their own URL shortener like Google did with youtu.be. For one of the best link-shortening analyses, see this report: http://searchengineland.com/analysis-which-url-shortening-service-should-you-use-17204.

Facebook fan page app providers Several companies offer services to help businesses optimize their Facebook fan pages, from basic apps right up to specialized enterprise-level customization:

Wildfire Interactive: www.wildfireapp.com

Involver: http://involver.com

Fan Appz: http://fanappz.com

Buddy Media: http://buddymedia.com

There is also a cottage industry developing around the management of marketing campaigns across social media sites and destinations. These applications come in a few forms:

- Sentiment monitoring (Radian6, Visible Technologies, Scout Labs, SocialTALK, Alterian SM2)
- Customer engagement (Objective Marketer, Spredfast, CoTweet, HootSuite, TwitManage)
- Research and influence (Rapleaf, Converseon, Traackr, BuzzStream)
- Configuration (Buddy Media, Involver, Clearspring, Widgetbox)

Many of these programs offer free trials—just be sure to do your homework if you are going to adopt a tool to help with your social media efforts.

Finally, a wide range of consulting businesses has emerged to help companies navigate all the self-serve options and popular tools. These companies are a particularly good option for people in companies who don't have time to learn and master social media marketing. Although the rise of social media has certainly democratized Internet marketing for the reasons we've pointed out in this book, it's still too complicated for a lot of people. Expect to see more companies emerge that specialize in helping people make sense of it all by providing "assisted-serve" products and services that are laser-focused on specific business goals.

Do keep an eye on our companion blog for ongoing resources and recommendations (www.facebookmarketinganhouraday.com).

The Future
of Facebook

B

As we mentioned *the introduction of the book, our goal was to create a real "practitioner's guide" to Facebook marketing in 2010. But where is Facebook heading in the future? If the past is any indication, the only thing we can say with any certainty is that Facebook will continue to aggressively evolve. So, we decided to ask a few industry experts their opinions on the future of Facebook. You know what they say, you have to skate to where the puck is going to be. We hope this appendix will give you some ideas that can further inform your Facebook and social media marketing campaigns.*

Appendix Contents

Dave Kerpen

Scott McCaskill

Lauren Cooney

Jesse Stay

Nick O'Neill

Kevin Tate

Dave Kerpen

Dave Kerpen is the chief buzz officer for theKbuzz.

You wake up on a Friday morning, roll out of bed, grab your "Facebook phone," and quickly scroll through your News Feed to browse the important world and local news of the day, weather, and what your closest friends are up to this weekend. You notice your favorite restaurant is having a special Saturday night that sounds scrumptious, so you make reservations. Oh, that suit you've been eyeing just went on sale, so you purchase it for delivery on Monday. It's getting late quickly, so you put down your Facebook phone and head to the bathroom to get ready for work. But as you're brushing your teeth, you feel a sharp pain coming from that tooth that's been nagging you over the past week. It's been way too long since you've been to the dentist, but that's no problem; it's back to your Facebook phone, where you type **dentist** in the search bar and find *two* local dentists that your friends have recommended, so you schedule an appointment with one of them for later today. TGIF.

This scenario might seem a little far-fetched as I write it in January 2010, but it's really not that far off. Facebook founder and CEO Mark Zuckerberg has always insisted that Facebook is a platform and that the website Facebook.com is really just the beginning. In his view and mine, Facebook will continue to grow its user base rapidly as it approaches 1 billion users worldwide and realizes its potential as the gateway to the social, mobile, interconnected Internet. But the most exciting growth of Facebook is in the platform: Mobile, Connect, and International are three key areas where Facebook will look to grow. Facebook's vision is to have an open, connected world, where individuals connect not only with one another but with companies, nonprofits, and even governments. People will connect on their own terms; for some that will mean Facebook.com, but for many others, that will mean access to the stream through a mobile device. 1800flowers.com (disclosure: a client of ours at theKbuzz) has been selling flowers on its Facebook page for months. The Limited in December of 2009 became the first company to sell products through a shopping cart directly in the stream. The future will bring a lot more companies conducting business within the Facebook stream and using Facebook Connect to allow their customers to bring their social graph with them when they visit the company website.

For you, as a marketer, it is essential to build your presence now, to engage your customers and prospects, and to grow your Facebook presence as Facebook itself grows. It is essential to determine how you can provide value to your customers and noncustomers, and you can use the Facebook platform to keep them engaged and to keep you on their minds. The Facebook platform includes Facebook.com, of course, and your fan page presence there, but increasingly in the future it will include your Facebook Connect–enabled website and Facebook stream and mobile-friendly applications. If you are smart—focusing on engaging, value-driven content that your target audience would want to see and not on telling people about your company—you will be light-years ahead of the plethora of marketers who currently still have a broadcast/push-marketing mentality.

Twitter and Google may be the only viable threats to Facebook's continued growth and ultimate dominance in the marketplace. Twitter grew rapidly in 2009, but its simplicity could be either a boon or a curse. Its growth has slowed down into 2010, and Twitter still has nowhere near the user numbers that Facebook has. Google has dominated the search market for years, and if it can somehow integrate an efficient social search product, it can retain its stranglehold on the search advertising market. There is the possibility of another social network coming along and overtaking Facebook, as Facebook did to MySpace and MySpace did to Friendster before that. However, that seems unlikely at this point. But all signs point to Facebook eventually winning this space.

The only other threat I see to Facebook's growth is Facebook itself. In its short history, Facebook has changed its product often and dramatically—sometimes much to the dismay of its users. In particular, concerns about privacy have haunted users, especially those users of older generations. Facebook would have you think everyone is open about sharing personal information online; however, the truth is, many people don't yet feel comfortable doing that. Still, with such a large share of the worldwide Internet-using population on Facebook, it appears highly unlikely that Facebook will self-destruct.

Social media in general and Facebook specifically allow you as a marketer to go much deeper in your relationships with customers and prospects and to tap into the social graphs of its hundreds of millions of users. Your Facebook marketing and moreover engagement efforts should absolutely be fully integrated into all of the marketing and communications that you do, online and offline. Whether you are a marketer for a Fortune 1000 company or a small business, a nonprofit or a government agency, a B2B company or a B2C company, your target audience is on Facebook waiting to engage with you. You must become adept at content creation and distribution, no matter what you are selling. Just as Facebook is open, your opportunity to grow your business using the Facebook Platform is wide open. Good luck!

Scott McCaskill

Prior to cofounding Social Agency, Scott McCaskill was CTO/CFO and cofounder of Small World Labs, where he wrote the original version of its social networking platform and helped grow the company from 2 employees to more than 30 full-time and contract employees and 100-plus clients. Before Small World Labs, Scott held roles at Dell, Boston Consulting Group, Singlecast, and Sapient.

Scott received a BS in computer science and history from Yale University and an MBA with a focus in finance and strategic management from the University of Chicago.

Facebook over the next three to five years will attempt to become the first and last place people go when online (a portal strategy), act as the profile "system of record" for the Web, and establish itself as an advertising powerhouse. On each of these goals, it will fail. Instead, its portal strategy will succumb to more interesting sites just as AOL did, an open source option to the social Web will eventually rise up, and Facebook will derive the bulk of its profits from games and charging for access to its APIs.

Facebook clearly wants to create an ecosystem that encourages users to spend as much time on it as possible, replicating the strategy first implemented by AOL and followed by Yahoo! and MSN a few years later. From applications to continuous updates to company fan pages (confusingly called *Pages*), Facebook fancies itself a site from which no one need leave. However, although Facebook is forever trying to find ways to be sticky, it will ultimately lose in its battle to become a portal. A new shiny object will siphon off users. Facebook's time-on-site will be driven by the games that make use of the platform, rather than intrinsic entertainment people continue to find on the site. Until Facebook begins charging for this access, the bulk of the profits will accrue to the game developers. Eventually, the games themselves could break out of the walls of Facebook, rendering the platform less and less relevant.

Facebook recognizes the limits of its portal strategy, to some extent, and is therefore pushing the Facebook Connect API. This single sign-on mechanism also forestalls the rise of a truly portable social graph, particularly if Facebook can get itself intimately involved in most/many high-traffic sites. In general, users would prefer a single profile that was portable across various social networks. Facebook obviously would prefer to not allow such data portability—thus its introduction and promotion of Facebook Connect. In the next two years, Facebook will continue to have tremendous adoption of this login mechanism. Over time, sites that use it though will gather more demographic information on their own and will implement other login tools. Eventually a mashup single sign-on site will develop, taking information from Facebook, LinkedIn, Ning, and any other site a user might have joined. That mashup, if sufficiently free, will become the system of record, undermining Facebook's stranglehold on personal profile data. At this point, Facebook will start to charge for the high-volume access to its APIs both through Facebook Connect and applications on Facebook.com. And those making significant use of the Facebook API will be happy to pay.

Although Facebook imagines itself to be the next Google and claims to make tremendous money already from advertising, it is unlikely that Facebook will really become the marketing behemoth that justifies its current valuation. In Facebook's favor is a cadre of smart people with an enormous amount of data at their fingertips. However, as many supermarkets will attest, data and smart people won't necessarily bring in tremendous sales. Currently the largest advertisers on Facebook tend to be the games developed for the platform. This makes sense; the games can directly sell virtual goods to Facebook members and surreptitiously sign them up for direct marketing deals. Their advertising dollars on Facebook bring high return. For regular advertisers, the case is less clear at the moment. Although the cost per click on Facebook is much lower than, say, AdWords, it is not clear that the conversion is the same. In fact, the most successful ads on Facebook simply drive usage to other parts of Facebook (applications, groups, fan pages). Can Facebook really drive conversions for products that don't include finding a date or buying a virtual sword? Not like AdWords can. Ultimately, Facebook continues to partner more and more with businesses to help it have a compelling presence on its platform—and charges big money for it, expanding its current offerings in this area. But the little guy won't necessarily have the money to play and will thus continue to work with the much lower-cost cottage industry of fan page configuration tools.

Finally, although Facebook won't be the final portal or social network or single profile system of record or the next Google, it will still offer a highly compelling place for businesses and customers to comingle in a fashion they have not in the past. This relationship building will be crucial for companies in the coming years; it is just questionable how much Facebook's cut will be during that time.

Lauren Cooney

 Lauren Cooney has 10 years of experience with product management, marketing, and building technical communities, strategies, and GTM plans for enterprise software companies across several different products, technologies, and languages. She joined Microsoft in May 2008 to lead the Web Platform & Standards team and focused specifically on driving change in Microsoft's web strategy, working on open source web initiatives and providing developers with the right products and tools to be successful when building web solutions. Cooney's team is responsible for the Microsoft Web Platform, the Web Platform Installer, the Windows Web Application Gallery, and www.microsoft.com/web. Before Microsoft, Cooney was a program director in the CTO office at IBM, focusing on strategy and community evangelism around Web 2.0 and open source technologies.

What is the future of Facebook? It's all about data.

When I worked at IBM two years ago, I had the privilege of working for the CTO of information management, Anant Jhingran. At that point in time, "mashups" were the next big thing, and almost every company out there, large and small, was in a race to get their product to market first. My team was building what would become the IBM Mashup Center—the first enterprise-ready mashup engine. In almost every meeting we had, Anant would reiterate to the team how data was king—and essentially by mashing up data we were providing corporations with essential information that they needed to run their business better. It's what all companies want more of—data of who their users are or who their customers are—and the information they get from this is how they can better reach more customers or serve specific customers.

Facebook isn't that different; it runs its entire business around data collection, utilization, and then the sale of that to advertisers. Mark Zuckerberg was smarter than all of us, though; he realized that data was king earlier than all of us. When he was sitting in his college dorm room creating what would become Facebook, I wonder, however, if he knew just how good his company would become at collecting data. You see, every time someone signs up for Facebook, they are prompted to enter almost every detail of their lives into this one website. From sex, age, occupation, and relationship status to favorite movies, books, and quotes—Facebook asks users for all of this information. And then when you download an application—you know, one of those fun apps that tells you your horoscope or whatnot—well, the people who make those applications collect your data as well.

What amazes me, however, is just how much data people are willing to provide about themselves, without even truly knowing how it is utilized. In this book, advertising is discussed extensively—and how you can drive people to your company/website/blog/product. See, that data doesn't just sit there and waste away. Facebook utilizes every *piece* of data it collects. Perfect example? I work at Microsoft. And almost any time I log into Facebook, there's an ad on the right sidebar of my profile that pops up; sometimes it's an advertisement for a new social networking site (I list social media as one of my interests), or perhaps it's the face of some random person attempting to prompt me to click their picture so I can get their resume because they want to work at Microsoft. It's truly fascinating how much manipulation Facebook does with its data—and how well it utilizes it.

How is data and people's privacy regulated? you might ask. Well, to be frank, it's really not yet. Privacy is something for large corporations to worry about, not "consumer" companies like Facebook is often made out to be. You're not providing a credit card number when you sign up for Facebook, and you're only letting friends view your profile, so immediately it's not a big deal. But what you might not realize is that Facebook, without letting companies or individuals see your data, is still selling it to them. Facebook allows its advertisers to segment who they want to advertise to-whether it be age group, gender, company, occupation, or more. So, you think your personal data is safe? Well, it's safe, but I wouldn't call it "safe" (unless you limit what you input about yourself, which I have self-regulated on my own Facebook page over the past few years).

What does this mean for the future of Facebook? And better yet, how are other companies out there going to be affected/changed by the way Facebook uses its data?

Facebook is better at collecting data than most companies. Microsoft and Google collect a decent amount through their search engines, but they're not able to tailor it as well as Facebook is currently. In the future, I think that these companies, as well as other ones, are going to start figuring out how to better segment and utilize their data. A great example is how Facebook can advertise to certain users based on age and gender. Right there as a potential advertiser, I am able to get a better use out of my marketing budget with a company that can better target my audience, because at the end of the day that will bring me more potential customers or users.

With this data collection, however, comes the risk of further regulation around privacy. Facebook has very specific privacy guidelines, and it lets you self-regulate your own privacy on its site by providing a nice little tab under "Settings" on your profile page where you can go in and choose your own settings for your privacy. That said, Facebook still collects all your data. Similar to the e-mail marketing revolution when it imposed certain regulations about how you had to include an "opt-out" button, I believe Facebook will probably face certain privacy restrictions as consumers get smarter about their data.

Facebook is very intelligent about how it is delivering on its business plan and executing on its revenue model. Data is king, and Facebook gets that. Facebook, as a company, has brought to realization what people who are driving information management have known for years: the more information you have, the more power you have...and the more money you can make. It's a different era, and the data revolution is just starting.

Jesse Stay

Jesse Stay is CEO and founder of SocialToo.com, a site that complements the social networking experience with useful tools and analytics. A speaker, author, developer, and entrepreneur, Jesse wrote two books, *I'm on Facebook—Now What???* and *FBML Essentials*, and was recently named one of 20 developers to follow on Twitter, as well as one of 10 entrepreneurs to follow on Twitter by Mashable.com. Jesse writes regularly on his blog, StayNAlive, and has contributed to the top two Facebook blogs, InsideFacebook and AllFacebook.

From Fishers to Farmers

A good friend of mine, Jeremiah Owyang, likes to talk about "Fishing where the fish are" (www.web-strategist.com/blog/2009/03/24/social-media-marketing-storyboard-1-fish-where-the-fish-are). Several years ago, Facebook brands would have to find new and unique ways of getting customers to come to them. To do so, they would use techniques such as SEO, advertising, pay per click, and other methods to bring as many customers to their websites as possible. Knowing what others were saying, and being able to interact with those mentioning or sharing their product elsewhere, was a near-impossible task. However, with social media, that all changed, and now brands are able to become virtual fishermen in ponds far away, in ways they were never able to before.

Now, and for the future, Facebook is working to take that even a step further. Through tools such as Facebook Connect, brands are now able to go from being "fishers" to "farmers," taking the interactions they have with their customers to their own website or turf. Now, as customers visit a brand's website, they will be able to interact with their friends there, instead of just on Facebook.com. Wherever a user goes on the Web, they will be able to share with their Facebook friends, which is a powerful concept!

With Facebook Connect, the power can be shifted from a single website like Facebook.com and move into the hands of the brand, and even further, the consumer. As the future of the Web holds, the consumers will be in control of their relationships, and brands will need to provide the breeding grounds for that to happen.

What Is Facebook Connect?

In its most basic form, Facebook Connect is a series of interfaces for programmers or brands to be able to access anything in the Facebook environment from their own websites or applications. The interface provides at a higher level HTML and JavaScript-based widgets that brands can copy into their websites to share things like a "Become a Fan" button or the ability to share content from their websites onto Facebook. At a lower level, a rich set of APIs is exposed for developers to access and build even more customized experiences for their customers.

The popular humor site JibJab.com is a great example of a brand that utilized Facebook Connect for success. With Facebook and Facebook Connect, JibJab was able to provide deep integration for their users, enabling them to bring in profile pictures, link friends, and share with others, all from the JibJab.com site using its Facebook login credentials. With this integration, JibJab boasted an increase of 1.5 million new users in just five months, something that took eight years to reach in the era of e-mail (www
.insidefacebook.com/2009/11/10/connect-brings-jibjab-1-5-million-facebook-users).

Huffington Post is another great example of success bringing the Facebook experience into its own environment. Huffington Post, a popular news website, sought to personalize the news-reading experience more and provided a deep integration into Facebook using Facebook Connect. Users, with a single login to Facebook, would immediately be presented with a list of their Facebook friends' reading activity—what their friends are reading, what they are commenting on, and what they like, all in a live activity stream. This way, readers could, instead of reading a chronological list of articles they may or may not be interested in, now see a list of articles they know their close friends are interested in, and more relevant content could be provided to each reader.

Huffington Post saw a boost of 48 percent in referral traffic, and the number of comments on the site increased, from 1.7 million to 2.2 million in a very short time frame. Huffington Post now boasts that 15 percent of its comments come from Facebook, and visitors went up 190 percent in just three months. They say those numbers are still growing (`http://paidcontent.org/article/419-huffpo-ceo-eric-hippeau-we-are-now-in-the-big-leagues`).

Brand after brand is utilizing the power of Facebook Connect, and there's a good chance if one brand isn't doing it, their competitor is. Facebook has also made it clear that it will further expand its offerings and that its future is "the open Web," not just the Facebook.com site. I think it's evident this is a tool every brand should be utilizing.

What's Next for Facebook?

Since we know Facebook's future is Facebook Connect, it's obvious brands should be considering it in their expansion strategies. However, what comes after Connect? What will we see two to five years down the road?

Developers are quickly working on new ways to identify customers and provide contextual experiences for them. I think the future will be in that contextual experience. Expect the future to be about the brand following the user where they go. Not only will the user see their Facebook friends when they visit a brand's website, but that brand will also follow them as they visit other websites and as they use other applications. When they visit Google.com, if they are an AAA member, they will see AAA images next to each participating AAA service that returns in their Google.com search results. Your brand will provide meaningful data for them as well.

I call this the Building Block Web (`http://staynalive.com/articles/2009/10/15/web-3-0-the-building-block-web/`). In the future, individual brands will be able to provide experiences, or bricks of application, on other brands' websites, and other brands will be able to provide experiences for the customer on individual brands' websites. The future will be all about the user, and the user will see what they want to see as they tour the Web.

As brands contemplate their strategy for the future, it will be important for them to find ways to till and cultivate in their own environment, while at the same time provide ways for others to till and cultivate that brand in another environment. This starts with Facebook Connect—brands should be bringing the Facebook experience, friends, and connections Facebook is good at building into their own environments. At the same time, each company should be looking into ways to bring its brand's experience into Facebook.com. Brands should be both fishers *and* farmers.

Nick O'Neill

Nick O'Neill is the founder and director of Social Times, Inc., a WebMediaBrands digital media company focused on covering the growing social web economy. He is a renowned social media industry expert, providing no-holds-barred commentary and insightful analysis on social networking and social media. Nick also speaks at conferences nationwide and has been written about in multiple national publications. With the opening of the Facebook platform, Nick saw a huge opportunity and has become fully dedicated to covering the social networking phenomenon via AllFacebook.com, eventually expanding beyond with SocialTimes.com.

Since Facebook's rapid ascent as one of the most important communication channels on the Web, businesses have been working to determine the best ways to reach their customers on the site. With new services like Facebook pages and Facebook Connect, and with more services to be announced in the future, what are the most important things for businesses to understand?

The World Is Becoming More Social

Although Facebook is commonly viewed as a destination website, Facebook should be increasingly viewed as an identity service. No matter where you go on the Web (and eventually off the Web), you will have the ability to connect with your friends and other individuals about your experiences. In a world where "social" is no longer a competitive advantage (and no longer an option), businesses need to be focused on developing quality content that engages the customers. Facebook is shaping up to be the company that is responsible for socializing the Web and the world. This means businesses must stay on top of the future products and services Facebook releases in order to remain relevant in this rapidly changing environment.

Listening Is Complex and Necessary

As users on Facebook (and other tools like Twitter) become more comfortable with sharing their information publicly, companies have the opportunity to find out what their customers are saying about them. Although the privacy of user data will continue to be a highly contested issue, it's becoming increasingly acceptable to share more personal information about our lives.

The Open Graph API

One of Facebook's new products that will soon be released is the Open Graph API. Although few details have been provided about the Open Graph API, the idea is that users will be able to become a fan of any page on the Web. All features that currently exist within the Facebook Pages product can be implemented elsewhere on the Web. The idea is that companies will be able to build communities around any product, service, or idea while having the ability to publish activity directly into users' Facebook streams. For 2010 and much of 2011, the Open Graph API will become one of the most important products for businesses.

Human Communication Has Been Redefined

One thing to keep in mind with Facebook as well as other technologies is that we are still part of the communication revolution. Never before have humans been able to communicate with one another so quickly. Additionally, the level of information being shared has become so detailed that many are becoming overwhelmed. Despite the issue of information overload, I believe that humans are empowered by these new tools of communication. While companies are looking to understand this rapidly changing environment, humans are also trying to figure out how to adapt. We are still at an extremely early phase of the communication revolution, and by reading this book you have signaled your intention to be part of this massive shift.

Kevin Tate

Kevin Tate is a founder and principal at StepChange Group, a Powered company. He has been creating online solutions for leading brands since 1996, first with I/PRO and then with Fort Point Partners and Kronos. He is a frequent speaker on the topic of social marketing and serves on the board of the Portland Advertising Federation. Kevin has a degree in international relations and economics from Stanford University.

Facebook has historically been referred to, derisively, as a "walled garden." This was and is mostly a fair critique, although that same "walledness" is what allowed Facebook to create a uniquely effective social marketing landscape. So, it's not all bad, and a lot of people can certainly benefit from it.

However, I believe 2010 will be the year that Facebook explodes beyond its "walls" and emerges as an ever-present social identity platform, no longer constrained to a specific, albeit large, corner of the Web.

The fact that Facebook has made public its plans for the Open Graph API in early 2010—which should effectively allow any web page/property to function as an extension of Facebook—lays some of the foundation.

And the Walls Come Tumbling Down

However, I foresee Open Graph as only the catalyst, not the end state. The important shift I foresee in 2010 is from "Facebook as a *hub* for social momentum" to "Facebook as an *enabler* of social momentum" anywhere on the Web. Here's what I mean...

Today, if you want your brand or campaign to participate in Facebook's reach and momentum, you have to put that program inside—or at least very close to (using Facebook Connect)—Facebook itself. Thus, the popularity of Facebook Custom Tabs,

Apps, and Connect implementations allows a brand to flow a program's momentum through Facebook (usually the Wall) in order to dramatically amplify the brand's exposure and engagement.

In 2010, with Open Graph and the likely extensions such as Facebook Connect as the enablers, marketers will be able to use Facebook tools to create that same amplification and engagement on their own turf (for example, their primary website or a microsite), rather than needing to always flow the momentum through Facebook.

This will effectively turn Facebook "inside out" and will dramatically expand the range of Facebook-powered, social consumer experiences—since those will no longer be constrained by the specific properties and attention landscapes of today's Facebook. The sky, rather than the "Wall," will truly be the limit.

The New Social Marketing Opportunity: Facebook-Powered Social Experiences

For marketers, this will open up a wide array of possible branded social experiences that leverage the reach and momentum of Facebook but that can be developed on their turf. This is significant because, although Facebook has offered tremendous reach, it has afforded somewhat limited brand influence and control. This has kept Facebook marketing, and most social media brand initiatives, focused "high in the funnel" (awareness and interest).

These new Facebook-powered properties—call them "social microsites," "momentum hubs," or "branded communities"—will play a new role lower in the marketing funnel, centered around high-value activities such as interest, education, evangelism, and conversion. For these to be effective, they will need to marry the reach and momentum coming from Facebook (and YouTube, Twitter, LinkedIn, and so on) with the content, commerce, and community that the brand provides. Companies that do this well will unlock a whole new area of measurable ROI from social media marketing.

The First Step: Creating Integrated Momentum Chains

As marketers start leveraging these new capabilities, the first and most visible examples will be companies that create momentum chains like these:

Advertising ⟷ Facebook ⟷ Communities ⟷ .com Sites

in which content and engagement can flow from one property to another, putting each to work in what it does best:

Advertising:	Reach
Facebook:	Engagement
Communities:	Content + context
.com Sites:	Conversion and support

Creating properties and programs that leverage this new, expanded momentum landscape will be an exciting area of innovation in 2010.

Glossary

A/B testing Approach for determining how different designs of a single part of a web page or landing page impact a desired outcome metric. A/B testing is generally used to tweak a site once a design or overall approach is already determined. See also *multivariate testing.*

ad approval Process undertaken by Facebook to ensure that ads created by advertisers meet Facebook's quality standards. All Facebook ads must undergo ad approval before being presented to Facebook users. The process takes as little as an hour or as long as a week, depending on whether the advertiser has created an ad before and/or whether the ad is similar to other ads that have run on Facebook. Failing to pass ad approval means the process starts over again, and the ad must still be approved.

ad copy Text used to convince Facebook users to click an advertisement at the upper-right part of different pages on Facebook. Ad copy is created in the Ads and Pages application on Facebook and is presented to the user after an advertiser bids to run ads in a campaign and enters payment information. In Facebook, ad copy is currently limited to 25 characters for a title and 135 characters for the body of an ad.

API Application programming interface; the code that is run by a social network or other platform company that allows developers to integrate third-party code with the platform. Facebook, Twitter, and a wide range of other Web 2.0 and social media services maintain a developer API.

approved app A Facebook application that has been reviewed by Facebook to assess whether the application meets Facebook's guidelines for acceptable standards, quality, relevance, and notifications. Once approved for inclusion, the app can propagate messages to the News Feed, and the app will appear in Facebook search results.

blog Web log, or self-serve publishing technology used by people and organizations to share thoughts, opinions, and reactions to current events. Facebook allows blogging via its Notes feature, which is available via the Facebook profiles or fan pages.

bounce rate Percentage of people who view a web page and immediately leave it, usually after not finding what they want. Bounce rates are usually calculated as a metric to indicate the overall success of an ad—clicks that are generated on an ad that result in a high bounce rate rarely provide the business metrics that are desired. A high bounce rate indicates that the traffic generated from an advertisement isn't "high-quality" traffic, while a low bounce rate conversely indicates that the ad does indeed target the right people.

business accounts Designed for individuals who want to use Facebook solely to administer fan pages and ad campaigns. For this reason, business accounts have very limited functionality. To create a business account, individuals must first create a Facebook ad or Facebook page. If a user already has a personal account, it is a violation of Facebook's terms of use to also create a business account.

campaign A marketing initiative that integrates a set of advertising, marketing, and/or public relations commitments aimed at achieving business goals.

click-through Also referred to as a *click*, a user who has seen an ad and clicked it to get more information.

click-through rate (CTR %) The frequency with which a user clicks an ad or family of ads. This is an important metric for determining the effectiveness of ad copy and images used to entice a user. Generally speaking, ads with a higher CTR % are more effective than ads with lower CTR % metrics, which indicate poorer response.

content audit Process undertaken to learn how much an organization has of specific types of content for future sharing or posting via a social network.

cost per action (CPA) The amount an advertiser will pay for a user to perform a very specific action, usually a sign-up on a web form or some other call to action that the advertiser wants. Facebook does not currently make CPA advertising available to customers but may in the future.

cost per click (CPC) The amount an advertiser will pay for a user to click an advertisement, irrespective of what the user does afterward. CPC advertising is currently an available option through Facebook advertising.

cost per mil (CPM) The amount an advertiser will pay for 1,000 impressions of an advertisement, irrespective of whether the user

clicks the advertisement or performs an action afterward. CPM advertising is currently an available option through Facebook advertising.

dashboard A summarized view of all important metrics that determine the success of a campaign or set of campaigns over time. Usually built in a spreadsheet, dashboards are important for recording numbers that are usually lost over time because social networks and other third-party sites do not keep exhaustive records long-term.

derivative metric The combination of two or more metrics that helps marketers analyze progress over time and opportunities for optimizing websites. Some examples of important derivative metrics are page views per unique user, daily moving average cost per lead/fan, effective CPM per week, and so on.

editorial policy Rules that an organization uses to govern the types of content and the frequency with which content is posted or shared via social media.

engagement ad Type of advertisement that relies upon users to perform an action—such as play a video, like an ad, and so on—and have that action appear visible to other friends on Facebook.

Facebook application A product created from a set of custom code that is designed to run and allow interactions inside Facebook. Applications come in a variety of forms—most notably social games, productivity apps, music/lifestyle-sharing apps, custom notification apps, notification apps, and so on. Facebook has its own set of applications, and there are hundreds of thousands of third-party applications.

Facebook credits Users may purchase credits to be used toward buying virtual gifts or interacting with certain applications.

Facebook Connect A set of technology provided by Facebook to web developers for integrating Facebook features with a third-party website. Facebook Connect includes embeddable single sign-on using Facebook authentication credentials, social comments, fan boxes and widgets, personalization opportunities, "share on Facebook" functionality, and other features.

Facebook Markup Language (FBML) The language used by developers to create Facebook applications.

fan A Facebook user who chooses to identify with a fan page and show support. As a result, fan page updates are shared on the fan's News Feed, and oftentimes the fan can post updates to the fan page directly.

fan box A Facebook "widget" that summarizes highlights of a Facebook fan page and is published to a website, blog, or other place on the Internet. Fan boxes may include the total number of fans for a fan page, small profile pictures of those fans, or the latest updates to the fan page.

"Friends of Connections" advertising An option in Facebook advertising that allows an advertiser to target people based on associations that friends have made. For example, an advertiser can target friends of people who join a group, are a fan of a fan page, or have installed a particular application.

Insights Facebook feature that exposes demographic details on users of a particular fan page or Facebook application. This feature is designed to give administrators an idea of the demographic groups that use the fan page or application, along with behavioral metrics and usage statistics.

landing page A page established on a website that is intended to isolate traffic from a single source, usually an advertising campaign. Landing pages are established by traffic source and are not replicated, so statistics on the effectiveness of the tactic can be isolated and measured against other tactics in the campaign.

live feed All Facebook activity from friends and fan pages in chronological order. Whereas the (default) Top News is a reflection of "popularity" according to Facebook's algorithms, the live feed (now called "Most Recent") is a straight listing of every post.

max bid The amount of money per click or per thousand impressions that an advertiser is willing to pay to advertise. Suggestions for bid price are provided by Facebook after considering demand for the advertisement and availability of impressions per criteria set by the advertiser. An advertiser will set a bid in advance of running advertisements on Facebook and other popular Internet advertising destinations.

moving average Average of outcomes for a particular metric over a period of time, usually a week or month. Moving averages are designed to smooth out the impact of holidays and weekends to provide a consistent trending view of data as a means to judge the overall health of a campaign.

multivariate testing Approach for determining how multiple design differences on a website impacts a desired outcome metric. Multivariate testing is generally used as a "scattershot" approach to quickly learn what features are responsible for the most well-optimized web destination that is possible. See also *A/B testing.*

networks Groups based around a workplace, high school, or college that users can join so they can connect with those around them easier. Facebook used to also have geographic networks but have phased out this feature.

News Feed Summary of the most important things that are shared by friends, fan pages, groups, and applications. Facebook's algorithms decide which posts users see and in what order. The more activity a post has from users' friends or joined fan pages, the more likely the post will appear toward the top of their News Feed.

Notes Application in Facebook that allows users to blog directly inside the Facebook platform. In Notes, Facebook users can "tag" each other, which sends a notification to the person being tagged. Along with generating their own note inside Facebook, users can use the Notes app to import an RSS feed, such as their own blog feed.

page view Statistic generated when a user visits a web page. Multiple page views are created when a user visits multiple pages in a single website. Generally, sites with higher page views are considered "stickier" than those with lower page views. Looking at page view statistics over time can determine whether changes to a site result in a stickier site or one that is less engaging.

privacy settings Part of Facebook that determines how users control incoming notifications, status updates, and personal data from other people on the Internet and on Facebook.

profile Arguably one of the most important features of Facebook, the profile is the place where users tell the world and each other about themselves. Demographic information, status updates, friends, and other customizations live in the Facebook profile.

publisher The box that appears at the top of every Facebook users' News Feed, personal profile Wall, and fan pages. On personal profiles, content can be published via the publisher by users and their friends, depending on privacy settings. On fan pages, the administrator can post content via the fan page publisher, and fans can also post content depending on the settings.

return on investment (ROI) The amount of financial gain that results from a campaign or other Internet marketing initiative.

search Users may search for any keyword or phrase by entering their query in the search box on Facebook. On the search results page, the filters on the left side of the page allow users to view specific people, fan pages, groups, and applications along with posts by friends or posts by everyone.

social graph The mapping of friends, friends of friends, and other connections that is the basis of Facebook and other social media platforms.

social media policy Rules and guidelines for the use of social media technologies and applications as it relates to a business or organization.

sponsored ad Advertising opportunity generally for organizations with larger advertising budgets to include a brief ad in the upper-right corner of the Facebook News Feed page.

status update The field to the right of any user's name on their profile or any fan page's name where up to 420 characters of text may be published. If the text contains a link, typically this will be posted on the Wall as a link, not a status update.

suggested bid Amount of money Facebook suggests that an advertiser "bid" to get the desired number of clicks or impressions in an advertising campaign.

unique user A visitor to a website that has not been to that site previously during the queried time period. Increases in the number of unique users over time indicate that marketing campaigns are successful at engaging with new customers, while those that see a decrease in unique users over time are perhaps engaging with an already informed customer base.

username A short name used to identify a fan page or profile on Facebook, using the convention www.facebook.com/*vanityname*. Vanity names are important for simplifying complex URLs that Facebook otherwise uses for fan pages and profiles. Users may create one username for their personal profile and one for any fan page they administer. Personal usernames can be changed one time; fan page usernames cannot be changed. To secure usernames, users should go to http://facebook.com/username.

vanity name See *username*.

Index

Note to the Reader: Throughout this index **boldfaced** page numbers indicate primary discussions of a topic. *Italicized* page numbers indicate illustrations.

A